TRANSGENDER NATION

★ ★ ★

TRANSGENDER NATION

Gordene Olga MacKenzie

Bowling Green State University Popular Press
Bowling Green, OH 43403

To the Gender Revolution

Acknowledgments

I want to thank the gender community for making me feel at home and providing me with invaluable resources and inspiration. In particular, I am grateful to Linda, Cynthia, Phyllis, Jessa, Dana, Donna, Virginia, and Merissa for the long and insightful conversations, the warm hospitality, valuable documents and their courage. I am also grateful to Diana, Joan, Darlene, Carol, Regina, Yvonne, Lorraine, Star, Misty, C.J., Ingenue, Wendi, Micky, Christine, Wendy, Michelle, Stephanie, Cee, Valerie, Cathy, Lee, Brian, "Louie," and the members of The Albuquerque Cross-dressers Support Group, Fiesta, and Boulton and Park for their insights and brevity. Thank you. I also want to thank my partner, Nicholas Tarnawsky, and my friend, Jane Caputi, for not only reading and helping edit the manuscript, but also for their support. Special thanks to my editors, Kathy Hoke and Pat Browne at the Popular Press. This book is dedicated to all the brave and courageous gender non-conformists whose gender essences I love.

Contents

Introduction

Everyday we do gender. The way we look, the way we act, dress, talk, walk, wear our hair, think about ourselves, communicate with others and desire comprise our gender schema. Gender is one of the most common daily rituals performed. It is also one of the most effective means of social control. From birth we are enculturated into a dual gender system, reinforced by all the major institutions. Most people don't think consciously about gender unless they are confronted with gender spectacles. In the U.S. and other western countries, gender spectacles, consisting of blatant visual displays of gender, are regularly transmitted in the mass media.

One of the most popular transmitters of gender spectacles in the U.S. is the afternoon TV talk show. A memorable image from 1992 was a tall, beautiful woman with long silky blonde hair, in a tight gold dress gliding across the stage of "Donahue's" afternoon TV talk show. As she approached her host, the camera panned to members of the audience who appeared mesmerized by such a blatant signifier of "femininity." Seductive images of Catherine Cossey, better known to the world as "Tula," in fashion layouts and photographs in *Playboy Magazine*, filled the television screen.

The audience's consumption of Tula's gender was interrupted only when TV talk show host Phil Donahue announced that "gorgeous" Tula was a transsexual who was born a male and had undergone extensive surgery to become a woman. As if to prove this point, a picture of Tula as a shirtless, flat-chested, male adolescent was flashed to the audience. For many spectators this was where their conditioned gender vision started to blur.

Donahue had just reinforced the widely believed misconception that sex-reassignment surgery is a magical elixir that transforms males into females and females into males. This is an impossibility. Such a notion is predicated on the misconception that gender, a psycho-social construct, can be biologically manipulated through genital surgery. More accurately, transsexual and transgender males can live as women and females can live as men with or without surgery. As such, we must question terminology that is not only erroneous, but is designed to convey the idea that to be "transgendered" requires that you buy into medical "treatments" which surgically reshape the genitals.

1

2 Transgender Nation

In order to think new ways about gender issues like transsexualism and transgenderism we need a new language reflective of that thinking. Throughout the book I use the terms *female-to-man* and *male-to-woman* to more accurately reflect the state of a genetic male or female living in the role of the other gender, part- or full-time. Refusing to use the widely accepted and medically derived terms *male-to-female* and *female-to-male*, commonly used to describe transsexuals, cross-dressers and transgenderists, questions the promise of biological transformation and the medical and cultural emphasis on the genitals as indicative of gender roles.

Another term I use throughout the book is *transgenderist*, coined by pioneer gender researcher and transgenderist Virginia Prince. I chose this term because it was self-generated, rather than medically applied. In that sense it can be a term of empowerment rather than disempowerment. *Transgenderist* as Prince originally intended designates an individual who lives full-time in the role of the "opposite" gender, without sex reassignment surgery. Recently, it has been suggested by members of the gender community that *transgenderist* be used to include transsexuals as a sub-category for legal purposes. Although this was clearly not Prince's original intent (pers. comm. 1993), the term has been widely adopted among members of the growing transgender community.

Tula, as a male-to-woman transsexual icon, helps indoctrinate American audiences into a transsexual ideology that reinforces cultural assumptions about what men and women are supposed to be. Transsexual ideology advocates the surgical "transformation" of transsexuals who are commonly defined as being in the "wrong body." Basic transsexual surgical procedures for the male-to-woman transsexual include amputating the penis and turning it inside out in order to create an artificial vagina, the chief cultural signifier of what a woman is, that is, what she is reduced to. The surgical procedures for the female-to-man transsexual at this time are far more complicated. From Trinidad, Colorado, dubbed "the Sex Change Capital of the World," to Mainland China surgical castration is but one part of the high price males who desire to be women must pay.

Highly orchestrated and sensationalized cross-gender scenes have become common rituals in the U.S.A. On any given day Americans can consume mass media created images and stories of cross-dressers (those who dress as the other gender), transgenderists (those who cross gender borders, usually full-time and traditionally do not desire surgical alteration) and transsexuals (those who presently are or are planning to live in the role of the opposite gender full-time and desire hormonal and surgical "treatment"). Transgenderists exist in all world cultures. Some have been revered as shamans. Most however, have been forced into the margins of their cultures. In the U.S. and other countries many transgenderists, expelled from the mainstream culture, have developed rich subcultures. Some of these subcultures provide a support system for disenfranchised transgenderists, cross-dressers, and transsexuals. The politics of these groups range from conservatives who wish to assimilate into mainstream culture to radicals who not only reject dominant cultural ideology, but also challenge the politics of current sex and gender organizations.[1] This wide diversity of individuals who make up the transgender nation is conspicuously absent in most mainstream media portrayals. The media saturation of transgender and transsexual images that peaked in the early 1980s on U.S. afternoon TV talk shows is still in its zenith. Unfortunately, most TV representations usually focus on misguided stereotypes.

The transgender emblems in popular culture function on multiple levels. Their presence in mainstream media both challenges and reinforces the bipolar gender propaganda we are continually blitzed with. Such propaganda flourishes in contemporary society and functions as reinforcement and inducement for gender behavior to conform to genital anatomy. "New" theories that argue that males develop "male rivalry" and "fierce struggles for dominance" as a result of "brawling sperm" (Small) to popular culture icons like Mattel's "mommy-to-be doll" and "My Bundle Baby," a pregnancy simulator designed so little girls can experience "the magic of being a mommy" (Albuquerque *Tribune*), are but more recent incarnations of gender propaganda.

Overall, this propaganda reinforces behavioral differences between the sexes based on anatomy. Dominant patriarchal ideology conditions males to become warriors and females to become breeders of warriors. Because their gender role is thought to be in "opposition" to their biological sex, transgenderists and transsexuals represent a challenge to a dominant gender ideology that insists on sex and gender conformity. Further, with their increasing visibility in the media, transsexuals and transgenderists are announcing their presence on the North American landscape. A benefit of this visibility is that viewing transgenderists and gender nonconformists who are "out" can inspire others to break "out of the closet." Hopefully, repeated exposure can also help viewers to appreciate differences and join the fight for transgender civil rights.

Unfortunately, more public visibility has also inspired a backlash. Conservative Republican and former presidential candidate Pat Buchanan opened his speech at the 1992 Republican National Convention by calling the democrats "cross-dressers" in an attempt to discredit them. Such bigoted rhetoric is designed to stir up a "cultural war" in which transgenderists, transsexuals, and cross-dressers along with feminists, lesbians and gays become targeted as the "enemy." Already conservative lawmakers, lobbied by Right Wing Christian fundamentalist groups, have passed and are drafting more legislation intended to deny transgenderists and cross-dressers their most basic civil rights.

Talk Show Tremors and Aftershocks

Three years before Tula became a media sensation, talk show audiences across America were exposed to in-depth interviews with family survivors of the late jazz musician Billie Tipton. Upon his death, Tipton was found to be a biological female. Billie Tipton had lived and passed as a man. Most talk show interviews with the family focused on how Tipton's wife never knew her husband, Billie, was really a female. Audience members, stunned by the fact that Billie was a transgenderist, fixated on the sexual orientation of Tipton's widow. Conditioned to believe that genitals determine gender roles and sexual preference, they attacked her, calling her a lesbian ("Sally Jesse Raphael"). Subsequent TV talk shows about Tipton, like "A Current Affair," elicited similar hostile and homophobic audience reactions. These negative audience responses toward Tipton may in part have been triggered by feelings of being "fooled" into believing Tipton was a male. But more importantly, the audience reaction mirrored cultural misogynistic attitudes in which female-men are more stigmatized than male-women, because of the pervasive belief that females can never be "real" men. Another factor that no doubt contributed to hostility among the audience, was that Tipton dared to live as a man without having surgery. Such an act defies the sex and gender order. As I argue throughout this book, all too often transsexual surgery upholds the bipolar gender system by encouraging assimilation and erasing difference. The recognition of such differences and variability in gender provides crucial evidence that the dominant and repressive gender hierarchy is built on propaganda and lies.

By comparison, recent audience response toward Tula seems to be getting more sympathetic. This is in part because not only has Tula undergone transsexual surgery, and is a heterosexual, but she is open about being born a male. In addition she fits the cultural ideal of "feminine" beauty. Nonetheless, the fact that both Tula and Tipton became public icons because of being cross-gendered registers one more tremor on the American fault line of gender, which, I might add, is on the verge of a giant quake.

That we as a culture desire to consume images of males who are transformed into women through surgical and/or cosmetic techniques represents a significant sociocultural phenomenon that provides a focal point for an analysis of gender bipolarism. Examining the role of the male-to-woman and female-to-man transgenderist in contemporary culture forces us to question what our cultural ideas about gender are, as well as where these ideas originated and where they are going.

As I write this, many of the brave transgenderists who once rejected surgical "solutions," hoping to create a safe social space for non-surgical male-to-women and female-to-men transgenderists, are opting for sex reassignment. This comes as no surprise in these backlash times when conformity and assimilation become ever more seductive.

In the early 1990s, transsexuals and transgenderists have emerged as a significant gender minority. Yet in spite of their high visibility on network, local and cable stations across the nation, few North Americans are informed about the reality of being a transsexual or transgenderist in a hostile world. In part this is because, like other minorities, televised transsexuals and transgenderists broadcast for mainstream consumption are usually stereotyped as all being alike. Currently, there is some evidence that these formulaic representations are undergoing a small change, due in part to a conscious manipulation of media images by political transgenderists and their supporters. Foremost among these are Linda and Cynthia Phillips, Donna Mobley, Mariette Pathy-Allen and Phyllis Randolph Frye. However, for the most part, transsexual and transgender persons are used by the mass media, particularly the electronic media, to draw audiences and boost program ratings. Besides being a hot topic for TV talk shows and the subject of recent films, transsexuals and transgenderists have also become the focus of new research in the social sciences.

Transsexualism is commonly referred to in the clinical literature "as a condition in which physically normal individuals feel themselves to be of the other gender and wish to change their body accordingly" (Grimm 66). In keeping with this, there is also a movement within the gender community to reject medical labels like *transsexual* and *transvestite*, using instead self-generated and non-stigmatizing terms like *transgenderist* and *cross-dresser*. In order to explore transgenderism in U.S. culture, it is essential to examine the clinical and psycho-medical discourses on transsexualism that influence cultural attitudes towards transgenderists and cross-dressers. These discourses enforce living as only one gender, in keeping with more traditional and repressive values. My working definition of *transsexual* includes any individual who self-defines as a transsexual, as well as those individuals who believe it is necessary to alter their body by hormonal and/or surgical means in order to live in the role of the "other" gender full time.

In the postmodern world, the "coming out" process for many transgender individuals is facilitated by two communication technologies: the telephone and the TV. Many transgenderists and cross-dressers report their first "coming out" experience was directly inspired when TV talk shows featuring transgenderists broadcast telephone numbers of local and/or national transgender organizations. Having operated the first open transgender phone line in New Mexico for more than five years, I know that the first phone call is often extremely hard to make. Many transgender callers' first attempt "to reach out and touch someone" is really an attempt to get in touch with themselves. Unfortunately, most transgenderists initially view themselves through the dominant gender ideology. Their phone conversations reflect such self-stigmatization. All too frequently first-time callers start out with: "Hello.... I have a problem and was wondering if you could help me.... I am sick and I need help...Do you know where I can get surgery?"

By rejecting medical definitions and categorizations that stigmatize them as having a "psychological disorder," transsexuals and transgenderists can shift the emphasis from a personal "disorder" to a cultural "disorder." This shift forms the nucleus of the Gender Movement.

In the early 1900s, psychoanalyst and cultural critic Wilhelm Stekel, a contemporary of Freud, observed that individuals diagnosed as psychologically "sick" or suffering from a "disorder" were the result of a "sick" or "disordered" culture. Stekel maintained:

As long as the world is sick there will be sick people...Diseases are manifestations of their times...the greatest group murderers are the state and society...if society wants to have more healthy members it must be healthy itself. (Stekel 460-61)

Over three decades later, Herbert Marcuse in his analysis of Freud's *Civilization and its Discontents* argued that psychological categories become political categories. He observed that

Psychological problems therefore turn into political problems: private disorder reflects more directly than before the disorder of the whole, and the cure of personal disorder depends more directly than before on the cure of the general disorder. (Marcuse xvii)

Following this line of thinking, the examination of the transgender individual requires an in-depth analysis of cultural attitudes that reinforce and encourage the medicalization of individuals who do not behave in accordance with gender bipolarity. Assuming Marcuse's and Stekel's observations to be accurate, the issue becomes how can we "cure" a sharply divided, hierarchical, oppressive bipolar culture.

My research on transgenderism and transsexualism grew out of a deep contempt for enforced gender roles. I was raised in a culture that expected hyperfemininity from females, a trait I saw many of my female friends and family members sacrificed to. Convinced that there were other ways to express yourself, I became interested in gender non-conformists. Attempting to better understand this phenomenon, and also curious about the social construction of women, I sought out female impersonators and local drag queens at the drag bars. These initial contacts in the early 1980s led to numerous others. Early on I became aware that many of the *girls* (a slang term used to refer to males dressed or acting like women) wanted not only to portray women, but to become "women." Out of the initial 25 *girls* I met, at least 20 were taking female hormones and four of them had undergone breast augmentation surgery. Over half expressed a desire to have sex-reassignment surgery in order to live as a woman full time.

From the 1950s through the early 1980s, medical and clinical theories about transsexuals dominated cultural perceptions of transgenderists and cross-dressers. I found it curious that hardly any work had been published on transgenderism and transsexualism in the social sciences or the humanities. Of the few published accounts available, most overwhelmingly endorsed medical and psychological explanations and "cures" for transsexualism and gender bipolarism. Even Janice Raymond's groundbreaking 1979 book, *The Transsexual Empire: The Making of the She-Male*, a radical feminist indictment of the medical empire, concluded with an endorsement of bipolar sex and gender roles based on anatomical assignment at birth. Discussing whether surgical male-to-women transsexuals who define as lesbian feminists should be allowed into separatist communities, Raymond argued:

Are they equal to us?...transsexuals are not equal to women and are not our peers...nor are they capable of meeting...the situation of women who have spent their whole lives as women. Women take on that self-definition of feminist and/or lesbian because that definition truly proceeds from not only the chromosomal fact of being born XX, but also...what being born with those chromosomes means. (Raymond 116-17)

8   Transgender Nation

Intentionally or not, Raymond's approach to transsexuals and transgenderists stigmatizes them.

Within the last six years, scholarly publications from the social sciences and the humanities on transsexualism and transgenderism have increased. Shakespearean scholar Marjorie Garber's book *Vested Interests* has gained national attention. Although Garber is overly zealous in including individuals in her cross-dressing pantheon, she does make several compelling arguments. Garber maintains that without cross-dressers there would be no culture. She also argues that the transvestite has contributed not only to the collapse of gender categories, but also categories of class, by their use of clothing which often had them mistaken for the wrong class. As I am writing, new theories on cross-dressing are emerging from other disciplines that will hopefully challenge orthodox gender theories. Radical groups like QueerCore are chipping away at Identity Politics and separatism. Postmodernist Jean Baudrillard in his new book, *The Transparency of Evil: Essays on Extreme Phenomena,* argues "that the sexual revolution has led not to sexual liberation but to a reign of transvestism, a confusion of the categories of man and woman." His conservative logic reveals not only a confusion of the categories of sex and gender but also a disdain for gender non-conformists. Perhaps more accurately, the sexual revolution has finally led to a gender revolution.

By far the most useful research on gender and transsexualism has been inspired by the contemporary Women's Movement, as well as the Gay and Lesbian Liberation Movement of the late 1960s through the 1970s. These movements raised important questions about traditional sex and gender roles that, until the Anita Hill/Clarence Thomas hearings and erosions of Roe v. Wade, seemed to have slipped into amnesia. In the ruins of the Reagan/Bush era, we are witnessing a backlash against civil rights, the sexual revolution, Women's Liberation and Gay and Lesbian Liberation. *Transgender Nation* returns to issues raised by these important social movements by exploring the relation of transsexual ideology to gender attitudes in America. Here transsexualism will be used as a lens to examine contemporary gender attitudes in America from the 1950s through the early 1990s.

In 1986 a major turning point in transgender consciousness occurred. CBS network aired "The Second Serve," a made-for-TV biography of transsexual tennis star Renee Richards. This mainstream media event brought numerous transgenderists, transsexuals and cross-dressers out of the closet. A month after the broadcast numerous local and national gay and lesbian helplines reported being flooded by calls from self-defined transsexuals, cross-dressers and transgenderists, looking for someone to talk to or transgender groups to attend.

Garland Harris, the then president of Common Bond, Albuquerque's gay and lesbian organization, contacted me. With the help of my partner, Nicholas Tarnawsky, Garland and I organized an open forum on gender identity, which included the showing of Lee Grant's 1986 documentary "What Sex am I?" Although the documentary endorses the medical model, it still provided a means of coming together.

As I looked around the room after the showing of the documentary, I saw small groups of transgender individuals expressing gender in a multitude of ways. A young drag queen wearing leopard print gloves, a black leather mini-skirt, tube top and hip-length platinum wig conversed with a 40-year-old female who passed as a professional-looking man in a suit. Across the room a 65-year-old, white upper-class man, who only dressed as a woman a few times a year with the help of his 62-year-old wife, discussed transsexual surgery with a latina male-to-woman transsexual who just had breast implants and was contemplating genital surgery. In the corner of the room a local businessman and self-defined transvestite, who had just "purged" all of his clothing and undergone extensive therapy, was talking to a former Hollywood actor and cross-dresser who passed as a woman until "she" spoke in a deep baritone voice. The former actor warned she had seen every well-known therapist in the field and advised the transvestite businessman to give up therapy and suggested "accept yourself and you'll be O.K."

This initial, well-attended forum led to the founding of the Albuquerque Cross-Dressers Support Group, whose purpose was and IS to provide support and a safe space to explore issues of gender. Initially, because they felt their goals were different, members requested the group be divided into two groups: a transvestite/cross-dresser and a transsexual support group. In 1988 the two groups, like many nationwide, rejoined to form an open cross-dressers' support and discussion group. While the Albuquerque Cross-Dressers Support Group remains integrated in these troubled times, groups are again splitting into those who are seeking surgical solutions and those who are not. Nationally, many cross-gender groups are struggling to stay integrated. Leaders in the struggle against gender oppression advocate uniting against the real enemies, like Senator Jesse Helms, evangelists Jerry Falwell and Pat Robertson, the Christian Coalition and others working against gender minorities, rather than ourselves.

From 1986 to the present, over 200 transgender individuals and their friends have been involved with the Albuquerque support group. Many of the observations made throughout the book are the result of my involvement as co-founder and former co-director of the group, as a gender activist and, most importantly, I hope, as a friend to the local and national gender communities. I have no desire to stigmatize transgenderists and transsexuals as sick or deviant. Therefore I purposely resist and refuse to categorize transgenderists and transsexuals as subjects or informants. Rather, I see myself as a political ally of the Gender Movement and hope my work will help to continue the breakdown of rigid gender stratification based on genital anatomy.

Particularly useful to this work was my being able to maintain long-term relationships ranging from 2 to 12 years with over 80 transgenderists, transsexuals and cross-dressers, locally and nationally. These relationships have been invaluable in allowing me to witness personal and social changes in consciousness as transgender individuals became involved in the gender community and the Gender Movement. Like any other group, there is great diversity and variety among members of the gender community.[2] In order to maintain records for my research, a number of my conversations were either taped, written, or remembered and later transcribed. Out of respect for confidentiality, when necessary, the names of transsexuals and transgenderists have been changed and information that would positively identify certain individuals has been altered.

In order to challenge "treatment" models and understand the sociopolitical aspect of transsexualism and its impact on gender attitudes in the U.S., a broad-based social-historical context must be developed. To my knowledge, no research has attempted to write the social history of transsexualism in contemporary America. This book attempts to fill the gap by asking what transsexual ideology, individual transsexuals, transgenderists and cross-dressers and the representations of transgenderists in the popular media reveal about contemporary U.S. gender attitudes. As such, this work is an examination of the interaction between the transgenderist and contemporary U.S. culture.

Transgender Nation is divided into five chapters. Chapter one includes a brief introduction and summary of some of the debates and problems involved in studying transsexualism and transgenderism from a sociocultural and sociopolitical perspective. Included is a sampling of social science and medical views, as well as a discussion of what the medical "treatment" for transsexualism involves.

Chapter two concentrates on the historical sexological categorizations of, contributions to, early medical "treatments" of, and popular attitudes toward transgender individuals from the turn of the century through the early 1950s when the term "transsexualism" first begins to appear in the medical literature. It also includes a look at other categories of transgenderists and cross-dressers who are frequently confused with transsexuals.

Chapter three focuses on the medicalization of transsexuals in America from the early 1950s to the present. This chapter also decodes major medical and psychological theories and theorists from Christian Hamburger, the physician responsible for Christine Jorgenson's "sex reassignment surgery," to contemporary theories, such as Richard Green's "sissy boy syndrome" and Gunter Dorner's essentialist proposal for endocrinological euthanasia. These theories are examined for what they reveal about cultural and personal attitudes toward gender.

Chapter four is an inquiry into popular culture representations and stereotypes of transgenderists in America. Included is an examination of transsexuals and transgenderists on the talk show circuit, on MTV, in rock-and-roll, throughout popular advertising, on prime-time TV, in print media and in popular films. This chapter examines the commercial exploitation of the transgender and transsexual image for shock, titillation and profit. It addresses the question of why the negative and demeaning stereotype of transgenderists as homicidal maniacs "dressed to kill" has such popular appeal. Incorporated throughout this chapter is a critique of how negative stereotypes perpetrate the gender oppression of transgenderists in America.

The final chapter returns to the question of bipolar gender roles and discusses transsexuals, transgenderists and cross-dressers as an oppressed gender minority that has joined forces to create the Gender Movement, a social movement fighting for civil rights. The book ultimately concludes that transsexualism is moving away from being considered a psychological "disorder" that is treatable with surgery and hormones to a grass roots civil rights movement.

Chapter One

Transsexualism in America:
A Tremor on the Fault Line of Gender

The increasing visibility of transsexuals on the daytime TV talk shows exposes on one level America's fascination with people who supposedly have changed or who desire to change their sex or gender. From the late 1980s through the early 1990s, popular daytime TV talk shows routinely featured interviews with transsexuals. Some of the most memorable include interviews with transsexuals and their wives and children, transsexuals in prison, transsexuals working for a call-girl service, transsexuals who are nuns, models and/or lesbians, transsexuals and their husbands and finally, transsexuals who have regretted their sex-change surgery and are now living according to their genital assignment at birth.

The end of the 1980s also marked the first time the term *transsexual* officially entered the English language dictionary. The 1987 *Random House Dictionary of the English Language 2nd Edition* includes in the definition of *transsexual*

1. a person having a strong desire to assume the physical characteristics and gender role of the opposite sex.
2. a person who has undergone hormone treatment and surgery to attain the physical characteristics of the opposite sex. (2012-13)

Such definitions imply that the "desire" for physical "transformation" is personally inspired rather than sociopolitically demanded. Such an idea negates the reality of being a transsexual in a bipolar gender culture. This in no way denies that the desire on the part of the transsexual may be so overwhelming to assume the physical traits and gender role of the "opposite" sex that frequently personal, social, psychological and economic resources are sacrificed in the process. In most cases, transsexuals attempting to live in the cross-gender role lose most if not all family and friendship support. If discovered, they are often fired from their jobs. As a result of personal, social and economic frustrations encountered while trying to live an "authentic life," some transsexuals are driven to a final solution of suicide.

The dictionary definition also implies that by undergoing prescribed medical treatments, transsexuals can attain the physical characteristics of the opposite sex. Nothing could be further from the truth. This medical promise that sex-reassignment surgery will provide physical characteristics of the "opposite" sex promotes unrealistic expectations about the physical capabilities of sex-reassignment surgery and ignores the hidden cultural agenda of a bipolar society.

"Sondra B.," a 39-year-old post-operative male-to-woman transsexual, expressed a belief in unreal expectations when "she"[1] confided, "I thought the surgery would change my body more than it did." When I asked her to clarify what her pre-surgical expectations were, she stated, "I thought I would get a smaller waist and my voice would become more feminine" (pers. comm. 1989). Because of the widespread belief in the medical ability to transform males into females, as well as an essentialist belief in the power of genitals to transform personalities and bodies, she believed that through genital reconstruction she would somehow attain other physical traits associated with the "opposite" sex. In a similar vein, psychologist Leslie Lothstein reported that a female-to-man transsexual standing 5 feet 4 inches and weighing 100 pounds asked if sex-reassignment surgery could make her 6 feet 2 inches and 185 pounds (Lothstein, *Female-to-Male Transsexualism* 141).

These unreal expectations, fostered by the widespread acceptance of medically generated definitions of transsexualism and a belief in the miraculous power of medical science to "heal" gender "deviants," are reinforced by the Western sex-gender code that links anatomical sex to gender identity and gender role to erotic object choice. Implicit in this symbolic code is a heterosexist, homophobic, and male bias. The Western sex and gender code reduces individual behavior to penises and vaginas. According to the gender code, individuals with penises are supposed to develop masculine gender identities and gender roles and choose individuals with vaginas for sex objects. Individuals with vaginas are expected to develop feminine gender identities, feminine gender roles and choose only individuals with penises for sex objects. In the U.S. and most other cultures, great personal, social and symbolic meanings are attached to the genitals. In fact, our entire external presentation to the world too often functions like a billboard advertising our anatomical sex.

Anatomy is Destiny—The American Way

Not all cultures believe that "anatomy is destiny." The role of the "berdache,"[2] accepted among some Native American tribes, reveals the valuation of a spiritual dimension of gender, whether one feels like a woman or a man, over the material dimension of gender based on anatomical sex assignment at birth (see Williams, *The Spirit and the Flesh*). However, in material-based mainstream American culture, gender behavior is usually dictated by sexual anatomy. Whether one possesses a penis or a vagina not only predetermines gender identity, gender role and erotic choice, but also largely controls the psychological, sociological and economic choices that are available to individuals in contemporary society.

In dominant U.S. culture, gender identity and sexual preference remain fused to biological sex. This paradigm has contributed to the idea that transsexuals are born in the "wrong" body. To begin to understand the plight of transsexuals in contemporary culture it is essential to separate the concepts of sex, gender and sexual preference. Male-to-woman transsexual Elizabeth Wells expresses the gender/sex dichotomy in this statement:

I am in the wrong body...I was a boy. My face, my body, my name, my birth certificate, all proclaimed my sex as male. How could I, in the face of such proof, deny it and insist that in fact I was female? But I was: and it was more than just a wish or a preference—I knew it. (Walters and Ross 10)

There are only two ways to express gender in mainstream society, masculinity and femininity and these are seen as diametrically opposed. In contemporary America one is labeled either a boy or girl or a man or woman. There is no real non-stigmatized or non-sensationalized category for a male-woman or a female-man. Gender researcher Ann Oakley observes that our society is organized around the differences rather than the similarities between the sexes. The term *opposite sex* reinforces dominant cultural stereotypes. In U.S. culture these stereotypes are derived from Judeo-Christian myths and values that over-emphasize the importance of reproduction and subsequently polarize and eroticize men and women and masculinity and femininity. Sex radicals and social constructionists such as Gayle Rubin, Jeffrey Escoffier and Pat Califia argue that conceptually separating gender from sex is crucial for understanding the sociopolitical meanings of sex and gender. By fusing sex, gender identity and sexual preference, Western gender ideology denies human variability and choice and advances biological determinism. Pioneer gender researcher and psychoanalyst Robert Stoller makes the following distinctions between sex and gender:

Sex is a biological term...with a few exceptions, there are two, male and female. To determine sex one must assay the following physical conditions: chromosomes, external genitalia, internal genitalia, gonads, hormonal states and secondary sex characteristics...

Gender is a term that has psychological and cultural rather than biological connotations; if the proper terms for sex are "male" and "female," the corresponding terms for gender are "masculine' and "feminine." These latter may be quite independent of (biological) sex. Gender is the amount of masculinity or femininity found in a person...both masculinity and femininity are found in everyone, but in differing forms and to differing degrees.

Gender identity implies psychologically motivated behavior. Though masculinity fits well with maleness and femininity goes with femaleness sex and gender are not necessarily directly related. (*Presentation of Gender* 15-20)

Stoller emphasizes that masculinity and femininity are beliefs, not incontrovertible facts. These beliefs are passed to us first by parents and later by other social institutions and reflect beliefs held by the dominant social order. Most importantly, Stoller observes "such convictions are *not eternal truths*; they shift when societies change." Unfortunately, most conventional medical wisdom treats gender as an expression of sex and as an eternal truth.

To begin to decode transsexualism along a sociopolitical dimension, it must be viewed as an issue of gender. On a medical level, transsexuals are defined as individuals whose gender identity is opposed to their biological sex. As such, transsexuals are stigmatized by themselves and society as violators of the sex-gender code. In contemporary culture they are routinely categorized as sick, deviant and perverse. A male-to-woman transsexual attempting to live in the cross-gender role and trying to keep her friends commented that she "felt the need to reassure them that I wasn't a danger to them or planning to overthrow society" (Walters and Ross 13). Because of the medicalization of anyone who defies bipolarized gender roles, transsexuals and some transgenderists are encouraged to view themselves as prisoners in the "wrong body." Through "sex-change surgery" (an early term predating the sex-reassignment surgery) transsexuals, as medical consumers, attempt to purchase genitals of the "opposite" sex.

Sex-Reassignment Surgery

From the 1950s, when surgical techniques learned during two world wars were established for sex-reassignment surgery, to the present, the medical and psychiatric models have dominated the field of transsexualism. Currently, there are a number of ongoing debates about transsexualism within the psycho-medical literature. One issue that has not been resolved within the professions is whether a transsexual who has had surgery should still be referred to as a "transsexual." Until recently, most post-operative transsexuals rejected the "transsexual" label, preferring to assimilate into the bipolar population. In an attempt to resolve difficulties with the term "transsexual," Norman Fisk introduced the term *gender dysphoria* in 1973 as a blanket term covering not only transsexuals but other individuals with so-called gender identity disorders who requested sex-reassignment surgery. This new term seems to have generated even more confusion. As critics have observed, the term *gender dysphoria* has become self-serving as a justification for referral of non-transsexuals for sex-reassignment surgery (Lothstein, *Female-to-Male Transsexualism* 59). From a sociocultural viewpoint, the suggestion that the cure for "gender dysphoria" is sex conversion surgery is appalling. *Gender Euphoria*, a transgender newsletter from Texas, deliberately puns on the term "gender dysphoria" to make the point that not all transgenderists want to be medically classified. In an October 1992 issue of *Gender Euphoria*, Sheila Mengert makes the compelling argument that, as transsexuals, "we are put in the position of having to appeal to a particular power group, the medical professionals, in order to validate our experience."

Terminology is not the only area of disagreement among researchers and transsexuals. There is also little agreement on how many transsexuals there are in America and how many transsexual operations have been performed in America. Estimates of how many transsexuals live in America range from a low of one in 10,000 (Walker) to a high of one in 500 (Lothstein, *Female-to-Male Transsexualism* 318). Like so much medical and psychological research on transsexuals, these statistics are unconfirmed. It is unclear whether they represent surgically or *non-surgically altered* transsexuals. (I use this term instead of *preoperative* because it implies the goal is surgery.) In the mid-1980s, *Science Digest* reported that three sex-change operations take place every day in America. In 1989 Colorado surgeon Stanley Biber estimated that there were well over 80,000 "female-to-male" transsexual candidates for sex reassignment surgery and at least that many or more "male-to-female" surgical candidates. "Christy," a male-to-woman transsexual who had genital surgery in 1987, stated that Dr. Biber, her surgeon, performed between 150 to 250 sex-conversion surgeries each year in Trinidad, Colorado (pers. comm. 1987). This seems to be a low estimate when compared with other reports on the number of transsexual surgeries performed by Biber at San Rafael hospital in Trinidad.

There are several other problems involved in trying to establish actual numbers of transsexuals in America. A large number of transsexuals not approved for surgery by gender identity clinics in the U.S. or not wanting to follow guidelines, can easily obtain sex-reassignment surgery in other countries, including Mexico, Denmark, Norway and Canada. Some U.S. gender centers advise transsexuals to get surgery in Brussels and Canada. Velma, who underwent sex-reassignment surgery in Canada in 1991, noted that at least five transsexuals a month from the Seattle area were traveling to Brussels for surgical sex-reassignment (pers. comm. 1990). Apparently, sex-reassignment surgery in Brussels is considerably less expensive than in the United States. Of course, surgeons abroad rarely offer statistics on the number of sex-reassignment surgeries performed. Currently, there are approximately 40 gender-identity clinics in the U.S.A. Most of these clinics claim to follow Harry Benjamin's guidelines for surgery, which include living in the role of the "opposite sex" from one to three years, undergoing psychological evaluations and taking hormones. Yet reportedly, there are many private surgeons, who, for the right fee, will perform sex-reassignment surgery on demand, without questions. These surgeons provide no statistics. Critics of transsexual surgery charge that even the clinics performing surgery do not want the actual numbers leaked for fear of shocking the public and gaining unwanted attention. Not providing actual numbers of individuals who desire to live in the "opposite" gender role also keeps them an invisible and politically powerless population.

In the age of increasing cosmetic surgery, opponents of elective surgery argue that unnecessary surgical procedures, such as sex-reassignment surgery, keep skilled surgeons from attending the sick and saving lives. Recent arguments to emerge from the First International Conference on Transgender Law (Houston) point out that attempts to better legislate cosmetic surgery, like being sure that doctors have surgical training, may help transsexuals obtain better care if transsexualism is de-medicalized and reclassified as a cosmetic surgery. In contemporary America, transsexuals who want to live in the "opposite" gender role are required to pay a high price, both physically and economically.

The actual surgical procedures involved in sex-reassignment surgery are complicated, painful, very expensive and in some cases extremely dangerous. For the male-to-woman transsexual, the most common procedures include surgical and hormonal castration, penectomy (removal of the penis), rerouting of the urethra, and turning the penis inside out to use as the lining of the artificial vagina. Usually, a catheter is inserted in the bladder and a vaginal pack in the neovagina. As healing occurs, the vaginal pack is surgically removed and the "patient" is instructed to insert a condom filled with foam rubber into the neovaginal cavity to keep it open. Three to five weeks after the surgery, the "patient" is instructed to use a rigid phallic-shaped vaginal dilator constructed of glass, wood, or plastic, or to practice heterosexual intercourse for 15 minutes at least two times a day. In addition, many male-to-woman transsexuals reportedly request other surgical procedures, such as breast enlargement, tracheal shaves, knee shaves, and face surgery to appear more "feminine."

For the female-to-man transsexual, sex-reassignment surgery is even more complicated, dangerous, expensive and less effective. Generally, the female-to-man transsexual undergoes several operations including a mastectomy, complete hysterectomy, closure of the vagina, phalloplasty (the construction of a penis), and the fashioning of a scrotum to house artificial testes. Until recently the neophallus was constructed from skin that had been removed from the patient's thigh or abdomen. However, more recent techniques remove skin grafts from the upper arm to provide skin for the penis. Besides being unattractive, the surgically constructed penis is usually dysfunctional in both urinary and sexual terms. The neopenis can only become erect by inserting stiff material into it or by having plastic tubes implanted into the groin, so that pressing a bulb will cause the penis to hydraulically inflate with fluid and erect.

The promise of sexually functioning genitals, virtually an impossibility for the female-to-man transsexual, is routinely promised to the male-to-woman transsexual. If the surgery is successful, a gynecologist is said to be unable to detect a genital difference between a genetic female and a surgically constructed male-to-woman transsexual. Such surgical promises and practices reinforce sexist overestimations of a functioning penis as a signifier of supreme "manhood" as well as the idea that males are more adaptable and can do anything, even transform into women. But female-to-men transsexuals, unable to obtain a fully functional penis, are not thought to be "real men."

This type of attitude also comes through in popular films like *Tootsie*. The 1982 box-office hit portrayed the stereotype that males can be better women than females. In the film, Dustin Hoffman, playing a male actor out of work, cosmetically transformed himself into a woman, Tootsie, in order to get an acting job. As Tootsie rises to fame, she becomes a model for females to emulate, confirming that males make better women than females do, a bizarre if logial supposition in a male-supremacist society. However, movies like *Tootsie* romanticize males cross-living as women as being successful, acceptable and popular. This movie illusion is very different from the actual social reality of males who live as women. As can be expected, the film concludes by reinforcing sex and gender biopolarism as Tootsie returns to his genitally assigned sex and gender. The final scenes show Hoffman as a male winning the love of a beautiful woman.

Such "happy" endings rarely occur for transsexuals who undergo surgery. Walters and Ross's 1986 study defines transsexuals as "people with genuine problems deserving of compassion, understanding...and appropriate medical and social management." Clearly, in American society and throughout much of the Western world, individuals desiring to live in the gender role "opposite" their biological sex are treated as sick, perverse, abnormal and are subjected to management in the form of medically prescribed "treatments" and "cures," including sex-reassignment surgery. Bringing a different perspective, transsexual Sheila Mengert cautions

we must not view the necessary aid we must obtain from medicine as the sole determinant of our identity as a people. Others must also seek aid of medicine...to live productive and happy lives, but that aid is only a part of who they are as individuals and as a people. (*Gender Euphoria* 4)

But does sex-reassignment surgery really benefit the transsexual? Personal dissatisfaction with sex-reassignment surgery ranges from one-fourth to three-quarters of those interviewed. In follow-up studies on post-operative male-to-women transsexuals, Walters, Kennedy and Ross reported that more than 35 percent were dissatisfied with their genital surgery. The most common reason was cited as "difficulty or pain with sexual intercourse" caused by a too small vagina and/or a fistula.

An important and well-recognized hazard of genital gender reassignment surgery is an artificial opening or fistula between the urinary tract (urethra and bladder) or rectum and the newly created vagina...Fistulae can be repaired by various operative techniques...Narrowing and eventual closure of the vagina inevitably occur if the vagina is not regularly dilated. (Walters and Ross 149)

If structural problems result from the surgery, the patient is advised that more plastic surgery may be required. Barbara, a male-to-woman transsexual and member of the Albuquerque Cross-Dresser's Support Group, had what she described as "botched" surgery in 1976 and suffered from numerous infections and problems related to sex-reassignment surgery. By 1991 she reported her urethra had almost closed up and she was suffering from a serious kidney infection. She made arrangements for corrective surgery. Although her insurance company assured the "well-known" Colorado surgeon they would pay the bill, she reportedly was turned away because she did not have the *cash* to prepay, the requirement for any transsexual surgery or repairs.

As I mentioned earlier, the promise of a functioning vagina is offered to the male-to-woman transsexual, but almost no hope of a functioning penis can be offered to the female-to-man transsexual. Critics aware of the high failure rate of genital surgery in sex-reassignment surgery for the female-to-man transsexual recommend

...until surgical techniques improve, phalloplasty should be avoided in female to male transsexuals...In our experience female to male transsexuals are most concerned about ridding themselves of the obvious physical manifestations of femininity—large breasts and a uterus that menstruates. While they also desire a phallus, most can accept not having phalloplasty until this surgical procedure is attended by a more successful outcome. (Walters and Ross 113)

Because of the poor surgical results and the enormous expense, many female-to-men transsexuals choose not to undergo phalloplasty. Female-to-men transsexuals who do undergo phalloplasty report numerous problems, including neopenises that have fallen off (see Lothstein, *Female-to-Male Trans-sexualism*). The majority of female-to-men transsexuals settle for an elongated clitoris, the result of taking male hormones, while a smaller number request a phalloscrotal prosthesis. In a society that defines men by the size and conquests of their penises, many female-to-men transsexuals feel inadequate. By buying into the medical model's "treatment" for transsexualism, transsexuals become dependent on medical caretakers throughout their lives for hormones and surgical repairs to the surgery that is offered as a panacea for their suffering.

Transsexualism as a Medical Problem

Paul Walker, a gender specialist and long-time advocate of transsexual surgery, maintains that when given the choice, "It is better to have a medical problem than a moral or psychological problem," (Walker, Interview on *What Sex Am I*). In other words, as long as transsexuals remain medically classified and "treated," society is supposed to respond with tolerance and sympathy. If transsexualism is viewed as a medical problem, whether caused by disease, injury, or a genetic and/or hormonal problem, the blame for "gender deviance" is removed from the transsexual, provided of course that person is under medical "treatment." Ironically, transsexuals undergoing "treatment" are forced to carry cards or letters from their doctors to explain to "an ignorant and uncompassionate world who we are" (Mengert 4).

This same type of justification was used at the turn of the century and during the early 1950s by proponents of homosexual reform. Hoping for social tolerance in a homophobic society, early reformers defined homosexuality as a medical problem; doing so was an attempt to remove blame from individuals. The results of medicalizing homosexuality can still be observed. Almost two decades after the 1973 declaration by the American Psychiatric Association that homosexuality was not an illness, homophobic attitudes stigmatizing gays and lesbians as "sick" are still widespread. Recent legislation funded in part by Pat Robertson's fanatical right-wing Christian Coalition and encouraged by the Republican party's bigoted rhetoric at the Houston convention threatens to take rights away from lesbians and gays.

Measure 9 in Oregon (narrowly defeated in 1992) defined homosexuality as "abnormal and perverse" and wrongly linked it to pedophilia. If it had passed, books with any positive reference to homosexuality would be banned from the classroom and removed from the library. Individual landlords and employers would have the right to "boot out 'abnormal' employees and tenants" (Cooper 16). Since the AIDS epidemic, violence against gays has dramatically increased and once again has linked the image of homosexuality to sickness. As Tere Fredrickson writing in *Gender Euphoria* warns "A lot of the gay/lesbian ordinances and executive orders *include* the gender community" (18). If gay and lesbian rights are denied there is no chance that transgenderists will attain equal rights. Classifying transsexualism as a medical problem has a similar effect of depicting all transgenderists as sick and in need of "treatment." It fosters a dependency on the medical and psychological establishments.

The serious medicalization of transsexuals *climaxed* in the 1960s when Harry Benjamin, an endocrinologist and the first person to make a career out of transsexualism, proposed surgery on the following basis: "Since it is evident, therefore, that the mind of the transsexual cannot be adjusted to the body, it is logical and justifiable...to attempt the opposite, to adjust the body to the mind." Benjamin's testimonial to the importance of the body as a cultural signifier in Western culture is still being used by advocates of transsexual surgery. Benjamin argued that hormonal and surgical intervention was "a life-saving measure" for transsexuals. If sex-reassignment surgery is a life-saving operation, why do surgeons demand a cash prepayment of fees beginning at $12,000? Follow-up studies do not confirm that sex-reassignment surgery is a life-saving measure. In fact, some studies indicate the suicide rate for post-operative transsexuals is extremely high (see Latham; Levine; and Lothstein, *Female-to-Male Transsexualism*).

Transsexualism and Social Constructionism

In contrast to the surgical "cures" advocated by proponents of essentialist ideology, social construction theories emphasize gender and sex as products of historical and social interactions rather than as fixed and unchanging biological products. Although radical feminist Janice Raymond vacillates between essentialism and social constructionism, she voices a constructionist concern when she asks how medicine and psychology can "cure" what is actually a sociopolitical issue. In the same vein, Raymond views transsexuals as "guinea pigs" for the medical establishment and questions surgical solutions that prohibit the examination of cultural gender stereotypes responsible for the creation of transsexualism in the first place. Sociologist Deborah Feinbloom also raises issues of concern to social constructionists when she observes: "The transsexual forces us to reexamine the standard definitions of male and female" (Feinbloom 246). Her statement implies that because the linear logic of the bipolar system held sacred by Western culture is disrupted by the existence of transsexuals, this fissure forces us to re-examine how "natural" it is to assume all biological males will act like men and all biological females will act like women. She further observes:

People are biologically male or female. For most the gender identifications, masculine and feminine (that is behaving like a male or female) are congruent with biological reality...The transsexual knows the biological reality but chooses to deny it as an "accident" of birth. (247)

In other words, transsexuals are not delusional. They are aware of their biological sex assignment, but believe psychologically they are of the "opposite" gender.

Perhaps even more disturbing than the medical peddling of genitals is the fact that many gender identity clinics also function as centers of "social control," specializing in the eradication of femininity in young males. These clinics routinely enforce stereotypical gender behavior on young gender "deviants" whose parents have turned them in for inappropriate gender behavior like cross-dressing and "feminine" mannerisms. "Treatment" consists of extinguishing feminine behavior through punishment ranging from losing tokens to physical abuse. Stereotypical masculine behavior is rewarded and reinforced. Donna Risley, a counselor and opponent of the above treatment, postulates that

Rigid sex-role stereotyping is not good for anyone, least of all any of our children; it may well be that gender dysphoric children to some degree represent part of the cost society pays for its present gender organization. (Walters and Ross 43)

The "treatment" of eradicating "feminine" behavior sounds an alarm for the gender attitudes commonly held toward women in contemporary society. By comparison, girls who imitate masculine behavior are not at this point, stigmatized as being ill, but are often rewarded, at least until puberty, when they are expected to magically transform into heterosexual "feminine" women. In contemporary culture, masculine is often perceived as "normal," feminine as the "abnormal."

To date, only a few researchers in the field of gender have challenged the complete medicalization of transsexualism. Most current work on transsexualism in the psychological and medical literature continues to reinforce surgical "treatment" and rarely challenges cultural bipolarism. Unfortunately, much of the new scholarship from the social sciences endorses sex-reassignment surgery and bipolarism. For example, anthropologist Anne Bolin, in her 1988 book *In Search of Eve: Transsexual Rites of Passage*, while appropriately critical of the outdated stereotypical therapeutic exchange between transsexuals and their medical caretakers, praises transsexual surgeons as "shamans" assisting transsexuals on their rite of passage into womanhood.

Gender Bipolarism and the Transsexual Body

In contemporary culture, there is not a permanent institutionalized role or safe social space for individuals who live outside of the dominant bipolar gender world. Even drag queens, as part of the gay subculture, live a peripheral and often threatened existence. In such impermanency, we see many of the political ramifications of gender. A biological male who desires to live in the gender role of a woman is continually psychologically harassed and physically threatened. That a male will give up manly privilege to live as woman upsets the status quo and inspires retaliation. These negative attitudes toward transsexuals and cross-dressers who desire to be women expose deeply embedded cultural misogyny and homophobia. In addition to exposing gender and sex bigotry, transsexuals and transgenderists can function as symbols of unification for sex and gender minorities, and women, inspiring a revolt against gender bipolarism and a Gender Revolution.

As stated earlier, that a female-to-man transsexual is denied a functioning penis because research in medical science has focused on the perfection of the artificial vagina rather than on the neophallus demonstrates a gender bias. Psychoanalyst Jacques Lacan observed that the penis "signifies" power in the patriarchy; unable to obtain an adequate penis, female-to-men transsexuals often feel incomplete and powerless.

Lacan suggested that in their search for truth through sex-reassignment surgery, the male-to-woman transsexual, a victim of bipolar ideology, confuses the organ and the signifier.

Transsexuals are the victims of error. They confuse the organ and the signifier. Their passion and their folly consists in believing that ridding themselves of the organ they can also be rid of the signifier which because it sexuates it also divides them. (Lacan qtd. in Millot 141)

The error, according to Lacan and psychoanalyst Catherine Millot, is in assuming that reconstructed genitals will lead to social acceptance in the chosen gender role. More often, as Millot reports, a surgically constructed female-to-man transsexual feels more like a monster after surgery than before. All too often the surgically transsexed body becomes a living cultural embodiment of bipolarism.

Social historian Jeffrey Weeks observes that the division of individuals along gender lines, founded on biological differences in the genitalia, has been reinforced through cultural ideology and various social practices. Medical "treatments" for transsexualism reward socially appropriate gender behavior with surgically made bodies to match. As Foucault observed, "Our relation to reality is organized through a series of gender discourses, concepts, and beliefs." For this reason, many transgender individuals, indoctrinated into essentialist gender beliefs that insist on body and gender matches, have opted for surgical "solutions," hoping surgery would allow them to disappear and assimilate into the stereotypical role of the "other" gender. In a world where land value has soared due to scarcity, development is frantically taking place on the human body. During the second half of the twentieth century, because of new developments in medical technology and cosmetic surgery, the human body is becoming even more colonized by bipolar gender ideology. Current gender beliefs and practices teach transsexuals and transgenderists to hate their body. As a result, the transsexual body in contemporary America is often brutalized, reshaped, and mangled to fit a rigid bipolar gender ideology.

In the 1990s, gains made by the contemporary Women's Movement and Gay and Lesbian Liberation, such as the right to control one's own body and the right to love someone of the same sex are under attack by a conservative backlash inspired by Clinton's election and the failing global economy. Bigotry and bipolarism have once again become fashionable. The pressure to conform to rigid bipolar gender roles is on the increase.[3] The transsexual of the 1990s functions on several levels. First, transsexuals, as people who feel they are born into the "wrong" body, politically and socially challenge the Western gender ideology that enforces biological and gender congruency. However, as long as transsexuals submit to surgical solutions, they reinforce gender conformity and control. Potentially explosive socio-political gender issues are often successfully amputated along with healthy genitals on the operating table. But, in attaining new surgically remodeled genitals, transsexuals fall prey to American consumer ideology. By throwing away old genitals and purchasing newly fashioned genitals, transsexuals become the ultimate American icon, the products of a capitalistic and deeply gender-biased culture.

Chapter Two

Historical Explanations and Rationalizations
for Transgenderism

Individuals who cross-dressed and/or attempted to live in the "opposite" gender role have always existed. However, the medicalization of these individuals only began in the 1800s, when early German and English sexologists began the classification of what they called the "sexual perversions."[1] In the U.S., by the mid-to-late 1800s, moral control over sexual behavior and gender roles shifted from the clergy to the new science of medical psychology. Medical theories of "disease" and "treatment" replaced religious threats of eternal damnation and/or exorcism previously applied to "deviant" sexuality.

Major theories about sex and gender at the turn of the century were derived from Freudian psychoanalysis as well as from attempts by early sexologists to categorize individuals on the basis of their sexual behavior. According to American interpretations, Freud's Oedipal complex, starting with the recognition of the anatomical differences between the sexes, set off the "castration complex" in males and "penis envy" in females, both of which supposedly culminated in a "normal" gender identification, masculinity for males and femininity for females and in heterosexual desire.

In order to understand the role of transsexual ideology in shaping and reflecting clinical and popular gender attitudes in American culture, it is necessary to explore the history of transgender and transsexual ideology and the gender attitudes these beliefs inspired. Here I will use historical sexological categorizations of transgenderists who felt themselves to be members of the "opposite" sex and/or desired to live in the role of the "opposite" gender as precursors of the modern category of transsexuals. These early sexological theories, primarily based on case histories, provide us with a glimpse into the unique historical relationship between transgenderists and their culture.

The term *transsexual* was reportedly first used in the medical literature in 1949 in America by the medical doctor D.O. Cauldwell. Cauldwell used the term "psychopathia transsexualis" to describe the case of a girl who wanted to change her sex. Prior to the 1910 publication of sexologist Magnus Hirschfeld's volume *Transvestism*, there were no separate medical categories or theories about cross-dressers or transgenderists. Rather, these individuals were routinely classified as "inverts," an early term for homosexuals, who at the time were considered with "sexual perverts."

Kenneth Plummer, a scholar who has written extensively about the social construction of homosexuality, demonstrates the historical damage labeling and categorizing have had on lesbians and gays. Plummer observes:

...the categories exist; they are applied...to millions of people throughout the world, and indeed are also today applied to large numbers of people throughout history...Certainly there is considerable political intent behind the making of such categorizations—to order, control and segregate in the name of benevolence.

Certainly too these categories have rendered—in the main—whole groups of people devalued, dishonorable or dangerous, and have frequently justified monstrous human atrocities and the denial of human rights. (53)

The same can be said of transgenderists and cross-dressers who have also been victimized and stigmatized by medical labels and categories.

Historically, transgenderists, cross-dressers and transsexuals were embedded within the category of homosexuality. Most early researchers argued that cross-dressing and cross-gender behavior were "symptoms of homosexuality." At the turn of the century, individuals engaging in same-sex relations were viewed with disgust and branded as "criminals against nature," because same-sex acts did not lead to procreation. Part of the categorical confusion is that no real distinction was made between sex and gender. Terms that seem to closely approximate the idea of gender, like "soul," "spirit" and "psyche," were commonly used by early sex researchers in an attempt to explain homosexuality. The lumping together of transgender behavior and homosexuality can be traced to early theories about homosexuality, many of which were really elaborate theories about gender.

In an attempt to explain same-sex attractions, a number of the early sexologists adopted Karl Ulrichs' theories on homosexuality, which confused gender and sexual preference. Ulrichs, a German lawyer and advocate of homosexual rights, in the mid 1800s refuted the dominant belief that same-sex acts were crimes against nature. Basing his theory largely on himself, Ulrichs proposed that male homosexuality was the result of a feminine soul in a male body and that female homosexuality arose from a masculine soul caught in a female body. Based on this hypothesis, Ulrichs argued "love directed towards a man must be a woman's love" and as such must not be considered a crime against nature (Kennedy 105-07).

Ulrichs' theory, based on a heterosexual model, raised many questions, including whether a non-transgendered same-sex partner was considered a homosexual. For Ulrichs, individuals who cross-dressed or expressed the gender role of the "opposite" sex were viewed as expressing their true "spirit," which was defined as a manifestation of homosexuality. Even though his theory was psychologically based, Ulrichs, a product of his time, believed in congenital theories of homosexuality which stressed genetic and/or inherited origins. Here Ulrichs' ideas resemble current popular theories about the origin of homosexuality which stress differences in brain structure.[2]

Ulrichs' "third sex theory," while attempting to liberate homosexuals from legal persecution and social ostracism, ultimately helped blur the lines between homosexuals and cross-gender-identified individuals. In retrospect, Ulrichs' definition of homosexuals as individuals whose biological sex contradicts their gender, (spirit, soul, psyche) is far more descriptive of the plight of transsexuals than homosexuals. "Elizabeth," a 42-year-old, non-surgical male-to-woman transsexual I spoke with in 1986, recalls Ulrichs' theories with her statement:

I have always had the soul or spirit of a woman. I have felt that I've had to masquerade as a man. When I am with a man sexually, my relationship to him is that of a woman. I was simply born into the wrong body. Nature made a terrible error and it is up to me to correct it. (pers. comm. 1986)

As categories, homosexuality and transsexualism share many historical antecedents. Homosexuality was defined and treated as a medical problem by the psycho-medical model until 1973, when it was deleted from the American Psychiatric Association's *Diagnostic and Statistical Manual of Mental Disorders* (*DSM III*). As of this writing, even though it is being challenged, transsexualism is still considered a psycho-medical problem that might be "cured" through surgery (*DSM III Third and Revised* [*DSM III-R*]). As a result of being medicalized, transsexuals, like homosexuals, have internalized medical labels, causing them to view themselves as sick and deviant. Because of the process of self-stigmatization, theorists like Plummer stress the necessity of viewing transsexualism as a political category, reflective of a repressive society, rather than as a "medical condition" requiring treatment. With the advent of Gay and Lesbian Liberation, many individuals with same-sex sexual and/or political preferences substituted their own terms, "gay" and "lesbian," thereby rejecting the medical label and the associated social stigma of the term "homosexual." As I mentioned earlier, inspired by the use of self-generated labeling as a fight against oppression, some transsexuals and members of the gender community are rejecting the use of the medical term "transsexual," using instead self-generated terms like transgendered, "transgenderist" and "cross-dresser."[3] But there is still a long way to go. The categories of transsexual and homosexual, as well as individual transsexuals, transgenderists and homosexuals have been and to a large degree still are confused by both the general and medical population. It is impossible to think clearly about transsexualism and transgenderism unless we make the distinction that the term *homosexuality* refers to sexual preference as compared to *transsexualism*, and *transgenderism* which refer to gender preference; therefore a transsexual may be lesbian, gay, heterosexual, bisexual or asexual and a lesbian or gay may be masculine, feminine or any combination of the two.

In his 1981 investigation of the category of homosexuality, Plummer raises four questions that can be applied to the categorization of transsexuality. First, he asks what is the nature of the categorization? Second, when and how did the categorization emerge? Third, how is the category conferred on certain people and behaviors? And finally, what is the impact on the people categorized? As Foucault observed, the history of sexuality becomes a history of historical discourses on sexuality. Further, Foucault maintained that discourses on sexuality, in which discourses on gender are included, are an ever-changing and expanding part of a complex growth of social control over individuals exercised through the apparatus of sexuality. Of course, Foucault overlooks the obvious—his own white, male and elite class privilege. As Emma Perez notes in her article, "Sexuality and Discourse: Notes from a Chicano Survivor," "He [Foucault] does not say...European white men hold political, social, racial and sexual power over women: and...use that power throughout history to control women and to sustain patriarchal power" (166).

Historic and Mythic Accounts of Transgenderists
Throughout history numerous reports of transgender persons attempting to live in the gender role of the "opposite" sex emerge. Among them are

members of European royalty, colonial governors in America, Native American healers, and others. Some of the earliest written accounts of transgenderists come from ancient Greece and Rome. Roman Emperor Nero was said to have murdered his pregnant wife by kicking her in the stomach. Arguing that his male ex-slave Sporum bore a remarkable resemblance to his dead wife, Nero ordered that he be changed into a woman.

After an operation probably consisting of penile castration, Nero and Sporum were married. Sporum reportedly was "delighted to be called the mistress, the wife, the Queen of Hiercolces" (Bulliet 79-80). He is alleged "to have offered half of the Roman Empire to the physician who could equip him with female genitalia" (Green and Money 15).

Transsexual desire is also found in ancient Greek and Roman myths. If we examine myth as a collective reflection of our cultural wishes, desires and fears, we can speculate why Sporum offered half of the Roman Empire to the physician who could create female genitals for him. In most ancient Greek and Roman sex-change myths, males are transformed into women as punishment. However, such punishment rarely works because the newly transformed male-to-woman reports much greater sexual pleasure in her new role.

One example is the ancient Greek myth of Tiresias, a Theban soothsayer. According to the myth, Tiresias came upon two snakes mating. He killed the female snake and as punishment was transformed into a woman. When Tiresias remarked that "a woman's pleasure during sexual intercourse was ten to man's one, he was changed back into a man" (Green and Money 13). Such sex-change myths and reports of subsequent superior sexual pleasure also contain a subtext of violence toward that which is female or associated with females. Nero's murder of his wife preceded Sporum's sex change, as did the murder of the female snake precede Tiresias' transformation. An ancient Roman myth follows a similar pattern. In the myth males who pillaged and destroyed Venus' temple were subsequently changed into women. The inscription of power to female genitalia can also be found in historical and contemporary sexological and clinical theories that maintain that female sexual pleasure is much greater than a male's and that female genitals, because of their reproductive potential, represent a power that males envy and also fear.[4]

Perhaps some contemporary analogues to these mythic and historical accounts of female devaluation, followed by male-to-women sex changes, do occur. In America, when the contemporary Women's Movement began naming injustices against women, sex-change surgeons were performing the first widely publicized sex-reassignment surgeries on male-to-women transsexuals at Johns

Hopkins University Hospital. In the early 1990s, during the Bush administration when women's rights were being eroded by Supreme Court decisions on abortion, Christian fundamentalists and neo-conservatives pushed for a return to "traditional" roles and "family values," which threatened women's rights. At the same time male-to-woman sex-reassignment surgeries were on the increase.

Not all historical personages who lived in the role of the "opposite" gender desired to have the genitals of the "opposite" sex. In 16th-century France, King Henry III was reportedly content just living in the gender role of a woman. Henry dressed as a woman and requested that he be referred to as "Sa Majeste," which means "Her Majesty" (Green and Money 16).

Perhaps the most famous transgenderist in history was the Chevalier d'Eon, a member of Louis the XV's court in 18th-century France. The Chevalier lived his first 49 years of life as a man and her last 34 years as a woman. The Chevalier undertook several secret missions to Russia as a woman and went undetected. Many believed the Chevalier's true sex to be female. However, an autopsy at death revealed her to be a biologically "normal" male, much to the distress of members of the court that wagered the Chevalier was a female.

Inspired by biographies of the Chevalier, sexologist and sex reformer Havelock Ellis coined the term *Eonist* to describe cross-dressers and transgenderists. However, not all *Eonists* enjoyed the privileged status that the Chevalier d'Eon did. Prior to the domination of the medical view on Western thought, socioeconomically privileged transgenderists and cross-dressers were tolerated as objects of curiosity. Religious and legal condemnation was generally reserved for less economically privileged transgenderists.

Turn of the Century Transgenderists

America at the turn of the century was not a good place to be if you were poor and transgendered. Violence was an all-too-common event in the lives of male-to-women transgenderists unprotected by wealth and status. Female-to-men transgenderists were also victimized. Historian Jonathan Katz observes that at the turn of the century there seemed to be an "irrational horror" that motivated a violent reaction to cross-dressers and transgenderists. Male-to-women transgenderists of the time commonly referred to themselves and each other as "men-women." Female-to-men transgenderists called themselves "women-men" (see Katz). An early 1900s newspaper account reflects the violence confronting transgendered persons. It tells of a man-woman who was found bludgeoned to death, her body salted down, then bent and stuffed in a trunk by her father, a meat packer. A transgenderist who knew the victim remarked:

In such strange ways a continuous string of both men-women and women-men are being struck down in New York for no other reason than loathing for those born bisexual. And public opinion forbids the publication of the facts of bisexuality, which, if generally known, would put an end to...these murders of innocents. (Katz 557)

This account bears a chilling resemblance to the hate crimes occurring almost 100 years later as we near another turn of the century. The term *bisexual* here refers to cross-gender.

From the 16th through the 19th centuries in America, scattered reports of transgenderists can be found in newspapers, legal records, medical journals and in the writings of the early sexologists. Accounts of Native American "berdaches," males who cross-lived as women, routinely appeared in the medical and sexological writings about cross-dressers at the turn of the century. Most accounts were usually derived second-hand from the diaries of Christian missionaries, travelers, and early explorers. Typically they were moralistic and racist diatribes against Native American transgenderists who were branded as "sinful sodomites" and "corrupt men with long hair" who wore women's clothing and performed women's work (see Katz; Williams, *The Spirit and the Flesh*; Roscoe).

Although thought of as deviants by European and American missionaries out to convert and/or destroy them, many Native American transgender persons were revered as sacred in their own societies and were thought to possess exceptional abilities. Author Will Roscoe maintains that because of forced assimilation into the dominant American culture, visible signs of males in women's clothing among Native Americans largely disappeared after World War II. However, he observes that the acceptance of transgender behavior remained. Today, some Native Americans who have been assimilated into the dominant culture define as transsexuals and seek transsexual surgery.

Fewer accounts of female-to-men "amazons," a term anthropologist Walter Williams coined for the female equivalent to "berdache," have been recorded. Paula Gunn Allen, a Native American writer, suggests that fewer accounts of cross-gender women exist because women have always been considered less important than men.

Concerns raised in early America about whether transgenderists were gay or lesbian are still with us and reflect the homophobia transgenderists are confronted with in addition to transgenderphobia. Sodomy was considered a serious crime, punishable by death. Accused sodomites were hanged, suffocated and drowned—torments and executions reminiscent of the witch trials (Katz 861).

While transgenderists and cross-dressers were being routinely tortured and sacrificed, sexologists at the turn of the century began the search for the etiology of cross-gender behavior. Rooted in biological explanations, early sexological theories cracked the door to public tolerance by replacing the image of transgenderists as "criminals" with the image of the transgenderist "sick" and in need of treatment. Unfortunately some of the treatments were as fatal as the criminal penalties for sodomy.

Most turn-of-the-century sexologists believed that gender was related to the sex organs. Therefore, injuries to the genitals were thought to cause transgender behavior. Sexologist Krafft-Ebing theorized that excessive horseback riding probably caused injury to Native American men's testicles, resulting in transgenderism and impotence since gender and sexual preference were thought to be related to the health of the genitals. Gay men and male-to-women transgenderists were thought of as "failed men," with diseased, injured and/or inadequate genitals. In addition theorists like Krafft-Ebing argued that "failed men" were more like females than males. Of course conversely, "failed" or genitally deficient females were not viewed as being like males. Rather, it was the highly accomplished and independent woman who was thought to be more manlike. Such attitudes suggest how deeply the superiority of males is rooted in Western sex and gender roles.

In 1881, the *Chicago Medical Review* reported that the first Colonial governor of New York, Edward Hyde, also known as Lord Cornbury, frequently appeared in public wearing women's clothing. Opinions among sexologists about Cornbury's behavior varied. Most conservative sexologists, like Krafft-Ebing, who thought the only reason males wore dresses was to attract other males, labeled Cornbury a homosexual. The more progressive sexologists seemed less concerned about sexual preferences and described Cornbury as a person who desired to live in the "opposite" gender role. Krafft-Ebing condemned Cornbury as an amoral homosexual

who was apparently affected with moral insanity; was terribly licentious and in spite of his position could not keep from going about the streets in female attire, coquetting with all the prostitutes. (Krafft-Ebing 438)

The diagnosis of "moral insanity" highlights how moral judgments disguised as medical facts were commonly used to condemn cross-dressers and transgenderists.

Captain Robbins, an American commander from Maine who had both a brilliant war record and a desire to dress in fine dresses and gowns, elicited the attention of the major sexologists. Depending on the sexologist's own values, Robbins was categorized as either a homosexual or a cross-dresser. Due to their elite status Governor Cornbury and Captain Robbins were never prosecuted.

Progressive German sexologist, sex reformer, self-defined homosexual and cross-dresser Magnus Hirschfeld expressed shock at Americans' reactions to cross-dressers. On a visit to America in the early 1900s he observed:

American newspapers report with unusual frequency the arrests of men who dress in women's clothing and women who dress in men's clothing...For example, one man who simply could not stop dressing as a woman was finally forced to wear a sign on his waist with the legend: "I am a man." (Katz 77)

Hirschfeld was used to fighting for the rights of cross-dressers and transgenderists. He even successfully petitioned the Berlin police to issue permits allowing transgenderists to cross-dress and/or cross-live (Katz 231). I am unaware of similar political action for transgender rights during this period in America.

In the U.S. cross-dressers and transgenderists were more likely to be stigmatized and tortured. Newspaper accounts reveal in New York, cross-dressers and transgenderists congregated at "Paresis Hall" to cross-dress and socialize. Is it just a coincidence that the name of the hall, Paresis, refers to a disease of the brain caused by syphilis? Perhaps the name of the hall is just a symbol of the social, medical and self stigmatization cross-dressers and transgenderists of the time were forced to endure? The "much hated" members of "Paresis Hall," thought to be "diseased," "insane" and "homosexual," were harassed and finally pushed out by the police (Katz 353).

Early Categories of Transsexuals

Contemporary transsexual researcher David King reminds us that even though transsexualism is a recent conceptualization, it is important to link it to its historical and cultural past in order to better understand the sociocultural and psychological consequences of early categorizations on transgenderists. Many early attempts to categorize transgenderists were inspired by the development of the case study, popularized by Freudian psychoanalysis. At the time most sexologists catalogued the so-called sexual aberrations in a formulaic style under major categories. These categories were substantiated by case studies and accompanied by personal documents, sexological analysis and diagnosis. Cases that today would be defined as "transsexual" were originally classified under the categories of homosexuality, sexual perversions, Eonism, androgyny, psychic hermaphroditism and transvestism. Each of these categories contained sub-categories such as cross-dressing, effeminateness, congenital sex inversion, antipathic sexual instinct, uranism, transmutatio sexus, transformation of sex and metamorphosis sexualis. This preponderance of categories within categories reflected the confusion of early sexologists in attempting to understand cross-gender behavior (Krafft-Ebing 302-95).

At the turn of the century a search for the cause of transgenderism and cross-dressing was launched in order to justify medical "treatments," "cures" and "prevention." Conservative theories espoused by most psychoanalysts and sexologists like Krafft-Ebing held that transgenderism and cross-dressing were "symptoms" on the road to insanity and a sexual abnormality. Proponents of this theory felt transgenderism and cross-dressing were deviant and dangerous behaviors that could bring a state of anarchy to established "norms" of heterosexual, monogamous, reproducing behavior. Because of the alleged threat transgenderists and cross-dressers posed to gender bipolarism, they were frequently subjected to popular "treatments" like cold sitz baths and intellectual retraining. Legal penalties for being a transgenderist were much harsher and included instances of cross-dressers being expelled from universities, committed to insane asylums and even put to death (see Katz).

Early Theories of Causation

Sexologists who supported the illness model of transgenderism and cross-dressing thought it was a symptom of homosexuality. Like homosexuality, cross-dressing and transgenderism were believed to result from a congenital, hereditary, or acquired condition. Congenital causes of transgenderism were thought to emanate from endocrinologic, glandular, and/or other physiological abnormalities. Krafft-Ebing staunchly believed that physiological abnormalities led to transgenderism and went to great lengths to prove congenital causes of transgenderism. He performed autopsies on the dead and measured the hips, ears, faces, pelvises, and skulls of the living.

The case of Count Sandor, a female-to-man transgenderist writer married to a female was one case Krafft-Ebing used to validate his theory. He thought that Sandor's "somewhat" masculine appearance might be a clue to a genetic basis for his transgenderism. Like other proponents of congenital theories of transgenderism, Krafft-Ebing seemed obsessed with the sexual preferences of transgenderists and cross-dressers. If they were gay, lesbian or bisexual, they were far more likely to be diagnosed as "sick." Krafft-Ebing categorized Count Sandor as a "congenital sexual invert" and included the following justifications:

She was 153 centimeters tall, of delicate build, thin but remarkably muscular on the breast and thighs. Her gait in female attire was awkward...The hips did not correspond in any way with those of a female, waist wanting...The skull slightly oxcephalic, and in all measurements below average...Circumference of the head 52 centimeters...Pelvis generally narrowed (dwarf pelvis), and of decidedly masculine type...labia minora having a cock's-comb-like form and projecting under the labia majora...On account of narrowness of pelvis, the direction of the thighs not convergent, as in a woman, but straight.

The opinion given showed that in S. there was a congenitally abnormal inversion of the sexual instinct, which, indeed, expressed itself, anthropologically, in anomalies of development of the body, depending upon great hereditary taint; further, that the criminal acts of S. had their foundation in her abnormal and irresistible sexuality. (Krafft-Ebing 436-38)

Heredity was another suspected cause of transgenderism that was investigated at the turn of the century. Theories of heredity stressed that the "sexual perversion" of transgenderism and/or cross-dressing was inherited from "insane" parents or relatives. As a precaution against inflicting their "insanity" on their offspring, transgenderists were warned not to marry or have children. Case histories used to validate this theory of transgenderism included lengthy family histories marked by insanity. In support of the heredity theory of transgenderism sexologist Havelock Ellis presented the case of a male-to-woman transgenderist who desired to become a woman. Ellis traced the transgenderist's desire to her father and reported: "...it is possible that T.S.'s father had a latent impulse of this kind...near the end of his life...he endeavored to put on his wife's clothing" (Ellis 110).

It was widely believed that congenital and inherited cases of transgenderism and cross-dressing were incurable. Therefore "prevention" was stressed. Such prevention included advising transgenderists not to masturbate or succumb to homosexual desire. Above all heterosexuality was encouraged! (Krafft-Ebing 450).

If congenital and inherited causes of transgenderism were given a poor prognosis by pioneer sex researchers, acquired cases of transgenderism were given a much better chance of recovery. Acquired causes of transgenderism and cross-dressing included excessive masturbation and/or being seduced by an "invert" and/or transgenderist. Popular remedies for persons "afflicted" with acquired cases of transgenderism included the use of hypnotic suggestion and prescriptions for heterosexual marriage. For cases of "antipathic sexual inversion," a category which included "men in women's garb and women in men's attire" who "psychically consider themselves to belong to the opposite sex," Krafft-Ebing advised hypnosis. Sometimes he prescribed the use of hypnosis in conjunction with hydrotherapy. A male-to-woman transgenderist who Krafft-Ebing believed was suffering from an acquired case of transgenderism was given the following suggestions every two or three days:

1. I abhor onanism, because it makes me weak and miserable.
2. I no longer have inclination toward men; for love for men is against religion, nature and law.
3. I feel an inclination toward woman; for woman is lovely and desirable, and created for man. (Krafft-Ebing 457)

Sexologists generally believed if patients could be rendered "sexually neutral" then medicine would have provided a service to society and the individual. In the early 1900s, Krafft-Ebing's views on transgenderism mellowed a bit. He suggested that patients with "antipathic sexual inversion" were "no worse than drunks" and in most cases did "not need to be confined to an asylum." Contemporary theories about transgenderism and homosexuality which stress hormonal causation can be directly traced to theories of the early sex researchers.

Instead of searching for physiological causes of transgenderism, the early psychoanalysts proposed possible psychological origins for cross-dressing and transgenderism. Delusions brought on by disruptions in the Oedipal complex, such as identification with the "wrong" parent at crucial stages and/or problems with the mother, were thought to be major causes of transgenderism. Wilhelm Stekl, a psychoanalyst and colleague of Freud, argued that separate categories for transgenderists and cross-dressers were unnecessary, since all were really cases of "latent homosexuality." Gutheil, Stekl's assistant, believed that "incest fixation" was the driving motive behind cross-dressing and transgenderism. In the case of Elsa, a female-to-man cross-dresser, Gutheil and Stekl theorized that Elsa became a man in order to identify with her beloved father and brother (Ellis 23).

The only case Freud published relating to transgenderism was "The Schreber Case" in 1911. Freud diagnosed Schreber's "symptom" to be the delusion that he was changing sexes and becoming a woman, "god's wife." Freud argued that Schreber's change-of-sex "fantasy" was related to his repressed homosexuality, delusions and psychosis and was not a case of transgenderism. Lothstein credits Freud's diagnosis of Schreber with alerting contemporary transsexual researchers "to the differential diagnosis between homosexuality and transsexualism" (Lothstein, *Female-to-Male Transsexualism* 54).

Before the 1910 publication of sex reformer Magnus Hirschfeld's *Transvestism: An Investigation into the Erotic Impulse of Disguise*, transgenderism was a sub-category of homosexuality. Hirschfeld, considered the leading expert of his time, argued that transvestism was clearly distinguishable from homosexuality and other groups of sexual "aberrations." The German sexologist, who was an openly gay cross-dresser, suggested that there were five separate categories of cross-dressers or "transvestites." His categories were based on sexual behavior instead of gender and included heterosexual, bisexual, homosexual, narcissistic and asexual transvestites. Although still placing more emphasis on sex instead of gender, Hirschfeld's transvestite categories at least opened the door for new categories of cross-dressers and transgenderists to emerge. Because of Hirschfeld's work, the term *transvestite* became widely used by sex researchers who used it to describe transgenderists, cross-dressers and transsexuals. As a category, transsexualism remained embedded in the category of *transvestite* until the 1960s, when the term *transsexual* first appeared in the *Index Medicus*.

Havelock Ellis, dissatisfied with Hirschfeld's categories of transvestites and psychoanalytic theories of transgenderism, was the first sexologist to make the distinction between individuals who simply enjoy dressing as members of the "opposite" sex and individuals who desire to live as or become members of the "opposite" sex. Ellis argued that Hirschfeld's categories failed to cover the wide spectrum of cross-dressers. Further, Ellis objected to Hirschfeld's sub-title of his book, "The Erotic Impulse of Disguise." Rather, he argued that for some transgenderists, the act of cross-dressing was an "emancipative act" that freed them from their social "disguise." Ellis argued that for those who believed they were born into the "wrong body," the act of cross-dressing confirmed their true self. His new category of "aesthetic inversion," under his category of "Eonism," delineated two types of aesthetic inverts that parallel today's transvestites and cross-dressers and transsexuals and transgenderists. He described the two categories as:

One, the most common kind, in which the inversion is mainly confined to the sphere of clothing, and the other, less common, but more complete, in which cross-dressing is regarded with comparative indifference but the subject so identifies himself with those of his physical and psychic traits which recall the opposite sex that he feels really to belong to that sex although he has no delusion regarding his anatomical conformation. (Ellis 36)

The "most common kind" refers to transvestites and cross-dressers, while the less common category of aesthetic inversion describes the plight of transsexuals and transgenderists. Years before the development of sex-reassignment surgery, Ellis described the case of a 35-year-old biological male who longed to be a woman. Ellis published her letter expressing a transsexual desire:

...it is as if the soul of a woman had been born in a male body...my secret ambition—to dress and live as a lady when I grew up...I really desired to be a woman, and not merely dress as one...I would undergo an operation if the result would be to give me a beautiful or attractive female form with full womanhood. (76-86)

Although Ellis distinguished the category of transsexuals and transgenderists from other cross-dressers and fought psychoanalytic assertions that cross-dressers were delusional and homosexual, it took almost 40 years before "transsexuals" were recognized as a separate category.

In sum, the category of transsexualism emerged out of the categories of homosexuality, cross-dressing and transvestism. In the late 1800s, as sex became increasingly medicalized, two major beliefs about transgenderists and cross-dressers emerged. The conservative ideology influenced by the writings of Krafft-Ebing and the early psychoanalysts did not make distinctions between types of cross-dressers. Krafft-Ebing viewed transgenderism as a path to moral insanity. The psychoanalysts argued that transgenderists and cross-dressers were really latent homosexuals, plagued by delusions caused by a failure to resolve the Oedipal complex. Advocates of both views sought to medically "cure" cross-dressers and transgenderists.

In comparison, sex reformers like Ellis and Hirschfeld recognized different categories of cross-dressers and transgenderists. Ellis' category of "aesthetic inversion," which emphasized the difference between transvestites and transsexuals, anticipated the modern category of transsexualism. Most significantly, Hirschfeld and Ellis placed less emphasis on "cures" and more emphasis on fighting for legal reform and public tolerance for cross-dressers and transgenderists.

Sex-Change Surgery 1920-1950

New experiments and technology in sex-change surgery from the 1920s through the 1950s helped further differentiate transsexuals from other cross-dressers. The first recorded modern attempt to surgically transform a male into a woman took place in Denmark during the 1920s. Lili Elbe, a male Danish painter, underwent a series of obscure genital operations, including the implantation of female ovaries. Even though Lili Elbe died soon after the operation, the event recorded in a book by Neil Hoyer impacted the consciousness of countless individuals in America who felt trapped in the "wrong body."

Since Ellis' category of "aesthetic inversion" was never widely used, the medical category of transvestite included not only individuals who felt they were members of the "opposite" sex, but also those individuals who wanted to be surgically transformed. As reports of sex-change surgery spread, the cross-gender identified "transvestite" became medically identified with the desire for surgical transformation. The case of Lili Elbe's change of sex published in the 1930s anticipated not only a future surgical "cure," but also a medically dependent relationship for the cross-gender identified transvestite.

The first official scientific sex-change operation reportedly was performed in Germany by Abraham in 1931. This technology was unfortunately used on unconsenting adolescent boys by sadistic Nazi doctors during World War II. One male-to-woman surgical victim desperately and without success tried to get the sex-change operation reversed (see Raymond). Another casualty of the Nazis was Hirschfeld's entire transvestite research records, burned along with his clinic. Hirschfeld himself was severely beaten and left for dead by the Nazis. He escaped to France, only to die while trying to rebuild his sex clinic. Transgender activist Phyllis Randolph Frye maintains that the majority of people who were murdered during the beginning of the Nazi Holocaust while wearing pink triangles were the transgendered of all sexual orientations.

After World War II, castration surgery, thought to "cure" homosexuals and transgenderists, became popular in the Scandinavian countries, particularly in Holland, Denmark and Sweden. U.S. males victimized by social condemnation and threats of violence often traveled abroad seeking castration surgery. Scattered reports of the "castration cure" appeared in America after the turn of the century, particularly in St. Louis, Kansas and Chicago. Both Ellis and Hirschfeld warned against castration surgery, claiming it would not inhibit sexual or gender desires. One rationale for performing castration surgery was a belief that transgenderism and homosexuality were inherited conditions.

Therefore it was argued that it would keep social "deviants" and "misfits" from procreating. Since gays and transgenderists were thought to be little more than criminals, it is no surprise that "castration surgery" was also routinely used in the Scandinavian countries and to a lesser extent in America as a punishment for sex offenders. Castration, and other genital surgery performed to alter behavior, reinforced the deeply ingrained idea that gender behavior and sexual preference emanated somehow from the sex organs.

McCarthyism, Alfred Kinsey and Transgenderism

American sexologist Alfred Kinsey, though not credited for it, made important contributions to theories of transsexualism and transgenderism. One year before D.O. Cauldwell allegedly coined the term *transsexual*, Kinsey had already used the term *transsexual* in one of his studies. In his 1948 study, *The Sexual Behavior in the Human Male*, Kinsey criticized the use of the term *transsexual* as a synonym for homosexual because it implied that homosexuals were "neither male nor female, but persons of a mixed sex." Few if any critics took notice of Kinsey's observation, which differentiated transgenderists from lesbians and gays. Instead, Kinsey's observation that 37 percent of all the males in his study engaged in a homosexual experience to orgasm set off a bomb in homophobic America, obscuring many of his other findings.

A major reason for the overt public reaction to Kinsey's finding was the social and political climate of the early 1950s. Most Americans in the U.S., fearful after World War II, tried to insulate themselves from the grim realities of the war by reviving outdated, "traditional" sex roles and creating "nuclear" families. The middle class fled to the suburbs and found salvation in consumerism. Meanwhile, a growing McCarthyism exploited this post-war fear and anxiety by creating the image of Communist "enemies" that had not only infiltrated the government but also the family. As the McCarthy hysteria grew, fueled by social and political anxieties, anyone perceived as different became targeted as a possible enemy.

In the early 1950s, the homosexual was targeted by McCarthyism as a "sexually perverted" bogeyman eager to betray the American government and harm the American family. A 1950 *New York Times* news story documents how homosexuals were targeted as the new enemy of America:

...Gabrielson, Republican National Chairman, asserted today that sexual perverts who have infiltrated our Government in recent years were perhaps as dangerous as the actual Communists. (Katz 141)

Homophobic members of the witch-hunt used Kinsey's report that most individuals were not exclusively heterosexual or homosexual but somewhere in between, to create a moral panic. They argued that the homosexual, like the Communist, posed a direct threat to both national and personal security. Foes of the "homosexual menace" tried to portray themselves as good heterosexual Americans. Most didn't even know what constituted a "homosexual." Frantic, they resurrected stereotypes of homosexuals as cross-dressers and transgenderists. As a result, persons suspected of violating mainstream sex or gender roles were targeted. As the most visually blatant, the cross-dresser and transgenderist were used as symbols of homosexuality. As a result, "masculine" appearing and/or acting females, as well as "feminine" appearing and/or acting males, regardless of their sexual preference, became major targets of the hysterical witch-hunt. Many were forced out of their government jobs.

Hate speech originating from Congress and the State department used the stereotype that all lesbians and gays resembled or wanted to be the "opposite" sex. Congressman Miller perpetrated this myth by describing gay males as: "...proud queens...not ashamed of the trick nature played on them. It is found the cycle of these individuals...follows the menstrual period of women" (Katz 154-55). In the same vein, lesbians were also commonly stereotyped as being "masculine": "...The mannish women...display themselves, strut around in fairy joints...on the make for the same girls the he-wolves are chasing" (154). As a result of the witch-hunt, thousands of transgenderists were forced into economic, social and personal ruin. In 1955 the *New York Times* reported 8,008 individuals were separated as "security risks" during the first 16 months of the security program. The records show "5912 individuals...dismissed or deemed suspect for reasons unrelated to disloyalty or subversion" and historians assume that the majority were accused of homosexuality (Katz 160).

McCarthyism fueled the raging homophobia in America, collapsing categories of sex and gender in the popular imagination. Kinsey's 1953 study on *The Sexual Behavior in the Human Female,* distinguished like Ellis before him, two types of transvestites. The "partial transvestite," the prototype for today's cross-dresser, was described as a male who on occasion adopted women's clothing and/or a feminine gender role. The second type of transvestite, the "true transvestite," is the blueprint description of the modern transsexual and/or transgenderist. Kinsey described the "true transvestite" as a cross-gender-identified person who desired to live in the opposite gender role full-time. True transvestites, Kinsey argued, were persons...who try to identify with the opposite sex in their work as well as in their homes, at all times of the day and through all days of the year. (Kinsey, Pomeroy, Martin and Gebhard 679-80)

Like other progressives before him, Kinsey did not think cross-dressers or transgenderists were "sick." He disdained "moral classifications," concentrating instead on whether members of sexual categories were accorded social advantages or disadvantages. Kinsey also pointed out that transvestites existed in almost all societies.

From the 1940s through the early 1950s, Kinsey began to focus his attention on the so-called sexual underworld of transgenderists and cross-dressers. In 1953 Kinsey proposed a wide-scale study of the actual occurrence of transgenderists in the United States. No doubt such a study would have differentiated transvestites and transsexuals and influenced our attitudes and beliefs about gender. To date, no study of this magnitude has been undertaken.

Unfortunately, in 1954, due to pressures from political conservatives and right wing fundamentalist Christian groups, the Rockefeller Foundation, responsible for funding Kinsey's sex clinic for 12 years, withdrew all financial support. It is hard not to draw a parallel between the Nazis' destruction of Hirschfeld's sex clinic and the end of Kinsey's research caused by conservatives and right wing fundamentalist Christian groups. An associate of Kinsey's, C.A. Tripp, commenting on the withdrawal of the $50,000 a year from Kinsey's research by the Foundation, reveals how they not only gave in to right wing fundamentalist pressure groups but also bought them off. Tripp charges:

At the same time, as if by some combination of apology and bribery the Foundation quieted one of the noisiest groups of critics...by making it one of the largest grants in its history—$525,000 to...Union Theological Seminary, to aid in the development of vital religious leadership. (Tripp 233)

Transsexuals, the U.S. and the 1950s

Transsexualism and transgenderism were introduced into American consciousness in the 1950s by two significant events. The first was Christine Jorgenson's return home to America after her "sex-change" surgery in Denmark. Not only was Jorgenson America's first publicly recognized transsexual, her story was also the most news-covered event of 1953. Secondly, Harry Benjamin, considered the American father of transsexualism, had his transsexual research generously funded by the Erikson Foundation. Newspapers and magazines were filled with photos and accounts of Jorgenson's story. The popular headline, "Ex G.I. George Jorgenson returns home as blonde bombshell, Christine Jorgenson" was circulated around the world. Even though Jorgenson was referred to as a "transvestite with sex-change surgery," the new category of transsexualism was about to emerge.

The same year that Jorgenson became a media sensation, endocrinologist Harry Benjamin presented a paper on transsexualism at a major American medical conference. He used the term *transsexual* to describe individuals who felt "trapped in the wrong" body. Although the term caught the attention of some members of the medical establishment, ultimately it was the media's popularization of the word *transsexual* that not only encouraged the widespread medical use of the term but also forever implanted it in the American consciousness. Jorgenson and Benjamin paved the way for the emergence of transsexualism not only as a distinct category, but also as a distinct identity. The 1950s marked the beginning of America's public and medical recognition of individuals who felt they were members of the "opposite" sex as a distinct category separate from other categories of cross-dressers.

Contemporary Categories Confused with Transsexualism

In the 1950s through the 1960s transsexualism was presented to the American public as a medical condition requiring treatment. Jorgenson's condition was explained by her doctors as a "hormonal problem." However, there is little evidence to back this diagnosis; rather, evidence suggests her physicians used the hormonal argument as a means of encouraging her social acceptance. Defining transsexualism as an illness served to elicit some public sympathy and curiosity. But it also reinforced in post-McCarthy America the myth that any gay male putting on a dress or acting "feminine" was a homosexual who really wanted to be a woman, implying surgery could cure homosexuals.

One way the U.S. and other countries have controlled so-called gender deviants is to categorize them. Doing so creates hierarchies of behavior under which individuals are classified and labeled. Although this approach may be useful from a diagnostic standpoint, i.e., for insurance purposes, it does not help most individuals understand themselves any better. The process of defining behavior in most cases operates more to confine behavior by relegating it to narrow categories. For example, in *DSM III* and *DSM III-R* transsexuals are distinguished from the category of transvestites on the basis of their desire for sex-reassignment surgery.

What happens when a transvestite decides to have surgery? Does it imply that he or she must adopt all the "symptoms" of transsexualism in order to be considered a serious candidate for surgery? As Anne Bolin suggests, strictly defined and enforced categories of behavior inhibit individuals from expressing or revealing behavior that is not included in specific categories. In the area of cross-dressing, it is simplistic to assume that all behavior will fit neatly into one category without overlap.

In my own research, I have encountered life-long transvestites, drag-queens, cross-dressers and transgenderists who sometimes cross gender lines into transsexualism. This is not to imply that a transsexual is lurking in the heart of every drag-queen, cross-dresser and transgendered person, but that in some cases cross-gender feelings may expand or change beyond the bounds of one category. I suggest that we view gender as a mercurial construct at the mercy of sociopolitical ideologies. As such, gender is always in a state of negotiation between the individual and society. America's dominant gender attitudes toward cross-dressers and transgenderists are heavily influenced by religious, psychological, and popular culture gender ideologies. As products of enculturation, cross-dressers and transgenderists often regard their own behavior as "sick" and "deviant" and experience great conflict, guilt and self-hate. Instead of locking individuals into narrow categories, it may be more useful to delineate the degrees of cross-gender-identity individuals are experiencing, as well as the social, psychological and political impact of their behavior. Although the category of *transsexual* signifies an individual with a cross-gender identity who desires or has had some medical intervention, numerous other categories and groups of individuals are confused with transsexuals.

Some of the biological conditions confused with transsexualism include "hermaphroditism" and "intersexed individuals." True hermaphrodites are rare. Most cases of hermaphroditism consist of individuals who are born with combinations of male and female genitals and/or secondary sex characteristics. Usually one sex is more dominant. The ancient Greeks and other cultures considered the hermaphrodite to be a sacred symbol. However, real infant hermaphrodites in most ancient western societies were routinely eliminated. Navajos in the Southwestern U.S. were an exception in their reverence toward the "Nadle," their male-to-women transgenderists, who they maintained were really hermaphrodites.[5]

Intersexed individuals are usually born sexually ambiguous at birth due to hormonal, gonadal, chromosomal, and/or genital contradictions. Some intersexed persons develop secondary sex characteristics of the "opposite" sex during puberty. In the U.S. transsexual surgery was developed from surgical techniques used on intersexed persons, who in some cases were raised as the "wrong" gender and after puberty had surgery to coincide with the gender of rearing.

Besides biological conditions, sexual preference is also commonly confused with transsexualism, particularly homosexuality and bisexuality. *Homosexual* refers to individuals with a sexual and/or political preference for members of the same sex. Many individuals with same-sex preferences refer to themselves as *gays* and *lesbians*, instead of the medically derived term "homosexuals." Like transsexualism, today, homosexuality was once thought to be an illness. Unlike transsexualism, homosexuality was deleted from *DSM III* in 1973. Bisexuals are individuals whose sexual preference includes males and females. Generally the desire for one sex is greater at particular times. Freud and others maintain that we are all basically bisexual.

In addition to biological conditions and sexual preferences confused with transsexualism, there is also a preponderance of media-created terms that have been used to describe cross-dressers and transgenderists. Some of the more common terms, though not all-inclusive, are *gender chameleons, gender blenders* and *gender fuckers*. These terms are usually applied to persons in popular culture whose appearances incorporate the "other" gender in some way. In *Gender Chameleons* Steven Simels illustrates how frequently heavy metal male rock icons appear in full "feminine" make-up and hair-dos. However, as a defense against being labeled "feminine" males they usually accent their "drag" attire with a "kick-ass" attitude. This image combines a "feminine" exterior with a "masculine" interior for maximum commercial appeal. The popular Seattle band, Nirvana, appear in house dresses (grunge drag) and proceed to trash the set in their 1993 award-winning music video "In Bloom." During the 1993 MTV music video awards ceremony, lead singer Kurt Cobain, when accepting an award for the music video, unzipped his pants and grabbed his penis, an affirmation of his "masculinity." Female rock and pop stars also incorporate degrees of gender-crossing into their public performances. Among the most notable at present is Madonna, known for combining elements of masculinity and femininity into her performances in order to push the audience's emotional buttons. Most recently she appeared in drag in a racist and sexist opening act "The Girlie Show" for MTV's 1993 video awards ceremony.

Gender terms, ranging from *flaming faggot, radical* fair (sic), *butch, femme* and *diesel dike*, evolved in the gay and lesbian communities to the more general term *androgyny,* all describe individuals expressing and experimenting with various psychological and physical representations of gender.

Androgynous refers to the psychological blending of culturally conditioned "masculine" and "feminine" traits. In the early stages of the contemporary Women's Movement, it was used as a concept implying movement toward equality, but was later discarded by feminists who complained it merely reinforced the bipolar gender system (see Heilbrun).

However, since the late 1970s the media has picked up on the term "androgyny," using it to describe individuals who blend cultural stereotypes of masculinity and femininity in their appearance. Entertainers dubbed by the media as androgynous in the mid 1980s through the early 1990s included Michael Jackson, David Bowie, Annie Lennox, Boy George, Prince, Grace Jones, Stephen Tyler, Axle Rose, and Madonna. Two of the more recent additions to the pantheon of media dubbed androgyny is k.d. lang who plays with images of male and female drag, much to the delight of her audiences and "supermodel" pop star RuPaul. Carl Jung's ideas about psychological archetypes, recycled in the 1960s and early 1970s, asserted that within every female is a man, referred to as the *animus* and within every male is a woman referred to as the *anima*. Jungian analysts suggest that these largely unconscious psychological constructs must be incorporated into the conscious mind in order for the individual to become a "whole," or well-integrated person.

Like the idealized androgyne, the Native American transgenderist is said to incorporate both "masculine" and "feminine" traits (see Williams, *The Spirit and the Flesh*; Roscoe). Anthropologists commonly use the term *berdache* to describe Native American males who choose to incorporate feminine traits and/or live in the role of a woman. Some current and past Native American cultures not only accept but revere transgendered male-women as sacred. Williams proposed the term "amazon" be applied to describe the less visible Native American females who reject traditional "feminine" roles and choose to live in the "opposite" gender.[6]

Transgenderists exist in most societies from the Siberian shamans to the Arab Xaniths, to the Hawaiian "mahus" and the Native American "berdaches" and "amazons." Unlike contemporary American drag-queens, cross-dressers, transgenderists and transsexuals who are frequently objects of scorn and attack, transgender persons in other cultures were and are often thought to possess magical powers. Some occupy the role of healers or shamans. Sometimes the gender role is a transitory one, as in the Omani who live on the Arabian peninsula. Transgender Omani males often dress and act as women when young. Sometimes they engage in prostitution with males in order to save money to marry females. In later life, some return to a transgender role. Some societies, such as the Hawaiians, allow only one or two males to occupy the "sacred" transgender position of the *mahu* (see Archer; Kellis).

Drag-Queens

In contemporary America, the two categories most related to and confused with transsexuals are drag-queens and transvestites. The drag-queen is probably the most recognized cross-dresser in America. Drag-queens became particularly visible in America during World War II when enlisted men in dresses, make-up, heels and wigs were paid to entertain the troops. Drag, the dressing up to varying degrees and/or incorporating the gestures of the "opposite" sex, has been traced back to ancient Greece and played an important role in rites of passage. Mircea Eliade documents that, on the wedding night, brides and grooms in ancient Greece switched clothing before consummating their marriage.

In America, the stereotypical drag-queen is a male acting or performing in varying degrees as a woman. Such drag often includes "big hair," a huge bosom, tons of make-up, flashy clothing, high heels, exaggerated gestures, voice alteration and extreme verbal agility and wit. Drag might also include cosmetic surgery, hormones, and/or electrolysis. Unlike the male-to-woman transsexual, the goal of most drag-queens is not to become a woman, but to impersonate a woman. Drag-kings, females who impersonate males, have just started to receive media attention. Some of the better known entertainers who incorporated drag into their performances included Judy Garland, Lily Tomlin and Judy Tenuta, known for her great Elvis impersonation. Popular drag in America ranges from amateur lip-sync impersonations in gay bars to professional female impersonators playing the straight clubs, to political camp.

Drag in the U.S. is usually associated with entertainment and/or comedy. Because it can potentially threaten traditional sex and gender roles, a crucial aspect of many male drag shows playing to mainstream audiences is to demonstrate their maleness, usually accomplished by pulling off a wig or exposing a male chest. Although viewed as threatening and thrilling to mainstream audiences, drag-queens and kings often exist peripherally within the gay and lesbian subculture and are treated with ambivalence. Queens are frequently judged harshly by gay males who accuse them of resurrecting the stereotype that all gay males are effeminate and really desire to be women and by women who feel drag is insulting to women for reinforcing stereotypes. Similar charges have been hurled at drag-kings and butch lesbians by the lesbian community.[7] As stated earlier, gay males dressed as women trying to attract men occupy a precarious position.

Gay folklorist Joseph Goodwin describes the loneliness that plagues drag-queens in contemporary America: "Gay men don't want us because we look real, and straight men don't want us because we aren't real" (Goodwin 59). "Cheri," a 28-year-old, local, well-known drag-queen who works at *glam drag*, a term meaning outdoing females at the glamour game and being concerned with the creation of the external appearance over the content of the act, lamented that most gay males didn't understand her. She observed that as a gay male dressed as a woman, trying to attract a gay male, she occupied a precarious position. Cheri shared her dilemma:

I really have problems with the gay men I pick up while doing drag shows at the gay bars. I always tell them that when I'm in drag that I'm creating an illusion. What they see is not what they get. Externally they see the illusion of Cher or Marilyn, but they don't see the foam rubber breasts duct taped to my chest, or the eight pair of panty hose with padding, or the pounds of make-up, or the fake eyelashes. When I greet them at my door dressed as a male they are disappointed. I want to be with a male as a man, not as a woman. (pers. comm. 1989)

In *Female Impersonators in America* Esther Newton argues that, because of the double social stigma of being gay and a drag-queen, most queens are relegated to a state of economic powerlessness. For many, the only "power" they feel is when performing.

A more aggressive and political form of drag is "camp." In camp, instead of relying solely on how one looks, humor is used as a weapon against sex and gender oppression. The Stonewall Riots of 1969, which ushered in the Gay and Lesbian Liberation Movement, were led by angry and campy drag-queens and lesbian butches, sick and tired of continual police harassment against themselves and their gay and lesbian bars. In *Persistent Desire* Joan Nestle points out that in New York and other cities it was not uncommon for cross-dressers to be arrested, brutalized, and sometimes raped for not wearing two or three pieces of clothing that were considered "appropriate" to their biological sex.

Joseph Goodwin calls *camp* an aggressive form of drag that "provides a way for the colonized to defy enforced sex and gender roles." Most significantly, on a political level, camp suggests that if males can pass as women and females as men, then gender may be an artificial category. Amber, a British drag-queen who does camp, underscores this point in her assertion that:

People should realize that the female image, like the male image is something that has been created. It's not a natural thing. When you're born you don't pop out wearing make-up and a dress do you, or a man's suit ? (Kirk and Heath 134)

Other terms related to drag are she-males and female impersonators. She-males are biological males who usually undergo differing degrees of electrolysis, breast implants, and/or other cosmetic surgery in order to appear more "feminine." Most stop short of sex-reassignment surgery, preferring to retain their penises. In street slang they are referred to as "hormone queens" because they take female hormones. Their existence is often more tenuous than glam and camp queens in the gay and lesbian community. Part of this tenuousness is because a number of she-males work as professional prostitutes. There are also class distinctions among female impersonators.

As anthropologist Esther Newton notes, most amateur queens are looked down on by the "pros," because of their excessive, loud appearances and life styles. Some of the professional impersonators in Newton's 1979 study called amateur queens "street fairies." Another difference between professional and amateur female impersonators is that the "pros" usually only dress while performing.

Transvestites

The cross-dressing and sometimes cross-gender-identified group most frequently confused with the category of transsexuals and perhaps their closest kin are transvestites. Since transvestism is a medically derived term, many members of the gender community prefer the term *cross-dresser* which is less stigmatizing. The *DSM III-R* diagnostic criteria for *transvestic fetishism* include:

Over a period of at least six months, in a heterosexual male, recurrent intense sexual urges and sexually arousing fantasies involving cross-dressing.

The person has acted on these urges, or is markedly distressed by them. (*DSM III-R* 164)

While this definition stereotypes transvestites as sick, fetishistic, heterosexual and male, a different interpretation of cross-dressing behavior is offered by transvestites themselves. Most male transvestites maintain that they cross-dress in order to relax and gain relief from the demanding male role and/or to express their feminine self. A large number also state that they cross-dress initially for erotic purposes. A major concern among most clinical researchers of transvestism focuses on their heterosexuality. This consensus among clinicians and some Tri-Ess (a national transvestite, cross-dresser organization) members is contrary to my findings. My research, gathered from over 100 local male transvestites and cross-dressers ranging in age from 25 to 58, indicated sexual preferences ranging across heterosexual, bisexual, asexual and gay and lesbian lines. However, most transvestites in the early stages of coming-out assert that they are strictly heterosexuals. Yet, some later report having fantasies of being with a male when dressed as a woman.

The idea that most transvestites are heterosexual has long been promoted by the "grand dame of transvestitism," Virginia Prince. Prince, a biochemist and self-defined heterosexual transvestite, launched a public relations campaign in the early 1960s in order to educate professionals and the general public about transvestism. One of Prince's motives was to make the transvestite more socially acceptable in the aftermath of McCarthy's homosexual propaganda campaign of the 1950s. In the 1970s, Prince described and defined the heterosexual transvestite as a "femmiphile," a "lover of the feminine." Prince differentiated reasons for cross-dressing among drag-queens and transvestites. She stressed that drag-queens dress to attract other males, while femmiphiles dress to express their inner feminine selves. Some cross-dressers accuse Prince of ignoring the erotic components of cross-dressing in her writings. Instead, Prince maintains, she focuses on clothing as a manifestation of an inner state and she suggests:

As long as we wear the uniform of one gender—clothing etc...we can only experience that half of the possible world that is appropriate to that gender. But when we change clothes...we can experience a whole new, previously unknown way of seeing and experiencing our world. ("Sexual vs. Genderal Identity" 89)

As the matriarch of cross-dressers and transgenderists, in the 1960s, Prince founded an organization for the expression of the "feminine" self, now known as Tri-Ess. Today, as a large national organization, Tri-Ess provides a safe environment where heterosexual cross-dressers can dress and socialize with other cross-dressers and their partners. In addition to Tri-Ess, numerous other groups for transgenderists, cross-dressers and transsexuals exist locally, nationally and internationally. *Tapestry*, a magazine written for and by cross-dressers and transgenderists, lists over 200 national cross-dresser and transgender groups. Organizations for cross-dressers also exist world-wide in countries including New Zealand, England, France, Canada, Australia, Japan and Egypt. Many of the U.S. groups sponsor nationwide social and educational activities for cross-dressers and friends of the gender community. One such activity, and the most attended annual "Texas 'T' Party" includes presentations of new research from the psycho-medical and academic communities, seminars for partners of cross-dressers, tips on how to pass, a safe environment to dress and be real in, political forums, and lots of entertainment. Jessa B., a local transgenderist who attended the 1991 'T' Party, reported the most important aspect of the event for her was the complete "atmosphere of acceptance where we were free to be ourselves" (pers. comm. 1991). Numerous events in the U.S., sponsored by the gender community, for and about cross-dressing, transgenderism and transsexualism from the "Fantasia Fair" to the International Gender Education Foundation's annual conference to The First International Conference on Transgender Law, all provide information, acceptance, and forums for new ideas for participants. As the featured speaker of the 1993 Texas "T" Party I was thrilled to see the level of political activism among many of the participants as well as the level of healthy individuals, many of whom were freed from "the closet" for a few days.

Unfortunately, many researchers investigating cross-dressing and transvestism ignore these growing social networks and continue to concentrate instead on the etiology of transvestism, hoping to find a "cure." Most psychological and medical studies about transvestism, though sparse, blame the mother or argue that transvestites were forcibly dressed at an early age. Evidence supporting the "forced to dress" theory advanced by Robert Stoller is very weak, reflecting more, perhaps, an internalized fantasy based on cultural taboos. This fantasy can be found in mass-produced as well as self-authored cross-dressing literature.

Another issue frequently ignored or trivialized by gender researchers is the existence of the female transvestite or cross-dresser. Few case studies of the female-to-man transvestite are documented. Most researchers contend it is generally an exclusively male phenomenon. Reasons usually cited for this assumption include that it is socially acceptable and even fashionable for a female to wear men's clothing; women's clothing is taboo for males; and finally, that women's clothing is highly eroticized in contemporary American culture. Although these issues are important, we must be careful to avoid a male-bias, which regards female behavior as unimportant. This bias can occur if one accepts dated cultural sex stereotypes, such as the idea that females are not as sexual or are not as easily aroused by visual stimuli as males are. Yet one of the self-defined female transvestites I know, "Mackie," observed that she became highly aroused while wearing Calvin Klein jockey shorts. But we must not become bogged down in psycho-medical definitions of transvestites. Looking only for patterns of arousal may obscure other important sociocultural aspects of transvestism and cross-dressing.

My research, largely drawn from the Albuquerque gender community and from numerous national contacts, confirms that there is a wide variation of behavior found among transvestites and cross-dressers. It is impossible and highly erroneous to say all transvestites are alike. However, there are a few characteristics many share. For most, cross-dressing began at an early age (5-9) with a relative's clothing and it was done in secret. At puberty most transvestites developed a strong masturbatory and erotic response to being cross-dressed. This erotic connection between the clothing and orgasm has led the medical model to view transvestites as 'fetishistic.' One of the difficulties involved in studying transvestites' behavior is that until recently, most of it was done in secret for fear of stigmatization. It is estimated that only a small proportion of cross-dressers join support or social groups.

The diagnostic criterion used in defining transvestism as sexually arousing fails to note that there are many arousing stimuli for most female and male adolescents. A more interesting aspect of cross-dressing may be that the more individuals cross-dress, the more likely they are to develop their cross-gender identities and their desire to cross-live. This may in part be due to finding an accepting environment in which to express the "true" self. Often the growing cross-gender identity is signified by the adoption of a cross-gender name. Cross-dressing among transvestites varies in frequency and amount. Members of the Albuquerque cross-dressers support group report dressing anywhere from twice a year to daily. Some members wear only women's lingerie or men's jockey shorts under their clothing, while others work hard to pass as members of the "other" gender. Some male transvestites and cross-dressers maintain they will never give up their "masculine" selves and view their "femme" personalities as occasional escapes from the rigid male role. Yet over a period of years, as their femme persona develops, many transvestites and cross-dressers attempt to live full-time in the "opposite" gender role.

Psychologist Richard Docter labels transvestites who desire to live more and more in the cross-gender role "marginal transvestites," who, he theorizes, will eventually become "secondary transsexuals." Docter has also begun to use the term *transgenderist,* originally coined by Virginia Prince, to describe those who choose to live in the "opposite" gender role full-time without surgery. Docter uses *transgenderist* to describe cross-dressers who desire only rarely to live in the gender congruent with their biological sex. What is disturbing here is that a self-generated term among transvestites is being used as a medically stigmatizing term.

Large numbers of cross-dressers are coming out of the closet nationwide in cross-dresser groups. As of this writing, Albuquerque has two such groups. The Albuquerque cross-dresser and transgenderist support group is open to all cross-dressers, transsexuals and transgenderists, regardless of their sexual preferences and "Fiesta" a local chapter of Tri-Ess started in Albuquerque in 1988. Fiesta is primarily a social group for heterosexual transvestites and their partners.

Although there are no exact numbers of how many cross-dressers exist, when the Albuquerque cross-dressers support group ran a one-day ad in the local newspaper classifieds advertising the group, the community center where the meetings are held reported over 60 phone calls in one day. "Ricky," a former member of the group who has since moved to another state, related the following incident as a measure of how many cross-dressers and transgenderists there might be in contemporary American society:

I was out playing golf with some of the guys I work with, when I stepped into a hole and broke my leg. In the ambulance on the way to the hospital all I could think about was being caught in 'female' underclothes...As the doctor cut through my trousers, exposing my black panties, he laughed and shook his head and said "you too?" (pers. comm. 1987)

Ricky interpreted the doctor's comment to mean that he was also a cross-dresser.

The most recent research on transvestism and cross-dressing to emerge from the psycho-medical model is Richard Docter's 1988 study on Tri-Ess members, in which he concludes that most transvestites and cross-dressers are heterosexual married men who experience gender envy because of social taboos prohibiting their dressing in women's clothing. Docter suggests that cross-dressing creates an altered state of consciousness that reinforces subsequent episodes of dressing, ultimately leading to a slow development of a female personality that in some cases completely "overthrows" the male personality, leading to secondary transsexualism.

In analyzing Docter's conclusions on a sociocultural level, we must question the way he uses the term *secondary transsexualism*. Within the context of his work, secondary transsexualism is presented like a dread disease that transvestites might catch if they develop their feminine gender identities too much. This suggests a hierarchical ranking in which being a transvestite is valued more than being a transsexual! Docter's insistence that most transvestites are heterosexual men is also suspect. Why is this aspect so important? Because of the fact that his population was drawn from Tri-Ess groups, which limit membership to heterosexual cross-dressers, his conclusion should come as no surprise.

I discussed Docter's findings with members of the local support group, which includes two individuals who participated in his study. Both expressed dismay with his findings. One member, Jerry, a 50-year-old male-to-woman cross-dresser from California, questioned Doctor's assertion that cross-dressing produces an altered state of consciousness. Jerry stated that:

I'm sick of the psycho-babble. Anything can produce an altered state of consciousness. It's a catch-all term. The bottom line of why I cross-dress is because it's fun. Period. (pers. comm. 1990)

This comment was followed by laughter, as other group members confirmed Jerry's comment and added "we dress to express who we really are, instead of who we are told to be" (pers. comm. 1990).

Transgenderism

Often we lose sight of the individual with clinical categorizations and rigid definitions. Historically, categories of sex and gender have operated on two levels. First, as Foucault and Plummer suggest, they have stigmatized, dehumanized, condemned and justified the barbaric torture of whole groups of people as "sick" and "deviant" simply because they did not conform to the status quo. Second, as gay activist Jefferey Escoffier asserts, the categories and definitions also helped mobilize and organize stigmatized groups to fight further stigmatizing, medicalizing, and stereotyping of their behavior. Ultimately, some of these stigmatized minorities have formed social movements, like Gay and Lesbian Liberation, to demand their civil rights. Most individuals identified with the different categories I have listed express the desire to have the freedom to explore their sex or gender roles. Being guided by everyone else's definitions of who they are does not allow this. As some members of the gender community observe, it is time to stop letting everyone from psychological and medical "experts" to television talk show hosts define us.

No doubt the most important categorization and labeling is self-generated. Empowering instead of disabling, Virginia Prince's term *transgenderist* accomplishes this. Members of the gender community first used it to define individuals who courageously cross socially defined gender borders full-time, although it is sometimes also applied to part-time gender-crossers. Members of the gender community also use the term *cross-dresser* as a non-stigmatizing and all inclusive term which unites members of the gender community. Such terms inspire the courage to be. Most recently Phyllis Randolph Frye, an inspiring transgendered activist, has suggested that transgendered be an umbrella term that includes transsexualism. However, there have been, should be and will continue to be struggles against allowing others to label and define transgenderists and their reality. Perhaps the category producing the most battle scars is the medical category of transsexualism. In the case of transsexuals who have been diagnosed and categorized, once surgically reassigned they cannot turn back. Much of the medical and legal pressure for sex-reassignment surgery is based on the persistent American belief that somehow gender emanates from the genitals.

Chapter Three

Transsexual Ideology:
The Medicalization of Gender in America

In *Sex by Prescription* Thomas Szasz refers to transsexualism as a "condition tailor-made for our surgical-technological age" (86). As a critic of the complete medicalization of transsexualism, he suggests that instead of supporting or opposing "sex change" surgery, sexologists would be better off "...scrutinizing the nature of transsexualism" (89). Pointing to the arbitrariness of defining transsexualism as a psychological "disorder," Szasz observes that

If a man cuts off his own penis psychiatrists call him a schizophrenic, but if he can persuade a surgeon to cut it off for him, then they call him a transsexual. (74)

Although Szasz's critique is insightful, it fails to take into account that self-castration is often considered a "medical symptom" of transsexualism.

The term *transsexual*, used by Cauldwell in 1949 and brought to the attention of the medical community in the early 1950s by Benjamin, was initially rejected for use by the medical profession. As Lothstein demonstrates, the American media's popularization of the word *transsexual* led to its subsequent clinical incorporation and acceptance. However, the concept and use of the word *transsexual* continues to be the source of great controversy among the different disciplines involved in transsexual research, as well as among transsexuals themselves. Much of this controversy centers on the medical relationship established between transsexualism and sex-reassignment surgery. The controversy includes the volatile issues of who should be sexually reassigned as well as whether sex reassignment surgery (SRS) is really rehabilitative.

Although there still exists much confusion about the actual meaning of the word *transsexual*, most members of the psycho-medical and surgical community involved with transsexuals use the basic definition popularized by

Benjamin and Hamburger. Both define transsexuals as individuals "trapped in the wrong body," but have no delusion as to what biological sex they are. Benjamin and other transsexual researchers maintained that a transsexual's gender identity contradicted his or her genital anatomy. As a result, transsexuals are portrayed as victims suffering from a serious body/mind dissonance that makes them deeply depressed and highly suicidal. Treatment, including the administration of cross-sex hormones and SRS, is rationalized as a prevention against self-castration and suicide.

Christine Jorgenson's meteoric rise to tabloid stardom after her famous 1953 "sex-change" operation helped usher in the surgical age of transsexuals. Although Jorgenson's initial surgery in Denmark was incomplete by today's standards, (she had yet to have an artificial vagina constructed) her dramatic "return home" inspired major medical hospitals in the U.S.A. to offer sex reassignment surgery. Throughout both the popular and the medical literature a melodramatic portrait of Jorgenson emerged as a "sick, abnormal" cross-gender-identified male, rescued by the "miracle" of modern "medicine." Medical reports of the time describe her as a "suffering woman...trapped in the body of a man" (see Hamburger). Christian Hamburger, Jorgenson's chief physician, reported that as a result of the widespread publicity surrounding Jorgenson's case, he was deluged with thousands of requests from individuals for SRS.

Such widespread media coverage of transsexualism, besides making "good copy," forged the link between transsexualism and SRS in the medical and public mind. It has only been recently, with the increasing visibility of cross-dressing, transgender and transsexual support groups, and new sociocultural research, that the relationship between transsexualism and the medical model has finally begun to be questioned. So at last we can ask what the existence of transsexualism reveals about contemporary American gender attitudes and beliefs.

The complete medicalization of transsexuals in America began in the mid-1960s when Johns Hopkins University hospital, aided by a private grant, opened the first official gender-identity clinic in America and began accepting applicants for surgical sex reassignment. Carefully staged as a major media event, the hospital's announcement of this decision was designed to elicit public sympathy and support for what was billed as "a research project" designed to help "unfortunate individuals, trapped in the wrong body." A carefully planned *New York Times* press release describing the "altruistic" project worked to swamp the hospital with hundreds of letters from self-described transsexuals desperate for the new SRS "cure" (see Green and Money). Many Americans expressed support for the research project that planned to "rehabilitate" transsexuals who were described as "deviant." As a result of the media coverage of such medical propaganda, the image of a transsexual in the early 1960s was that of a suffering and damned person whose only salvation depended on medical intervention.

America in the mid 1960s had become a "therapeutic society." Blinded by the promise of new cures for everything and worshipful of the new trinity of medicine, psychology, and technology, few dared to question the ethics of SRS for what was described as a psychological condition. Meanwhile, the American landscape shook with the great social quakes of the Civil Rights Movement, the Anti-War Movement, the Sexual Revolution, the Contemporary Women's Movement and the beginnings of Gay and Lesbian Liberation, movements that raised questions about injustice and inequality. While contemporary feminists were rediscovering and articulating theories of sexism and gender oppression, members of the 1960s counter-culture were enraging mainstream America by blending masculinity and femininity in their external appearance. Seemingly oblivious to these cultural movements, medical teams comprised almost solely of white upper-class men in white coats searched for suitable candidates for sex-reassignment surgery. It should be no surprise that the first officially recorded sex reassignment surgery at Cook County hospital in Chicago was performed on an African-American male-to-woman transsexual. Throughout the 1960s to the mid-1970s, the transsexual remained the sole property of the medical profession.

In order to find candidates for SRS, gender-identity teams undertook the task of defining the ideal SRS candidate. Most agreed that Benjamin's concept of "primary" transsexuals who were defined as individuals who, from their earliest memories, recalled feeling like members of the "opposite" sex and consequently desired SRS would be ideal candidates for SRS. Benjamin, influenced by Kinsey's scale of sexual preference, devised a scale of cross-dressers which ranged from the periodic cross-dresser to the primary transsexual. Benjamin argued that the primary transsexual was a "real" transsexual, who could benefit from sex reassignment surgery. By the 1970s "secondary" transsexuals, the closest to primary transsexuals on the scale, who, according to Benjamin became aware of their cross-gender-identity at a later age than the primary transsexual, were also thought to be good candidates for SRS.

Today, most applicants for SRS are considered to be secondary transsexuals, as primary transsexuals are thought to be exceedingly rare.

However, primary transsexuals are still idealized as the best candidates for SRS for several reasons. First, since primary transsexuals claim they have always felt like members of the opposite sex, clinicians feel there is less of a chance that they might change their minds after surgery and sue. Second, by choosing subjects who report feeling like members of the opposite sex since their earliest memory, researchers hope to find an underlying "hidden biological" cause for transsexualism that would once and for all justify gross medical and surgical invasion into the transsexual body. However, not all primary transsexuals are eligible for SRS. In gender clinics adhering to Harry Benjamin's codes for surgery, additional proof such as the ability to live and work in the role of the "opposite" gender and psychological evaluations are required.

Numerous studies have been undertaken and millions of dollars have been spent trying to find a biological cause of transsexualism. To date, no biological etiology has been found. The most consistently popular theory, originally advanced by Hamburger and Benjamin, suggests that transsexualism is the result of prenatal cross-sex hormones. Typical of the numerous studies attempting to prove a prenatal hormonal cause in male-to-women transsexuals are the studies done on males whose mothers were injected with female hormones while pregnant. The hypothesis is that the cross-sex hormone would cause feminization of the fetus's brain resulting in a "feminine" brain trapped in a male body. However, gender researchers Kessler and McKenna report studies attempting to prove this theory show no indication that sons of mothers injected with female hormones while pregnant exhibit excessive "femininity" or are cross-gender-identified.

Similar studies launched to prove an endocrinological basis for female-to-men transsexuals have failed to do so. Yet the search for a bio-endocrinological explanation for transsexualism continues today. In the tradition of the medical model of disease, a search for a cause is undertaken in order to initiate stamping-out the "disease" through "treatment" and/or prevention. Therefore, we must seriously question whether transsexualism is a "disease" requiring medical intervention or whether it is a cultural symptom of the *dis-ease* evoked by challenging the traditional Western sex and gender code.

Although my concern here is not with finding an etiology of transsexualism, I am concerned with analyzing why so much time and research in America has been devoted to finding a transsexual etiology and what this pursuit reveals about contemporary U.S.A. gender attitudes. Some critics of transsexual surgery suggest that the search to find a biological cause for transsexualism is motivated by a desire to justify hormonal and surgical treatments. An analysis of transsexualism must take into account the role of the psycho-medical and surgical models in the construction of contemporary transsexual ideology, as well as the effect of that ideology on transsexuals themselves. Toward this end we must review the medical and surgical literature as a conveyor of, and justification for, *contemporary* gender beliefs and values. The majority of these studies conducted from the early 1950s through the present fixate on finding a cause for transsexualism, and/or with how artificial genitals look and work sexually. Overall, the idea that transsexuals are born in the "wrong" bodies is widely accepted without questioning or examining the sociocultural implication of such an assumption. Unfortunately, many social scientists fall prey to medical propaganda and fail to question transsexual ideology.

To try and understand the cultural implication of reinforcing the idea that transsexuals are trapped in the "wrong" bodies, we can draw from the theories of semiotics, "a science devoted to the study of meaning" (Solomon 9). Jack Solomon, author of *The Signs of Our Time: Semiotics: The Hidden Messages of Environments, Objects, and Cultural Images*, writes that semiotics is concerned with the social and political significance of meanings. Solomon devised principles of semiotics as analytic tools to explore cultural meanings and motivations behind the signs. Solomon advises:

1. Always question the 'commonsense' view of things because 'commonsense' is really 'communal sense.'
2. The 'commonsense' viewpoint is usually motivated by a cultural interest that manipulates our consciousness for ideological reasons.
3. Cultures tend to conceal their ideologies behind the veil of 'nature.'
4. In evaluating any system of cultural practices, one must take into account the interests behind it.
5. We do not view our world directly but view it through the filter of a semiotic code or mythic frame.
6. A sign is a sort of cultural barometer, marking the dynamic movement of social history. (10)

To begin to semiotically decode the medicalization of transsexuals in contemporary society, we must first ask what the idea of being born into the "wrong" body means. Common sense dictates that the idea of "wrong" bodies assumes the existence of "right" bodies. Right bodies, according to transsexual ideology, must match the gender of the individual; accordingly, masculine-acting people belong in male bodies and feminine-acting people belong in female bodies, thereby reinforcing sex and gender congruence demanded by contemporary American society. Accepting the premise that one could be born into the wrong body means accepting the hidden moral agenda concealed in the term "transsexual." This agenda presupposes that certain gender behaviors are allowed on the basis of whether you inhabit a male or female body, determined by genital anatomy. As gender researcher Sandra Bem observes, gender schematicity derives from

the society's ubiquitous insistence on the functional importance of the gender dichotomy even in situational contexts where sex needn't matter at all, from the culture's insistence that an individual's sex matters in virtually every domain of human experience. (310)

Ultimately, the assumption that one can be born in the wrong body reinforces sex dichotomization found in dominant ideology. Where does sex dichotomization come from and how is it reinforced by the clinical model of transsexualism? In the U.S. sex dichotomization can be traced to Judeo-Christian hierarchical and patriarchal values, upon which American culture is largely based. As such, sex dichotomization is passed from generation to generation and forms the Western sex and gender code. The code makes no distinction between sex and gender. Operating largely on an unconscious and to a lesser extent conscious level, the Western sex and gender code functions as a cultural prescription for a linear relationship between the sex organs and gender behavior. As Gayle Rubin observes, individuals are coerced into conforming to the code by the promise of economic and social reinforcements, which include being seen as a "normal" individual rather than a social outcast or member of a stigmatized minority. According to the Western sex and gender code, "normal" individuals are supposed to develop a gender identity, a gender role, a sexual preference, and a life based on the sex of their genitals.

In capitalistic America the material—that which can be seen, possessed, manufactured and sold—is valued above all else. Therefore, genitals as material objects are accorded primary importance in transsexual ideology. The biological sex of the genitals determines the realms of experience individuals will be allowed to participate in.[1] As I established earlier, according to the Western sex and gender code, possessing a vagina is supposed to inspire the development of a "feminine" gender identity and role, culminating in the selection of a member of the "opposite" sex to procreate with in an already overpopulated world. In a like manner, according to code, if you possess a penis, you are expected to assume a "masculine" gender identity and role culminating in heterosexual and procreative acts and desires. Through sex-reassignment surgery, genitals can be reshaped and manufactured to appear like the genitals of the "opposite" sex, theoretically providing transsexuals access to experiences they have previously been barred from. However, it follows that according to transsexual ideology, once surgically altered, one is expected to act according to the code. With the overt emphasis on the appearance and the sexual function of the genitals dominating the psycho-medical and surgical literature, transsexuals are reduced to their genitals. Satisfactory adjustment as a surgical transsexual, for example, is all too often based on whether or not one can achieve an orgasm through heterosexual intercourse.

Social constructionists have criticized the Western sex and gender code for not differentiating between sex and gender (assuming gender, like anatomy, is somehow biologically determined). Most clinical views on transsexualism, while espousing that gender is the result of biology *and* environment, resist the implications of social constructionism and still seek some hidden biological cause. This biological-determinant ideology has vast social implications in all areas. The positing of a biological and genetic base for gender behavior (determined by the appearance of sex organs) fosters inequality between the sexes and guarantees heterosexuality as the norm. It leads to the devaluation of women, perpetuation of homophobia, and an intolerance for gender minorities.

Medicalization of Transsexuals

Leslie Lothstein, author of the impressive and first serious study of the male-to-woman transsexual, observes that since the last century transsexualism "has been transformed from a purely cultural phenomenon into a medical-surgical entity" (Lothstein, *Female-to-Male Transsexualism* 302). He laments that in over 40 gender-identity clinics nationwide, "gender dysphoric" transsexuals reportedly at odds with their anatomy and described as suffering from a profound psychological disturbance in their gender identities and/or roles, are being treated hormonally and surgically, rather than psychologically or culturally. The exception seems to be the preventative psychological "treatment" offered to "pretranssexual" children (see Green, The "Sissy Boy Syndrome").

In order to examine contemporary American transsexual ideology, it is imperative to trace the medicalization of transsexuals in America from the 1950s through the present. This requires decoding transsexual "treatments," the medicalization of the genitals, and an examination of the contemporary medical transsexual ideology.

An examination of major medical influences, theories and movements in American transsexual ideology reveals major themes that challenge and/or reinforce the Western sex and gender code. The most insidious among these is the depiction of transsexuals as sick and abnormal and in need of hormonal and surgical "treatment" and/or rehabilitation. Accompanying this view is the never-ending quest to prove the bio- and psycho-endocrinological basis of transsexualism. The core of transsexual ideology almost always contains transgenderphobic, homophobic, sexist, misogynist and sexually dimorphic attitudes and beliefs. These attitudes and beliefs are rarely questioned, but are quickly absorbed and passed on as contemporary transsexual ideology. As a result, in the techno-surgical process of SRS, not only are genitals amputated, manufactured and sold, but simultaneously, a gender ideology is manufactured, reinforced and transmitted. This deliberate transmission of gender ideology, both on a conscious and unconscious level, has been and continues to be a source of sex and gender oppression both culturally and globally.

Only recently have studies questioned the reported 68 percent - 86 percent success rate claimed for sex-reassigned transsexuals (see Lothstein, "Sex Reassignment Surgery"). All too frequently these high percentages are based solely on external appearance and reported functioning of the reconstructed genitalia. Psycho-social and socioeconomic aspects of post-operative transsexuals tend to be overlooked in the majority of American medical studies. Conversely, cross-cultural studies on transsexuals in Poland, the Soviet Union, the Scandinavian countries, Singapore and mainland China show a reverse trend (see Ruan, Tsoi). Instead of concentrating solely on external appearances, heterosexual function of the genitals, and etiological explanations, studies from these countries often explore psycho-social aspects of transsexualism, such as interpersonal family and social relations, as well as job performance and relations to co-workers. Many cross-cultural studies examine transsexuals as part of their culture rather than as aliens. This attitude toward transsexuals seems to extend to European popular culture, where transsexuals are accorded a certain respect. For example, in Spain a popular television personality, a male-to-woman transsexual, is looked on as a professional, rather than as an oddity.[2]

Is the overemphasis on the artificial genitalia a distinctly U.S.A. phenomenon reflective of a materialistic consumer culture whose primary focus is on market value? If so, have artificial genitals become just another commodity? And are transsexuals just consumers involved in business transactions with medical corporations and doctors who function as sales representatives? Although it is tempting to reduce the medicalization of transsexuals to a by-product of consumer capitalism, the transference of gender attitudes and maintenance of rigid sex and gender stereotypes (by-products of medicalizing transgenderism) must also be examined. That we "treat" individuals who do not fulfill cultural stereotypes of sex and gender, while culturally obsolete sex and gender stereotypes are left "untreated," exposes a frightening aspect of American gender attitudes. The implications of this treatment are far-reaching.

All individuals are to some extent vulnerable to cultural attitudes about sex and gender, since these attitudes form the basis upon which one's entire identity is constructed. Medical interactions with transsexuals are extremely complex and vastly understudied. Within the medical community, arguments of whether surgical sex reassignment is ethical or even "rehabilitative" continue. Within the last decade more studies have begun to question the safety of hormonal treatment and sex-reassignment surgery for transsexuals (see Johanes et al.). Major figures responsible for contemporary transsexual ideology, including Robert Stoller, have predicted that sex-reassignment surgery will one day be abandoned. To date, however, the search for an underlying transsexual etiology continues. The number of self-defined transsexuals is accelerating as rapidly as new techno-surgical techniques for reshaping the genitalia. To date, little sociocultural analysis has been done on the relationship between the psycho-medical, techno-surgical model (clinical model) of transsexualism, the transsexual individual and American culture.

Major Events in Transsexual History: 1950-1990s

Major medical events in transsexual history have significantly influenced the direction of current transsexual research. Further, these events can be interpreted as both a reflection and shaper of contemporary American gender attitudes. Harry Benjamin, considered the father of transsexualism, and an ardent supporter of sex-reassignment surgery for transsexuals, justified transsexual surgery on the following basis:

If the mind cannot be changed to fit the body then perhaps we should consider changing the body to fit the mind. (Green and Money 268)

Benjamin's statement has since become the motto for advocates of sex-reassignment surgery, who view transsexualism as synonymous with SRS. For almost three decades, advocates of transsexual surgery have tried to define the ideal candidate for surgical sex reassignment.

An examination of the *Index Medicus*, a yearly index of published medical and clinical studies from the 1950s through the present, reveals historical trends in clinical transsexual ideology that have been instrumental in reflecting and shaping cultural attitudes toward gender. As a result of Johns Hopkins University Hospital and other experimental sex reassignment programs established in the 1960s which exposed more clinicians to transsexuals, the number of articles on the subject multiplied. With the substantial increase in transsexual literature, "transsexualism" emerged for the first time in 1968 as a separate and legitimate category in the *Index Medicus*. From 1953 to 1968, articles on transsexualism, provided clues to what was considered important. During this period most articles on transsexuals were listed under the categories of "Sexual Deviation, Sexual Perversion and Transvestism." The medicalization of transsexuals in America escalated throughout the 1970s, as an estimated 20 new gender-identity clinics opened nationwide in response to the rising number of individuals seeking SRS.

Consequently, in 1973 Norman Fisk introduced the term *gender dysphoria syndrome* to cover the wide range of applicants seeking sex-reassignment surgery (Fisk). A much more inclusive term than *transsexual*, *gender dysphoria syndrome* included "transsexuals, as well as transvestites, homosexuals and some psychotics who desired SRS." Fisk noted that "by conceptualizing our patients as having gender dysphoria syndrome we have obviously liberalized the indications and requirements for sex conversion surgery" (386-87). Outraged, critics of Fisk's new diagnosis charged it was "self-serving for the medical profession to justify the referral of non-transsexuals for sex reassignment surgery," opening the door for potential abuses (Lothstein, *Female-to-Male Transsexualism* 59). Perhaps the most blatant abuse of the new diagnosis of gender dysphoria syndrome concerns a bizarre experiment in which five incarcerated psychopaths were surgically sex reassigned in an attempt to cure their "character problems." Lothstein observes that the SRS apparently did not work.

By the 1970s the articles on transsexualism in the *Index Medicus* had expanded beyond earlier topics of: "Drug Therapy" (usually hormones), "Etiology...Surgery" and "Therapy" (usually SRS) to include new focuses of clinical interest in such areas as "Complications...Prevention and Control...Family & Genetics" and "Psychology." This shift in interest reflects the growing concern not only with bio-psychic theories of transsexual etiology, but also the justification for the "treatment" of a new population, "pretranssexual" children. Studies during this period that single-mindedly searched for a biogenetical etiology added fuel to the nature vs. nurture argument. Authors of these studies advanced popular socio-biological arguments, while paying lip service to environmental influences. One such study asserted that biology ultimately influenced all gender behavior by acting like a "backstage coach" (Bolin 43). Sadly, even psychological studies of the time fell back on socio-biological theories of causation.

Studies on the effects of elevated testosterone levels, prenatal hormones, H-Y antigen anomalies and temporal lobe disorders were in abundance. Most psycho-socio-biological theories concentrated on the influence of dominant, overprotective mothers, absent fathers, and the role of the family in reinforcing "pretranssexual" behavior. An indicator, no doubt, of intent, studies on surgical techniques by far outnumbered all other categories of transsexual research published during the 1970s. These studies overwhelmingly focused on the latest techniques for creating artificial genitalia, particularly the vagina. On one level this reveals the American obsession with the genitals, as well as the growing medical notion that the body consists of replaceable parts. In study after study the transsexual's body is compared to a machine. Several follow-up studies on surgically reconstructed transsexuals even ask "how they are running" (see Edgarton). We must ponder what the implications are of thinking of the transsexual body as a machine and a series of replaceable parts.

Most medical follow-up studies by the mid seventies, though small in number and questionable in conclusions, reported satisfactory outcomes in post-operative transsexuals, suggesting "to date...sex reassignment surgery does indeed improve the condition of the afflicted individual" (see Lothstein, "Sex Reassignment Surgery"). Lothstein and others question the high numbers of "satisfactory outcomes," noting that they completely ignore new reports of post-surgical transsexuals who revert to living as their former sex or transsexuals who suffer psychotic breaks or commit suicide. When clinicians overlook these statistics, they participate in objectifying the "patient" and the patient's body. If the body is viewed as a machine, then a break-down in parts does not have to be taken seriously. This is demonstrated time and again by the numerous surgical procedures many transsexuals are subjected to in order to correct "improperly functioning parts."

Glowing reports of "satisfactory outcomes" in the studies of the 1970s through the 1980s call into question the methods used to measure outcomes. Most of these studies were primarily based on self reports. Predictably, participants in the studies were asked a disproportionate number of questions about the appearance and sexual functioning of their reconstructed genitals and

editions of *DSM III* are permeated with dimorphic myths and misinformation in the "Gender-Identity Disorder" sections. Typical of the latter is the warning in *DSM III* that extensive and persisting "childhood femininity in a boy or childhood masculinity in a girl" can increase the likelihood of adult transsexualism (263). Longitudinal studies conducted in the mid- to late 1980s on boyhood femininity contradict this assumption. Categorizing "Gender Identity Disorders of Childhood" as mental disorders encourages the so-called treatment of young gender "violators," often referred to as "pretranssexuals." Dimorphic myths include reports that male transsexualism occurs more frequently than female transsexualism, and that "female-to-male" transsexuals are more stable than their "male-to-female" counterparts, claims disputed by transsexual researcher Leslie Lothstein.

Of more interest here is what effect such misinformation and myths have on transsexuals, transgenderists and cross-dressers, as well as transsexual "treatment" and contemporary gender attitudes. Do their alleged diagnostic criteria also function as a mandate and reinforcement of cultural bipolar sex and gender roles? This in no way is intended to deny the suffering of transsexuals, but to question how much of this suffering is generated by a clinical transsexual ideology that reinforces cultural gender bipolarism. Because transsexualism is viewed as a personal problem rather than a sociocultural problem, "cures" become the responsibility of the individual rather than the culture. Clinical studies have yet to address this concern or the debilitating effects of gender bipolarism.

With the 1980 classification of transsexualism as a mental disorder, publications defining the role of the clinician, the role of the transsexual, tips on passing as the "opposite" gender, SRS and standards of care appeared, contributing to further homogenization of transsexuals and clinicians. During the late 1970s through the 1990s, clearinghouses of transsexual information like the Janus Information Facility (JIF) formerly the Erikson Education Foundation, and the Harry Benjamin International Gender Dysphoria Association, Inc. (HBIGDA) distributed how-to pamphlets considered of interest to clinicians and transsexuals.

Among the most circulated photocopied pamphlets are Money and Walkers' "Counseling the Transsexual," *Guidelines for Transsexuals* (from JIF), and "Standards of Care: The Hormonal and Surgical Sex Reassignment of Gender Dysphoric Persons" from the HBIGDA. These photocopied pamphlets advise clinicians on how to manage the transsexual client, do surgical referrals, family counseling and word insurance policies. The information pamphlets for transsexuals read like an "owners' manual" and offer advice on how to find sympathetic clinicians and surgeons, how to pass, tell your family, change legal documents and have heterosexual intercourse with reconstructed genitalia. *Guidelines for Transsexuals* suggests choosing a surgeon who "will be interested in vigorously pursuing your insurance claim" and includes the following economic advice:

Claims...should probably not define...treatment simply as "transsexual surgery" or "cosmetic surgery": applications under these categories are consistently rejected. Best results have been obtained when the condition...is presented as a "neuroendocrinological or psychohormonal disorder," absolutely requiring and responsive to surgical and hormonal treatment. Another effective classification is "gender dysphoria." (JIF, *Guidelines for Transsexuals* 27)

From the late 1980s through the early 1990s, while glowing reports of new genital surgery techniques, including phalloplasty, expanded, scattered reports citing deadly effects from hormonal and surgical "treatment" published in the clinical journals were hardly noticed. These studies included growing incidences of breast cancer in estrogen-treated "male-to-female" transsexuals (see Prior, Vigna and Watson).

At the present time the requests for SRS and the number of surgeons performing it are at an all-time high, indicating that even though SRS is still an experimental procedure with uncertain results, it is more popular than ever. Currently, gender researchers are continuing the search for what they postulate to be the hidden biological cause of transsexualism, a cause advocates claim will justify "treatment." But exactly what is being "treated" and, perhaps more importantly, why and at what cost?

To address these questions we must again return to the major tenet of transsexual ideology, the idea that transsexuals are born in the "wrong" body. Where did this idea come from? Certainly, as I demonstrated in the previous chapter, case studies from the early sexologists as well as personal accounts from cross-gender-identified individuals included references to being trapped in the "wrong" body, a claim also made by many contemporary transsexuals. This claim is rooted in a dualistic belief that right and wrong bodies exist. But the modern medicalization and subsequent acceptance of the technological transformation of the genitals is a result of a clinical transsexual ideology created by the major transsexual theorists, reinforced by dominant ideology and left largely unchallenged. The two pioneering figures most responsible for the creation of modern clinical transsexual ideology are the Danish Christian Hamburger, responsible for the Jorgenson case, and the German-born American, Harry Benjamin. Both men were trained as endocrinologists and were responsible for creating the theoretical framework on which modern clinical transsexual ideology is built.

"Wrong Body" Theorist
Christian Hamburger

Christian Hamburger was the physician responsible for the sex reassignment of Christine Jorgenson. He was also the man "Christine" Jorgenson named herself after. In the 1953 case study of Jorgenson published in the *Journal of the American Medical Association,* Hamburger theorized about symptoms, etiologies and treatments for the "problem" of transsexualism, which, at the time, he referred to as "Eonism" and "genuine transvestism." Concerned primarily with the "male-to-female" transsexual (Eonist), Hamburger wrote the following description: "Eonists are persons with a fundamental feeling of being victims of a cruel mistake—a consequence of the female personality in a male body" (391). Hamburger believed the "abnormality" of being a transsexual could lead to "possible suicidal attempts" as well as "attempts at self-castration." He argued against psychotherapy as a treatment for transsexuals. Hamburger maintained it was impossible to make a "genuine transvestite" (primary transsexual) wish to have his mentality altered to bring "it into harmony with his physical appearance." His argument against psychotherapy was influenced in part by his strong belief that Eonism was constitutionally conditioned by prenatal hormones. To this he added, if there was no cure for "genuine transvestism" (primary transsexualism) then medical ethics decreed: "...if a disease cannot be cured an attempt should be made to improve the stress and inconvenience of the patient in order to make his life as tolerable as possible" (391). Toward this end, Hamburger suggested that the patient be allowed to appear as a woman in public and be legally recognized as such. Hamburger's treatment for Jorgenson became the model for the contemporary "treatment" of transsexuals in America. First Hamburger injected Jorgenson with estrogen to cause hormonal castration and the development of "feminine" features. Next he amputated her penis which Hamburger justified in this way: "from a eugenic point of view it would do no harm if a number of abnormal men were castrated and deprived of their sexual libido" (395). After penile castration, Hamburger surgically reconstructed the scrotum to give the "patient's" genital area a more "feminine" appearance.

Hamburger did not complete the final stage of sex reassignment surgery, the construction of an artificial vagina, because he apparently considered to do so would encourage the practice of homosexuality. His attitude was the reverse of the American idea, espoused by Benjamin and others, who felt surgery would curb homosexuality because of their belief that a vagina made one a woman, so sex with males was thought to be heterosexual. Hamburger rationalized his position by suggesting that most "genuine transvestites" (primary transsexuals) rarely desired sexual contact. Finally, Hamburger cautioned that his therapy for transsexuals should be implemented only in "suitable cases without violating the interests of society" (396). While Hamburger and others performed surgery abroad, endocrinologist Harry Benjamin was busy administering hormones to transsexuals in America.

The Father of Transsexualism

Hailed as the father of transsexualism, Harry Benjamin, trained in Steinach's technique of the cross-sex transplantation of gonads in guinea pigs, became the greatest advocate of SRS for transsexuals who he felt were members of the most "neglected sexual minority." He viewed transsexual surgery as a "salvation to poor...pitiful...unhappy...abnormal transsexuals" (Green and Money 14). Benjamin and Hamburger, like their predecessors, passed on more than just a theoretical foundation on which modern transsexual ideology is based. An examination of their theories on transsexualism reveals that many sex and gender values and beliefs were transmitted along with their "scientific" theories.

Benjamin and Hamburger contributed to transsexual ideology the belief that hormonal and surgical treatments for transsexuals were therapeutic and life saving. Benjamin claimed that if denied hormonal and surgical treatments, at least 20 percent of "male-to-female" transsexuals were at risk of performing self-castration and were highly suicidal. Convinced that hormonal "treatments" were necessary for transsexuals, Benjamin maintained that withholding hormones and SRS from transsexuals was like withholding insulin from diabetics. He argued that the cross-sex hormones functioned like "transsexual tranquilizers" to calm transsexuals down. This tranquilizing effect, Benjamin believed, was due to the promise that estrogen would feminize the male-to-woman transsexual by redistributing body fat, softening the skin, reducing body hair and creating some breast development. Benjamin "treated" female-to-men transsexuals with androgen and other male hormones which produced a thickening of the vocal chords, resulting in a deeper voice, increased facial and body hair, a decrease or end to menstrual periods, and an increase in muscle mass. Because he viewed male and female transsexuals differently, it is not clear whether Benjamin thought hormones for the female-to-men transsexuals functioned as tranquilizers. It appears that he felt only the male-to-women transsexuals needed "calming down." Such noticeable body changes coupled with the promise of SRS in the future, Benjamin felt gave transsexuals hope that they could be "cured." Prior to the establishment of gender-identity clinics in America, Benjamin routinely referred transsexuals abroad to have SRS. Benjamin's optimism about transsexual "treatments" obscured reports of negative side-effects resulting from the prolonged use of hormones or possible surgical errors during SRS. Instead, his treatment model contributed to the absolute medical dependency of transsexuals.

The Transsexual Phenomena, Benjamin's 1966 book, provided the first comprehensive "treatment" guide for transsexualism. Commonly referred to as the "transsexuals' Bible," it also became a guidebook for transsexuals seeking surgery. Numerous researchers, including myself, have observed self-defined transsexuals presenting case histories taken directly from *The Transsexual Phenomena* as their own in order to convince clinicians that they are serious candidates for SRS. This often-unconscious fabrication of individual case histories attests to the great influence transsexual ideology has on transsexuals. Fabricating a case-history in order to obtain SRS can lead to disastrous results. Lee Grant's documentary "What Sex am I?" illustrates this point in an interview with "Clifford," a dissatisfied surgical transsexual, who describes how "he" (gender he feels he belongs to now) memorized a case-history in order to convince clinicians that he was a viable candidate for SRS. Deeply regretful about having surgery, in the interview, Clifford reveals he was a "homophobic" homosexual who believed surgery could make him more socially acceptable. When interviewed, Clifford had reverted back to living as a man, mournful that no surgery could restore his penis. Other transsexuals dissatisfied with SRS have resorted to more dramatic means than Cliffords' failed lawsuit, including a homicide attempt on the SRS surgeon and suicide (see Millken).

Anne Bolin, in her 1988 work *In Search of Eve: Transsexual Rites of Passage,* substantiates how common it is for transsexuals seeking SRS to borrow textbook case-histories out of a fear of being rejected as candidates for SRS. Perhaps this would not be the case, Bolin argues, if SRS candidates were not forced to present outdated stereotypes which have undergone little or no change in the last 40 years. This inhibits the development of new knowledge and understanding of transsexuals. If traditional transsexual ideology remains unchallenged, it perpetrates not only antiquated ideas about transsexuals, but also gender.

In addition to a surplus of homophobia and sexism, Benjamin's book is also an indictment against psychotherapy as an effective transsexual "treatment." Unfortunately, these ideas have become a part of contemporary clinical transsexual ideology and have been incorporated into "treatments." Although most key transsexual theorists profess to have a liberal attitude toward homosexuality, their work indicates otherwise. The idea of being "trapped in the wrong body" is all too often viewed synonymously with having the "wrong" sexual desire. Underlying Benjamin's view of transsexual surgery as providing a service to society is the notion of transforming "unacceptable" homosexuals into more socially acceptable transsexual *heterosexuals*. Such an idea reeks of genocide.

Benjamin claimed surgically reconstructed "male-to-female" transsexuals with a sexual preference for males are no longer considered to have the "wrong" sexual preference. Through SRS, the perceived homosexual "threat" to society is amputated along with their genitals. Benjamin emphasizes over and over that surgical transsexuals are "satisfied with their ability to be a normal sex partner" which for him meant being in a heterosexual missionary position which he refers to as face to face with their spouse or lover (see Green and Money; Benjamin).

As a zealot for transsexual surgery and an advocate of gender and law and order, Benjamin argued that:

I have become convinced from what I have seen that a miserable unhappy male transsexual can, with the help of surgery and endocrinology attain a happier future as a woman. In this way the individual as well as the society can be served. (135)

A surgically constructed male-to-woman transsexual parroted the homophobia embedded in transsexual ideology with a remark to Benjamin: "I didn't go through all of this [sex-reassignment surgery] so I could have sex like a homosexual" (Benjamin 256). Instead of examining homophobia within a broader cultural context, Benjamin and others used it as an inducement for SRS. Additionally, the transsexual theorists of the late 1960s consistently devalued and reduced women, lesbians and gays to their genitals and sexual preferences. While genitally fixated American advocates of transsexual surgery on one level viewed it as a possible "antidote" to homosexuality, arguing that if they outfitted a genetic male with a neovagina, sex with males would be "heterosexual," their European counterparts, also homophobic, had a vastly different perspective.

Hamburger did not believe in the power of an artificial vagina to transform males into the "opposite" sex. His recommendation against vaginoplasty for Jorgenson may have been rooted in not wanting to add the volatile issue of sexual preference to the already bubbling controversy of "sex change." If Danish transsexual researchers approached the construction of a neovagina with caution, American researchers couldn't wait to construct artificial vaginas in male-to-women transsexuals. Not surprisingly, the final phase of Jorgenson's "sex-change," the creation of the neovagina, took place in America several years after her return from Denmark. Enthusiastic about the possibilities of the artificial vagina, Benjamin stated: "The artificial vagina is very close to the anus, and the girls just throw their legs up a little higher and the man thinks he is entering the vagina" (267).

The distinctly American emphasis on the importance of heterosexual intercourse as a symbol of "normalcy" is manifest in the above statement. Clinical publications on transsexuals from the 1960s through the 1970s graphically display the American fascination with reconstructed genitals in an excess of detailed diagrams, descriptions and close-up photographs of artificial vaginas. Benjamin's genital-obsessed research became incorporated into contemporary transsexual ideology in the United States, where gender identity is still confused with genital anatomy and sex. As a result of such an association, the ultimate criterion of being able to pass as a member of the "opposite" sex is overwhelmingly reduced to the appearance of the genitals and capacity for heterosexual intercourse, a somewhat bizarre criterion. Annie Woodhouse, a feminist gender researcher, observes that gender is primarily observed and announced through "various visual and vocal signals such as hair, clothes, body shape, and movement, gestures and facial expressions, voice and speech" rather than through the appearance and function of the genitals that are concealed beneath these gender "facades" (Woodhouse, *Fantastic Women, Sex, Gender and Transvestism* xiii).

Surgically Constructing "Good Citizens"

The renowned transsexual surgeon Stanley Biber, an heir to the homophobia embedded in contemporary transsexual ideology, is one of the first surgeons who decided to operate on male-to-women transsexual lesbians. Biber, who boasts of having performed over 3000 SRSs in his small town of Trinidad, Colorado, reports that he used to believe that operating on transsexual lesbians was unjustified. Although Biber denies charges of homophobia, his statements still resonate with homophobia. He announced during an interview that

several years ago we started doing them...we got taken in. Then we started looking at their lesbian lifestyle and started thinking about it, and they were living very good lives, were very productive and were doing fine. So little by little we came to believe, so what the hell, if there's homosexuality in the normal population, why shouldn't there be homosexuality in the transsexual population. So little by little we advance and I don't hold it against them...

We've had a few that came in and thought they were lesbians, and after the surgery, they changed and are not lesbians any more. They went straight. (Pierce, "Interview..." 80-81)

Even though Biber's statement suggests a belief in the social construction of gender, he, like his predecessors, appears concerned with how SRS can be used to create better citizens. Biber observes that transsexuals "have gone through a lot of psychological stress, and if we can help make them good citizens, I like that" (Pierce, "Interview..." 82). Biber's statement implies that transsexuals who do not undergo SRS surgery are not good citizens, which could be translated to mean good Americans. Whatever his intent, the word "citizen" implies not only allegiance to the government but also protection from the government, a right transsexuals and transgenderists rarely have. According to this type of conservative transsexual ideology, SRS provides a valuable service to society by creating good citizens out of gender "violators."

Of course, not all transsexuals who apply for SRS are accepted for treatment. Though estimates vary, most statistics from the gender-identity clinics suggest that only one or two out of ten SRS applicants actually undergo genital surgery, a statistic that may in part be related to the high costs of surgery. Contrary to popular belief, most transsexuals do not go through gender-identity programs, but obtain SRS from a growing number of endocrinologists and surgeons abroad willing to perform requested procedures without screening.

Fisk offers one explanation for the acceptance of the medicalization and surgicalization of transsexuals in America by observing,

it is certainly much more acceptable and less socially stigmatizing to have a legitimate medical illness than it is to suffer from a supposed sexual perversion, sexual deviation or fetish. (389)

Over a decade later, Paul Walker reinforced the medicalization of transsexuals when he suggested that, if given a choice, transsexuals would rather have a medical problem, because it is much more socially acceptable, particularly if it is surgically curable.[3] Conceiving of transsexualism as a medical problem prevents looking at the cultural etiologies of cross-gender behavior.

The Disavowal of Psychotherapy

For more than a quarter of a century, there has existed an uneasy and complex relationship between transsexuals and psychotherapy. There is also a deep contradiction in that transsexualism is considered by the medical profession to be a mental disorder, not treatable by psychotherapeutic intervention, but responsive to surgical techniques. As Lothstein observes, traditional transsexual ideology dismisses psychotherapy as a useless treatment for transsexualism. The only exception is the use of psychotherapy with pre-adolescent cross-gender-identified children, where, until recently, "femininity" in young boys was viewed as a precursor to adult transsexualism. As early as 1968, psychoanalyst Robert Stoller pronounced adult transsexualism to be an irreversible malignant condition, resistant to psychological methods. Yet he proclaimed it "may be treatable and reversible in the small child" (Stoller, *Sex and Gender* 40).

It follows that with few exceptions, psychotherapists have played a secondary role in the actual treatment of adult transsexuals, even though the most widely accepted guidelines for transsexual "treatment" require two psychological evaluations before obtaining SRS. However, most psychological contact with transsexual clients is geared toward the goal of SRS, rather than toward allowing the clients to explore their feelings about gender. Since what is thought to be the real life test, the period during which the transsexual assumes the role of the "opposite" gender for six months to two years, is considered the most reliable measure of whether one will benefit from SRS, more time is spent in psychological consultations advising transsexual clients how to live in the cross-gender role than exploring issues of gender. Critics of transsexual surgery have complained of the confusion manifest in treating a "mental disorder" with surgical techniques. Commenting on the "confused condition of transsexualism," psychotherapist Jeremiah Dolan notes that in modern society, offering "hormones and surgery might be seen as an easier management solution to the problem" of transsexualism than psychotherapy.

The few claims of psychotherapeutic "cures" for transsexualism usually consist of little more than therapists imposing personal and cultural sex and gender values on their clients. This type of "therapy" consists of conformity to cultural sex and gender stereotypes, without regard for the personal consequences. Most "treatment" consists of convincing transsexuals to accept gender roles "congruent" with their biological sex, which the therapists typically argue is their "natural" role, suggesting that gender is inborn.

A well-known advocate of this "treatment" through psychoanalysis, Charles Socarides asserts:

The sexual pervert, including the transsexual, has been unable to pass successfully through the symbiotic and separation-individuation phases of early childhood...The function of transsexualism is to achieve "femininity" through radical surgical and plastic procedures and endocrinological manipulation designed to remove all traces of true anatomical gender and to promote enactment of a synthetic and assumed feminine role in the general environment and in the sexual act. (347)

Socarides, like his psychoanalytic predecessors at the turn of the century, claims all transsexuals are really delusional homosexuals wanting "to freely engage in homosexual activities" (Socarides 348). He views transsexualism as a solution to anxiety and guilt associated with homosexual desire. Socarides advises his transsexual clients to abandon their "delusional" desire and develop a bipolar sex-and-gender identity "congruent" with their genitals. Other reported "cures" for transsexualism include conversion to fundamentalist religions that zealously espouse bipolar sex-and-gender roles (see Shore).

The widespread dismissal of psychotherapy as viable "treatment" for transsexualism in the Western world may in part be based on treatment failures as well as the unproven assumption that transsexualism is biologically caused. Historically, traditional psychotherapeutic techniques applied to adult transsexuals have failed for a multitude of reasons. Reasons for failure include trying to mold patients into rigid stereotypes by denying their personal reality, and ignoring cultural etiologies.

As I noted earlier, popular psychotherapeutic treatments from the 1950s on have often incorporated drastic medical techniques used to force transsexuals into gender conformity. Endocrinological therapy was often used in tandem with psychotherapy. Male-to-women transgenderists and transsexuals were injected with testosterone. Female-to-men transgenderists and transsexuals were shot up with estrogen. They were told these administrations of hormones would "cure" their "abnormal" feelings and desires. The results were often disastrous, since the hormones amplified undesirable secondary sex characteristics, creating great anxiety in the transsexuals and transgenderists. These same treatments were routinely applied to homosexuals. Operating on the assumption that gender identity and sexual preference were hormonally generated, it was assumed that injections of same-sex hormones would "normalize" transgenderists' and transsexuals' gender identity and homosexuals' sexual preference. Treatment in some cases proved fatal (see Katz).

An overlooked factor of why psychotherapy fails is that very few therapists are trained to deal with transsexualism. As a result, most therapy either ends up endorsing standard medical treatment or attempting to brainwash transsexuals into gender conformity. Standard "treatment" rarely focuses on helping transsexuals understand and accept themselves. Leslie Lothstein's work is the exception.

Objecting to the traditional medical devaluation of psychotherapy encouraged by orthodox transsexual ideology, Leslie Lothstein wisely observes that one reason it may have been so easily dismissed is because transsexuals often make therapists uncomfortable by forcing them to examine their own sex and gender identities. Lothstein's studies reveal that members of the mental health profession commonly describe transsexuals as the most difficult patients to work with. He further observes that therapists who are unfamiliar with, or feel threatened by, working with transsexuals are often more than eager to relinquish them to medical and techno-surgical "remedies." The "myth" of the ineffectiveness of psychotherapy for an alleged "mental disorder" has been embraced by some transsexuals as well. Many transsexuals view traditional psychotherapy as a waste of time and money. All too often transsexuals wind up paying therapists while educating them about transsexualism. A worst case scenario occurs for many transsexuals when they encounter bigoted therapists, confused not only about their own sex and gender identities, but also unclear about what transsexualism is. Unfortunately, reports of disastrous therapy situations abound.

One such incident happened locally when "Marsha," a 28-year-old male-to-woman lesbian transgenderist with a Ph.D, had a horrific "therapeutic" encounter with a local psychiatrist. Marsha was assured in a phone conversation by the therapist that his specialty for over 40 years was working with "transvestites, transsexuals and homosexuals." During the first few minutes of their session, Marsha expressed her desire to explore the possibility of cross-living as a woman and the possibility of future SRS. Without asking any questions, her psychiatrist shocked her when he advised her to: "Go to a gay bar, get picked up and have anal intercourse, then you will understand what being a woman is all about" (pers. comm. 1989). Marsha reported feeling deeply insulted, offended and confused by his insensitive, homophobic and sexist suggestion.

Several other self-defined transsexuals and transgenderists have reported similar horror stories with the same psychiatrist and have warned others to avoid him. From his comment it is clear the psychiatrist defined and differentiated males and females by their roles in heterosexual intercourse. Once again, medically generated transsexual ideology overestimates the role of the genitals and underestimates the role of gender in cross-gender identity. While I do not believe it was the psychiatrist's intention to challenge dominant cultural assumptions about sex and gender, I cannot resist deconstructing his suggestion from a psychoanalytic and feminist perspective. His prescription to experience womanhood by being anally penetrated exemplifies how women in a patriarchy are culturally and literally "fucked." As long as transsexual ideology condones cultural sexism and homophobia, personal and cultural bigotry will continue to be passed off as "treatment."

Money, Stoller and Green's Contributions to Transsexual Ideology:

The great social movements of the late 1960s and early 1970s including civil rights, the sexual revolution, feminism and gay and lesbian liberation, seem to have had little impact on clinical transsexual research. Critics like Anne Bolin have observed that transsexual research remains frozen in time. The three most influential figures and major contributors to the clinical model of transsexual ideology from the 1960s to the present are John Money, Robert Stoller and Richard Green. As authors of more books and articles than other transsexual researchers, they are regarded as experts in the field and have been the inspiration for much transsexual research.

All three are trained in psychology and psychiatry. However, their theories embrace the endocrinological etiology theories advocated by Benjamin and Hamburger. Like their predecessors', the theories of Money, Stoller and Green are filled with contradictions. Their theories focus on the acquisition of gender identity and contributing family dynamics as well as theories on prenatal hormones in the etiology of transsexualism. These theories both refute and support sex-reassignment surgery as "rehabilitative" for transsexuals. Perhaps the most curious aspect of all three researchers is that each has projected that one day SRS may be obsolete.

John Money, the co-founder of the Johns Hopkins research project on transsexualism and sex-reassignment surgery, developed his theories on gender by working with hermaphrodites. Money observed that in some cases of hermaphrodites, the gender of rearing contradicted secondary sex characteristics which developed at puberty. Further, he hypothesized that the gender identity hermaphrodites developed, although in contrast with their biological sex, at some point became fixed. Because they developed a "fixed gender identity," Money recommended that hermaphrodites and sexually anomalous individuals be surgically sex-reassigned in accordance with their gender identity. Based on his observations and follow-up of these cases, Money concluded that there was a "critical period for gender identity differentiation" and this period coincided "with the critical period for acquiring language" (Money and Tucker 109). Money's early research suggested that "gender role," a term he coined in 1955, may be based on social and environmental factors, rather than biology (Money, "Propaedeutics" 16-17).

In a seeming testament to the power of sociocultural variables on the acquisition of gender identity, Money cited his popular case of the "castrated twin." Basically, the study concerns an identical male twin who at seven months old was accidentally castrated by an electric cauterizing needle during a routine circumcision. He was reassigned as a girl after surgical castration and feminization of his external genitalia. The "girl" twin was described by Money at age five as having successfully adopted the "female role." Money applauded her:

fussing over her brother... "like a mother hen," while he in turn, takes up for his sister if he thinks anyone is threatening her...unlike her brother, the girl was neat and dainty, experimented happily with styles for her long hair, and often tried to help in the kitchen. (Money and Tucker 97-98)

As Foucault and other social constructionists caution, cultural gender stereotypes are dependent on historical periods of time, as well as the culture of rearing. In stark contrast to social construction theory that stresses the fluid and changing aspects of gender, Money and other influential transsexual researchers assume that once developed, gender identity remains fixed. In the case of the reassigned twin, the gender team recommended the use of female hormones and the construction of an artificial vagina at puberty for the "girl" twin. Money suggested: "If she waits until shortly before she is ready to begin her sex life, sexual intercourse will help keep the vaginal canal elastic and unconstricted" (Money and Tucker 97).

While the twin case suggests that gender identity might be learned, the researcher's gender attitudes contradict this idea when he suggests fitting transsexuals into rigid, fixed cultural stereotypes. The little girl is praised for maternal behavior, attention to her appearance, and other "feminine" stereotypes, like helping her mother in the kitchen. Further, because her gender-identity is defined as "feminine," it is assumed that her sexual preference will be male.

She is already being defined by her yet-to-be-constructed neovagina by Money. Throughout transsexual ideology, heterosexual intercourse is routinely prescribed to help keep the neovaginal canal open. Time and again, covert gender attitudes are conveyed along with transsexual ideology. These gender attitudes serve to keep the dichotomous Western sex and gender code intact. In the twin study, becoming a "girl" means being reduced to a not-yet-constructed sex organ and subservient social and sexual relationships to males. These covert sexist and homophobic attitudes appear throughout the clinical literature, remaining largely accepted and unchallenged. For example, in the-now famous 1979 Meyer report, the measure of transsexual adjustment for cohabitation is blatantly heterosexist and homophobic. Meyer writes: "if the patient is male requesting reassignment as a female, a gender appropriate cohabitation or marriage means that he lives with, or marries a man as a female" (Meyer and Reter 1011).

Long after the Gay Liberation Movement began and the American Psychological Association decreed homosexuality was not a mental illness, transsexual ideology continues to resurrect and reinforce homophobia (see Tripp). For example, a 1986 article evaluating endocrine levels in male-to-woman transsexuals refers to any animal behavior or human behavior not resulting in penile-vaginal contact, or what Masters and Johnson refer to as the "coital connection," as "abnormal sexual behavior" (Futterweit, Weiss and Fagerstrom 76).

Money's recent works deliberately advocate confusing the concepts of sex and gender. Money, appearing at first to be on the side of sociocultural influences on transsexualism, proposes combining gender identity, which he defines as the private definition of the self as male or female, and gender role, which he describes as the public definition or social stereotype of self as male or female, into the gender identity/role (G-IR) paradigm (Money, "Propaedeutics" 17). Money maintains that most likely the G-IR paradigm has "its origin in the same hormones that in prenatal life program the differentiation of the genitalia" (19). What at first appears to be an interesting concept of gender identity and gender role is ultimately used to support a socio-biological argument for sex and gender dimorphism. Money provides bipolar examples that he argues are not dimorphic but just more common in one sex than the other. One example he cites is parentalism. He asserts that:

Parentalism is sex shared insofar as it is exhibited by the father as well as the mother, but is threshold dimorphic insofar as an infant or child evokes it more readily and more frequently in the mother, than the father. For example, the sleeping mother is typically more sensitive to the stirrings of the neonate than is the sleeping father. (20)

Further, Money indicates that these behavioral dispositions are biologically based rather than socially constructed, which negates the "sex shared" parameter and winds up reinforcing sex and gender dimorphism. Behavioral dispositions Money lists as sex shared but more dominant in one sex than the other include describing males as more athletic, prone to competitive rivalry, territorial, likely to fight and responsive to erotic visual imagery. Money suggests females cuddle, rock and cling more and exhibit a greater prevalence for domestic neatness.

Money's platitudinous remark that these behaviors may be sex shared is abandoned as the study proposes an endocrinological explanation for gender differentiation. Money's speculation of an endocrinological base for gender differentiation, compounded by his view that at some point gender becomes fixed and unchangeable, contradict his theory of sex shared behavior. In interviews Money has consistently observed: "It is society and its pressures that create the situation which fosters gender abnormalities" ("Propaedeutics" 21). What sounds like a needed call for a critique of culturally constructed stereotypes of gender is contradicted when Money states that there is no distinction between sex and gender. As I stated earlier, if sex and gender are not separated, a political critique of gender is impossible. Money, completely aware of this, suggests that there is a "hidden political agenda" in the nature/nurture ideology of sex differences and argues:

Formulated in terms of reductionist biology, nature is a political strategy of those committed to the status quo of sex-differences...Conversely, neglect of biological determinism is the political strategy of the advocates of the political and social liberation of the sexes from historical stereotypes. ("Propaedeutics" 14)

Money proposes that the two strategies can be combined in the biology of learning which he calls "neuroscience." However, a deeper analysis of his work reveals his own "political agenda," designed to discredit and inhibit socio-cultural research. He, like other socio-biologists, draws many of his assumptions about human gender behavior from studies on animal sexuality. This method of research not only generalizes from other species but also blurs the separate categories of sex and gender and as such has been highly criticized by social construction theorists and liberal socio-biologists.

Money's search for an endocrinological etiology for transsexualism is decidedly socio-biological in that he is involved in finding the biological basis...of social behavior. In a piercing critique of socio-biology, Ashley Montagu cautions:

what sociobiologists do not fully understand is that as a consequence of the unique history of human evolution...Humankind has moved into a new zone of adaptation namely culture. (Montagu 9)

Montagu also maintains that if gender research continues to focus on biological determinism, human responses to the challenges of the environment will be overlooked. Further, many social constructionists and liberal socio-biologists caution that socio-biological theories operate to conceal a "New Right Movement" and agenda (see Adkins).

Psychoanalysis or Mother Blaming

Psychoanalyst Robert Stoller, a proponent of a possible biological etiology for transsexualism, has emerged as a harsh critic of sex reassignment surgery. In his 1985 work, *Presentations of Gender*, Stoller notes that he was one of the first to work in depth with "sex change" patients in the 1960s and not share in the sweeping enthusiasm for hormonal and surgical "treatment." Stoller asserts,

Little good has come from the social experiment of "sex change." We do not know how many patients...were helped...Perhaps we have been witness to...a lunatic fad. (169)

What goes wrong in "sex change" treatments?...there are no statistics about the frequency, severity, or mortality; the usual morbidities and mortalities associated with anaesthesia and extensive surgery (for example, hemorrhage, anuria, cardiac arrest, embolus), perforation of viscera, failure of the grafted phallus to take in females, scarring of the artificial vagina in males with loss of some or all of potency, chronic cystitis, strange-looking genitals, abnormal urethra with resulting abnormal urinary stream, sloughing off of skin grafts, chronic infections (of vaginas or postmastectomy), paranoid psychosis, psychotic depression, chronic though non psychotic depression, suicide, hopelessness, regret at the "sex change," lawsuits. (168)

In addition to the above, Stoller condemns his colleagues' data as unreliable. He laments their failure to discuss the long-term effects of cross-sex hormones and to provide results of how many patients require further surgery to correct complications "as if it were beneath the dignity of the treating physician to study...in order to report" (168). Despite his dissatisfaction with traditional transsexual "treatment," Stoller believes that primary transsexuals, the "most feminine of males and most masculine of females do better with sex change than without" (169).

Stoller's psychoanalytic theory has become a cornerstone in American transsexual ideology. It attempts to explain the origin and manifestations of "masculinity" and "femininity," an essential task for psychoanalysis starting with Freud's theory of the Oedipal Complex. Concentrating primarily on the cause of male-to-woman transsexualism, Stoller's theory is that "too much mother and too little father yields femininity in boys" (*Presentations* 28). He challenges the traditional concept of conflict essential to traditional psychoanalytic theories of gender development by asserting that "non-conflictual gratification can lead to developmental arrest" (*Presentations* 26). According to Stoller, the period of non-conflictual gratification for the male-to-woman transsexual is the uninterrupted period of "blissful" mother-son symbiosis which Stoller feels is the critical period for the formation of gender identity. Much of Stoller's writings on transsexualism focus primarily on blaming and psychopathologizing their mothers. His frequent references to the "feminine" male as a "gross aberrance" (26) indicates a bias not only against females but "femininity" as well.

Stoller believes a "biopsychic force," comprised of innate traits set into motion by family dynamics, is the major factor responsible for transsexualism. He also thinks there is a possible biological base for gender behavior. However, most of his hypothesis rests on a psychological determinism with origins in early family experiences. Specifically, he asserts that mothers are the major catalysts responsible for causing male transsexualism. According to Stoller the pattern begins with a "harsh" maternal grandmother, who, because she has no love for her daughter, turns her into a "psychological" transgenderist. The daughter tries to turn to her father, but Stoller observes that the father's unavailability makes her feel that being a woman is worthless. Rejected by her mother and abandoned by her father, the daughter wishes to become a male and, in some cases Stoller maintains, "prays to God for a penis." Instead of becoming a male she usually winds up marrying a distant and passive man for, as Stoller states, "It is unlikely a more manly man would marry such a woman."

Stoller believes the mother, who he postulates still wants to be a male, is responsible for creating a transsexual son. According to his logic, her infant son becomes the "beautiful phallus" she has longed for. Mother and son become involved in a "blissful symbiosis," resulting in the son becoming "feminized." When the son begins to cross-dress, his mother not only encourages it but degrades "masculinity." Once again the father is "distant and passive," failing to intervene to separate mother and son or serve as a "masculine" role model. Stoller believes that the male "primary" transsexual never goes through the Oedipal complex, thereby avoiding any conflict. Object relations theorist Paulina Kernberg is in agreement with this theory and adds that the mother of "pretranssexual" boys

does not consider the child as a narcissistic object, but as an idealized version of herself...The mother...would reenact an O-R (object relations) in which she herself plays the role of her own mother, this time enchanted with her daughter-boy; namely her feminine son. (Stoller, *Presentation* 31)

Person and Ovesey, critics of Stoller's "non-conflictual" theory of gender identity, charge that there is no symmetrical explanation for the female-to-man transsexual. Like other major transsexual researchers, with the exception of Lothstein, Stoller basically dismisses female-to-men transsexuals as part of a "continuum of butch homosexuality," and speculates that their sexual preference is only for "feminine" heterosexual females.

As so often happens in transsexual ideology, gender is either abandoned, confused, or replaced with heterosexist ideas or values about sexual preference. Stoller's heterosexist and heterogender paradigm does not acknowledge diverse gender behavior such as female transgenderists living full time as men who identify their relationships with males as gay. Such diversity suggests that gender and erotic object choice are far more complex than the clinical model, tainted with cultural prejudice, allows for.

Stoller claims his theory differs from Freud by emphasizing symbiosis as opposed to the Oedipal complex as the determinant of gender identification.

According to Freudian theory, becoming "feminine" is a much trickier process for the girl than becoming "masculine" is for the boy. Freud argued that maleness and masculinity were the primary and more "natural states." Traditional Freudian analysis views the girl as not only having to shift her object of desire from her mother to her father, but also having to shift her sexual pleasure from her clitoris to her vagina, acts that supposedly renounce both her bisexuality and "penis envy," transforming her into a "normal" feminine heterosexual. According to Freud, "the vagina becomes valued...as an asylum for the penis" (Freud, *Sexuality and the Psychology of Love* 175).

Stoller differs with traditional Freudian theories of gender identity by arguing that the boy, not the girl, has a more difficult time establishing his gender identity, since his first gender identification is with his mother. Accordingly, in order to develop "normal" masculinity, he must separate himself from his mother. This is a much more difficult task Stoller argues, since "masculinity" in our culture consists of the negation and denial of all that is "feminine," starting with the mother. According to his hypothesis, after separating from the mother the "normal" girl's "femininity" remains intact. However, after the boy separates from the mother, he must renounce his "femininity" in order to develop his "masculinity." This act, according to Stoller's hypothesis, makes him more vulnerable to the "perversions," because his first identity with his mother is both desired and hated. Stoller's work incorporates both homophobic and sexist values and attitudes throughout and ignores social reality.

By blaming mothers of primary transsexuals for *poisoning* their sons with "femininity" during "blissful symbiosis," he not only denigrates women and "femininity" but ignores the fact that not all primary caretakers are female. An interesting study to test his theory would be the examination of male transsexuals whose primary caretakers were male. Feminist psychoanalysts Dorothy Dinnerstein and Nancy Chodorow believe the misogynist renunciation of "femininity" and females resulting from mother/son symbiosis may in part be remedied by having more males involved in primary caretaking roles.

In *Presentations of Gender* Stoller again demonstrates male bias in his pronouncement that there are few, if any, female transvestites, an assumption he even admits is based on little or no contact with this population. Like his ideas about female transsexuals, this assumption is also erroneous. Contrary to Stoller's assertions, the Albuquerque Cross-Dressers Support Group, reflective of a nationwide trend, has experienced a steady growth in the number of female transvestites, most of whom reject clinical labels and prefer to be called cross-dressers or transgenderists. Clinicians all too often assume if people don't come in for treatment they don't exist. Nothing could be further from the truth. Many transgenderists don't buy into the clinical definitions of themselves. Why should they?

The reason Stoller cites for the scarcity of female transvestites sounds like it came out of a fashion magazine. He argues that because women are allowed to cross-dress, and are even considered fashionable for doing so, there are few if any female transvestites. What his assumption fails to take into account is that complete cross-dressing transcends the realm of "fashion" and incorporates the construction of secondary sex characteristics. Although "masculine" clothes may be in vogue for women, it is an altogether different matter when a woman stuffs a sock in a jock strap to simulate a penis. By doing so, she parallels the male cross-dresser's construction of breasts, an act that, *far from making a fashion statement*, often culturally condemns her to a peripheral nether world.

Theories like Stoller's too often accept "masculine" violence as normal. "The boy's normal contempt for women," often a precursor to violence toward women, is a result not of genital differences but the boy's "pathological and defensive reaction to maternal omnipotence," feminist psychoanalyst Chodorow maintains (Chodorow, "Oedipal Asymmetries and Heterosexual Knots" 243). Further, because women mother, Chodorow observes, heterosexual relationships are rarely fulfilling.

Stoller's psychoanalytic theory of gender identity reinforces and perpetrates the essentialist, heterosexist, bipolar Western sex and gender code. He views "normal" gender identity amendable prior to preadolescence when the hormones kick in and, as John Money asserts, "the gender gates close." Therefore, Stoller suggests "inappropriate" gender identity can be psychologically "treated" in preadolescents. By overemphasizing biology and/or family matrixes as causes of transgenderism, Stoller and other researchers become obsessed with the manipulation of hormones and/or Oedipal complexes, and ignore the existence of well-adjusted transgenderists.

A heinous error in medical and clinical generated transsexual ideology and a great cause of needless oppression and suffering is the assumption that males own "masculinity" and women own "femininity." Thankfully, this hideous logic is being challenged by the growing transgender movement. Researchers who continue to ignore the gender movement reveal themselves to be more interested in controlling than trying to understand gender behavior. While Stoller offers a useful critique of sex-reassignment theories, his insistence on a psychological etiology for transsexualism works to stigmatize women and maintain repressive bipolar sex and gender roles. This is evident in his "treatment" for "feminine" boys, which consists of using rigid behavior modification techniques to develop "masculinity." Such "treatment," adopted by Richard Green and others, raises the question of whether the punitive enforcement of rigid gender stereotypes under the guise of "treatment" is ethical.

"Masculinity" is regarded as an achievement in Stoller's paradigm. Such gender bias not only negates anyone considered "feminine," but also fosters the hatred and devaluation of women. If only Stoller and other creators of transsexual ideology would heed their own advice and see the proverbial ideology embedded in their own assumptions. A rational Stoller advises:

Let us not fool ourselves. Research on "transsexualism" or "sex change" is as soggy with morality and righteousness as rum cake is with booze. (*Presentations* 160)

Unfortunately, many of Stoller's own transsexual theories are also soggy with morality.

The Sissy Boy Theorist

A long time advocate of Stoller, psychiatrist Richard Green conducted a longitudinal study designed to identify and treat pretranssexual boys. His results, published in his book *The "Sissy Boy Syndrome" and the Development of Homosexuality*, culminates his 15-year study of boyhood "femininity," which Green and others believed led to adult "male-to-female" (male-to-women) transsexualism. His sample was made up of "feminine" boys turned in by their parents to a gender-identity clinic for exhibiting "feminine" behavior. Such behavior included cross-dressing, playing with "girl" toys, preferring a female peer group, avoiding rough-and-tumble play and desiring to grow up to be a girl. This small group of males was reportedly matched with a control group of "masculine boys," selected for exhibiting stereotypical masculine behavior.

A disturbing and predictable development took place during his study. Green seemed to abandon his search of how gender identity is formed and became preoccupied instead with the role of gender in determining sexual preference, an all-too-common occurrence in studies of gender identity. His results, repeated in other studies (see Zuger), assert that boys with a cross-gender identity grow up to be adult homosexuals. Seventy-five percent of the "feminine" boys in the Green study reportedly grew up to be bisexual or gay. Only one participant became a "transsexual." All the "masculine" boys were described as growing up to be heterosexual with the exception of one gay male. To my knowledge, no serious study has been conducted to find the cause of heterosexuality.

That his study veered from its original purpose and ended up proposing a possible etiology for gay males is significant. Besides confusing sex and gender preferences, the study also resurrects the stereotype that all gay men are "feminine." Throughout his study, Green reminds the reader that he has a liberal view of homosexuality. He attempts to prove his assertion by noting that he was on the American Psychological Association's committee that voted to delete homosexuality as an illness. Green's study, steeped in contradictions, raises serious questions, one of which is if he is so accepting of homosexuality why does he advocate "treatment" to prevent and control in preadolescent boys cross-gender behavior, which he maintains is a precursor to adult "homosexuality."

Green's writings focus mainly on the treatment, prevention and management of non-mainstream gender behavior. In *Human Sexuality* he recommends that "it is important to remember that the supreme goal of clinical management is to reduce social and interpsychic conflict" (Green, *Human Sexuality* 161). How is this possible with "treatment" that is policing and enforcing cultural gender and sex stereotypes? Even though such "treatment" for preadolescent "feminine" boys attempts to avoid hormonal and surgical solutions which have been blamed for physical malignancies, the results of these treatments may prove to be just as or more malignant and disabling on a personal and cultural level.

Green's rationale for the gender torture of young "feminine" males has its origin in Stoller's idea that boyhood "femininity" results from "too much mother and not enough father." Other ideas influencing Green's theory and treatment can be traced to cognitive developmental theory which stresses differences in adult and child thinking and labeling based on genitals, and social learning theory which emphasizes the social network as a shaper of attitudes through reward and punishment. Although he maintains that gender identity and sexual preference "can embrace physiological or psycho-social theory," Green clearly is on the side of physiological theories of gender. An advocate of the prenatal cross-hormone theory of sex and gender, Green maintains that

cross-gender behavior in childhood and homosexual behavior in adulthood are age-dependent expressions of the same underlying, evolving pattern of female sexual identity. (*"Sissy Boy Syndrome"* 371)

Ignoring feminist, lesbian, gay and transgender scholarship on the social construction of gender, Green posits a *gender contagion theory* of how a young male becomes "feminine." Basically, Green believes that the "feminine" boy catches "femininity" much like a disease by having too much contact with women and girls, resulting in his "interests, skills, and attitudes" being shaped by them. Therefore, Green posits, his "romantic needs and erotic patterns" mirror his female social network, causing him to "seek males" as erotic partners (Green, *"Sissy Boy Syndrome"* 371). Such a heterosexist and reductive assumption implies females only choose males as objects of desire. His belief denies the diversity of erotic object choices, again reinforcing a misguided dominant belief that all gays are "feminine" and can only be erotically attracted to "masculine" males. He doesn't even consider the possibility of homogender object choices. Green thereby negates such possibilities as "masculine" males being attracted to other "masculine" males, or "feminine" males erotically aroused by other "feminine" males or "feminine" females, or the idea that "masculine" females could be attracted to other "masculine" females and/or "masculine" males. A serious flaw in his and similar studies *is assuming that we are attracted to people's sex, rather than their gender.*

Psychoanalytic, social learning and endocrinological theories on male-to-women transsexualism and transgenderism all promote the ideas of *female contamination* and mother blame. Far too often psychoanalysts blame the mother for smothering and restricting her son's movements. Social learning theorists argue "feminine" males get "contaminated" by being around too many females and their "toxic" by-product of "femininity." Endocrinological theorists blame females for secreting too many female hormones prenatally which allegedly condemn their sons to "boyhood femininity." Each theory depicts the "feminine" male as a victim of female persons, hormones, or femininity. In this paradigm all females are viewed as potential *typhoid Marys*, as carriers and contaminators of "femininity," a dread "disease" causing *dis-ease* for gender enforcers. The value of studying clinical transsexual ideology lies not in cure rates, but in what it reveals about cultural gender attitudes. Green justifies his "treatment" for "sissy boys" as a necessary intervention to prevent them from being socially isolated and/or violently attacked. The enculturation of the "feminine" boy is difficult, Green observes, because

Early grade school brings social distress. Without "masculine" skills, without the capacity for full participation in the rough-and-tumble play of early boyhood, with "feminine" mannerisms and with minimal input from the father, it is difficult for the boy to move off the "feminine" developmental track. He is labeled "sissy." There is increased isolation from males...The feminine boy is less attractive to teenage girls. (*"Sissy Boy Syndrome"* 380)

Never bothering to address the dual cultural hatred and fascination with the "feminine," Green's "treatment" contributes to the cultural devaluation of "femininity" and females by insisting that young males get rid of all that is considered feminine. If, as Green contends, "feminine" boys are not attractive to teenage girls, why do millions of teenage heterosexual females idolize the "femme" males in rock music?

To some extent we are all raised to despise the feminine. Recently, one of my female students, "C.C.," in her mid-30s, reported that she felt an aversion to her five-year-old son's curiosity about "femininity." Apparently he liked to watch his mother put her make-up on. One afternoon C.C. found him playing in her make-up and reported it made her "feel physically sick" and unable to stand the thought of him "touching her things," a feeling she had never had before. Worried about how her response might affect her son, she is trying to understand her actions. At last report C.C. stated she went out and bought her son his own make-up! While she is trying to understand and modify her response to her son, I am reminded of a similar incident confided to me by a friend, "M.M.," who had a preadolescent "feminine" son who mimicked her actions. Because it so disturbed her, she sought "professional" help. Her male therapist told her to voice her hatred toward her son. Nearly every day for several years in an attempt to scare the "feminine" out of him, she told him she hated him for trying to be like her. Ten years later, he is still a "feminine" young man, but extremely depressed and confused.

If the "feminine" male is stigmatized in America, the preadolescent "tomboy" manifesting "masculine" behavior remains safe from most public ridicule. Will this still be the case after Green completes his current study on tomboys?

Parents rarely bring "tomboys" to gender clinics for treatment. However, at puberty, most "tomboys" are expected to automatically transform into "femmes" and devote their lives to *finding a man*. Sex researchers observe that most tomboys comply with cultural pressures to conform. The "feminine" boys in Green's study also reportedly stopped most cross-gender behavior by adolescence, no doubt in response to escalating threats of violence and attacks from therapists and peers. However, Green observes, they have not stopped being gay. Many gays and lesbians are forced to hide their sexual preferences as are most transgenderists. However, it will be interesting to see if Green follows up with the "feminine" males when they reach their 30s, a time when living a gender facade for most transgenderists becomes unbearable.

In order to reinforce "masculinity" Green insists on using male therapists as models for "feminine" boys, reminiscent of Robert Bly's prescription for his men's movement. Much of the so-called treatment for "feminine" boys consists of nothing more than scare tactics, threats and physical punishment. A five-year-old "feminine" boy in treatment with Green was warned "that as he grows up, and continues to do sissy things that he won't have many friends, and people will make fun of him, and that he'll be very unhappy" (Green, *"Sissy Boy Syndrome"* 274).

Such advice no doubt was used to scare his "patient" out of femininty and into masculinity. Green advocates involving the whole family in the "therapy" process where he separates mothers, fathers and "feminine" boys into separate group therapies. His foremost goal is to destroy the mother/son bond. He advises that "You've got to get these mothers out of the way...Feminine kids don't need their mothers around" (Green, *"Sissy Boy Syndrome"* 223, 275). Once the mother is moved out of the picture, Green encourages fathers and sons to bond. He theorizes that fathers of cross-gender boys avoid them because their sons avoid "masculine" pursuits. Green posits the avoidance of "masculine" behavior may be biologically based. So he advises fathers to engage in non-aggressive "masculine" activities to counteract the "femininity" in their sons.

If, as Green has often publicly asserted, parents are not responsible for the behavior of their "feminine" sons, why does he advise parents to conform to stereotypical gender roles and interactions with their sons. In one particularly disturbing case, Green prescribed that a mother quit her professional career and adopt a more "traditional and submissive relationship" to her husband and son in order to avert her son's "femininity" (see Green and Money). The feminine boy, according to Green is considered cured when he rejects femininity and develops masculinity. "Rejecting femininity" in this case means developing negative gender attitudes and possible acts of violence toward anything considered "feminine" or female, including women and his "feminine" self. The following excerpts from an interview with a "feminine" boy in "treatment" illustrate this point. In a profoundly disturbing interview with Green, a ten-year-old boy denounced his former "feminine" behavior as "a big fat girly problem." Green's "patient," on his way to mental health and gender conformity, provided an account of his new found "masculine" behavior, which included *violence to* and *avoidance of* "girl" things, including throwing his female "dolly" away. He described the incident:

a couple weeks ago—a little dolly. It was real ugly. I just got so mad I threw it away—cause I ripped all the hair off of it. I threw the whole thing away. (*"Sissy Boy Syndrome"* 277)

The motive for the boy's violence and rage toward the female doll may have been elicited in part by his parents who were enlisted by Green to serve as *pseudo-therapists/gender police* to monitor and censor "femininity" in their young son. Green describes how his treatment works:

parental attentiveness or disinterest was used to positively or negatively reinforce specific "masculine" or "feminine" behaviors, such as playing with boys' toys or girl-type toys. At home, a token reinforcement program was instituted. Kyle received blue tokens for "desirable" behaviors, such as play with boys' toys or with boys and red ones for "undesirable" behaviors, such as doll-play, "feminine" gestures, or playing with girls. Blue tokens were redeemable for treats such as ice cream. Red tokens resulted in loss of blue tokens, periods of isolation, or spanking by the father. (*"Sissy Boy Syndrome"* 295)

We must ask what the long-term consequences of a masculinity conditioning program that fosters violence and rage toward anything associated with femininity and females, and a strict separation between the sexes might be. Allegedly designed to ward off negative social reactions to "femininity" in boys, Green ends up incorporating similar negative social reactions such as social isolation, threats and physical violence in his "treatments." His "treatment" program is an all-too-real reflection of contemporary society in which the endocrinologically based and culturally embraced assumption that "femininity" belongs to females makes both "feminine" males and females targets of violence. Recent crime statistics confirm an alarming rise in violence against females, which former NOW president Molly Yard has called a reflection of "gender inequality." Less reported, but alarmingly common also, is the violence toward "feminine males," sometimes resulting in death (see chapter 4).

Do treatments that inhibit "femininity" help contribute to negative attitudes and actions against anything associated with femininity? And are treatments that routinely punish boys for playing with girls or "girl" things ethical? In addition, we must ask what the long-term consequences of such behavior modification may be both individually and culturally. At age 15, Kyle, the former "feminine" boy treated by Green, was described as having developed a "normal male identity" and "normal aspirations for growing up to be married and have a family" (Green, *"Sissy Boy Syndrome"* 295-96). Obviously for Green, "normal" behavior means conformity to rigid cultural stereotypes prescribed by the Western sex and gender code.

In a follow-up interview with Kyle at 18, Green notes that Kyle had "primarily homosexual drives" and had attempted suicide because he did not want to be gay (Green, *"Sissy Boy Syndrome"* 315). The issue of suicide seems to be taken lightly by Green as he proposes a heterosexual antidote. Green told Kyle that "it's not that you have exhausted the potential for finding a woman of your choice." Kyle was further advised by Green that there were "probably seven thousand unmarried, unpregnant women" on the UCLA campus (Green, *"Sissy Boy Syndrome"* 317-18). A prescription to get married and prove your manhood by procreating sounds suspiciously like the hideous Christian fundamentalist "repairitive" therapy that promises "miracle cures" to homosexuals and has been proven ineffective. Green's advice to find a woman to Kyle is thoughtless and frightening. Kyle and other clients whose treatment included ridding oneself of anything "feminine" could be very dangerous or possibly lethal to females.

Treatment programs like Green's, whose goal through behavior modification is to transform "feminine" boys into "masculine" heterosexuals, should be eradicated. Concerned that, in Kyle's case, treatment "did not abort his development of homosexual arousal," Green suggests that a "deficit" in masculine identification may occur at a "critical developmental period beyond which the deficit cannot be remedied" (Green, *"Sissy Boy Syndrome"* 319). Such a conclusion recalls psychoanalytical and endocrinological theories proposing that at some point gender identification becomes fixed.

Recent studies on "feminine" boys, inspired by Green, concentrate on "the prevention of adolescent transsexualism" and adult homosexuality. These works typically employ a bio-psychological approach, arguing that "constitutional factors...cannot be excluded," so they propose modifying the family's interactions (see Wrate and Gulens). Most clinical studies on transgenderists and transsexuals are so obsessed with the subject's sexual preference that the issue of gender becomes obscured. For example, in 1989 Zuger launched a study to find out if relatives of "feminine" boys were "sexually deviant." Although Zuger's findings suggested a social construction rather than a hereditary base for gender, it demonstrates the researchers' obsession with the erotic choices of transgenderists. In addition, these studies reveal the confusion caused by not viewing sex and gender as separate constructs.

Not surprisingly, Green acknowledges the Right Wing has already issued several homophobic books, inspired by Green's research, advising parents how to raise their children "straight." Green's theories of "feminine" boys reflects the confusion generated by a clinical transsexual ideology, where sex and gender are increasingly confused and endocrinological theories are advanced as etiological explanations.

To date, the studies on "feminine" boys, which speculate that cross-gender identity in childhood is often an indicator of adult homosexuality, are suspect and must be examined for their underlying cultural agenda. Is the confusion between sex and gender a convenient way for the medical profession to covertly "treat" homosexuality, which is supposedly not considered a mental "disorder," unless the individual deems it so, such as in "Ego-dystonic homosexuality," itself a highly suspect category (*DSM III* 281-83).

An article by Lawrence Mass in the May 1987 issue of *The Advocate* observes that Green does not present any gay perspective. Mass also points to other serious problems among which are that the solution to the

problem of the traditional victimization of "effeminate" males by their sexist and homophobic peers is to help teach them to conform more convincingly and consistently to traditional gender roles. (56)

Comparing Green's homophobic solution to racism, Mass argues it would be less troubling if accompanied by a

more outspoken commitment to and documentation of an active program to minimize homophobia in childhood environments. It's a little like trying to teach highly ghettoized blacks how to behave more "properly" (don't jive too much, straighten your hair)...so they won't get traumatized by racists—without going after the racists. (56)

Green's patent response to any criticism of his "therapy" has been to argue that his patients look back favorably on their "treatment," adding that at least no one has been harmed by it!

By enforcing gender conformity and control, so-called "treatments" like Green's provide an incentive for *psychological euthanasia*, wherein gender "violators," viewed as suffering from an incurable disease, are forced to suppress behavior, not harmful to the self or others, because it has been socially stigmatized. In the late 1960s through the early 1970s, Green was instrumental in using aversive shock therapy on transgenderists and cross-dressers. Tiana, an extremely gifted male-to-woman transgenderist, recalled that while she was a student at UCLA, Green routinely subjected her to shock therapy for cross-dressing. This treatment, she observed, did not work. Tiana stated that at the time what was even worse for her than undergoing the shock treatment was the humiliation of finding that Green had placed a huge sign reading "Gender-Identity Clinic" above the bench in his waiting area. Tiana related that each time she sat on the bench, with the large sign above her, she felt more stigmatized, isolated and abnormal.

In reflecting on psychoendocrinological gender theories like Green's, critics have observed that gender is reduced to a fixed set of psychological traits that prohibit any serious consideration of the ways gender is used to structure distinct realms of social experience. Since medically generated transsexual ideology influences and informs all other views of transsexuals and gender, that ideology must be challenged. By insisting on endocrinological etiologies, researchers are creating a medical smoke screen to keep the Western sex and gender code intact. The result is a culture that views technology as salvation and accepts without question the *medical invasion into gender*. Therefore it is essential to remove the mesmeric grasp endocrinological and biological theories of gender have on transsexuals and the general public. The bio-endocrinological theories of extremist Gunter Dorner, who proposes an *endocrinological euthanasia* for transsexuals and transgenderists, people he views synonymously with gays and lesbians, represents not only a threat to the separate political existence of sex and gender, but also a threat to the very existence of gender and sex minorities.

Dorner's Endocrinological Euthanasia

A critique on biological theories of "homosexuality" by Wendell Ricketts can also be applied to biological theories of transsexualism. Ricketts warns that "biological research on homosexuality shows the ineluctable taint on 'objective' science of personal beliefs and cultural prejudices" (66). The peril of insisting that gender is biologically determined is demonstrated in the theories of endocrinologist Gunter Dorner, who directed the Institute of Experimental Endocrinology at Humboldt University in the former East Berlin. For over 20 years Dorner has been attempting to prove that homosexuality is biologically determined by prenatal hormones in the womb. Transsexualism, according to Dorner, is "an extreme variety of homosexuality," or, as Wendell Ricketts observes, to Dorner homosexuality is a "muted form of transsexuality" (78). Dorner claims he developed his gender theory, which confuses sex and gender, when he viewed "The Ballet of Vienna" on television. Dorner observed that "there were some homosexual dancers with typical female behavior" performing "gestures that couldn't possibly be performed by heterosexual males" (Murray 100).

Reasoning that homosexuality and transsexuality are probably the result of prenatal hormones, Dorner designed a "treatment" to eliminate both gays and transsexuals. In an interview with Dorner, Linda Murray concludes that he believes that

the hormonal imbalance results from stress in the pregnant mother. He claims he can tell, based on amniotic fluid samples, if the fetus is at risk for being born homosexual, and he can "correct the abnormal" condition in the uterus by injecting supplementary androgens or masculizing hormones. Furthermore, Dorner has announced that in the near future he may be able to turn adult gays into straights with an experimental drug. (102)

To justify his proposed genocidal "treatments," Dorner cites his research on the LH (lutenizing hormone) positive feedback approach. He observes that the LH positive-feedback approach is largely responsible for female ovulation at puberty. It results from estrogen triggering a brain hormone (LHRH), which releases LH. Dorner maintains that an injection of estrogen can artificially trigger the release of both hormones. Operating on this basis, he injected homosexuals and heterosexuals with estrogen. According to his theory, which erroneously assumes all "feminine" males are gay, "gay men should respond the same way females do," because, Dorner argues, their brains are "feminized" prenatally due to a lack of androgens, "particularly testosterone" (Murray 102). Dorner claimed that when gay males are injected with estrogen they show a significant rise in LH levels, "as if the shot of estrogen were signaling a phantom ovary" (102). Conversely, he argued, when heterosexual males are injected with estrogen, their LH levels "fall or stay flat" (Dorner 102).

In 1984, an American team replicated Dorner's LH findings, which Dorner says proves his case. However, Dutch researchers subsequently not only disproved both studies, but added that in their opinion the LH hormone originates from the testes and not the hypothalamus (Murray 102). Dorner's work, which was funded by the former German Democratic Republic, has met with mixed reactions in the U.S. John Money warned if Dorner administers androgens to pregnant mothers they may cause unwanted secondary sex characteristics like the development of "deep voices and facial hair in the mothers" (108). Further, Money cautioned the administration of hormones in the womb may be carcinogenic to the child. The director of the Kinsey Institute, June Reinsch, expressed concern over the genocidal aspect of his proposal, and warned that "we don't know the consequences of eliminating homosexuality" (127). Other critics of Dorner fear if a so-called treatment to eradicate homosexuality, transgenderism, and transsexuality in the womb exists, who will be entrusted to make the decision?

Will the decision be left up to the parents at all? What if society or government decides it wanted to "cure" homosexuality in the womb—perhaps as a desperate measure to control the spread of AIDS? (128)

Outraged by Dorner's proposal, the National Gay Task Force thought that fanatic groups such as the Christian right and right-wing extremists might try to use Dorner's theories to promote endocrinological euthanasia. In 1987, it was widely believed that Dorner had already put his ideas into practice. UCLA endocrinologist Gorski,[5] an advocate of Dorner, stated if Dorner

could pinpoint just the right critical period and just the right level of androgens you could probably reduce the incidence of homosexuality. (Murray 128)

Such a comment indicates that Gorski might endorse espects of Dorner's treatment.

In contemporary American society, where clinical gender research currently focuses on identifying and "treating" young gender "deviants," is Dorner's proposal so far-fetched? As long as researchers subscribe to hormonal bipolar theories of gender that blur sex and gender and continue to taint their research with personal and cultural prejudice, endocrinological euthanasia may in the future replace the current transsexual treatments.

Do Money, Stoller and Green's endocrinological based theories of transsexualism anticipate a future endocrinological elimination of transsexualism and transgenderism, particularly since they all project that in the future sex-reassignment surgery may be obsolete? While SRS is currently the medical "treatment" of choice for transsexuals, it may in part be a reflection of living in the age of plastic and cosmetic surgery, where the body is reduced to a series of mechanized, replaceable parts. As reports of dissatisfaction and disastrous results, such as lawsuits for inadequate vaginas or transsexuals changing their mind become increasingly common, SRS may be replaced with new endocrinological "treatments." These new treatments, like SRS, will reflect personal and cultural biases. If put into practice, Dorner's endocrinological "treatment" will not be concerned with personal and social liberation, but with a slave class of cloning heterosexual gender conformists.

Some of the more liberal socio-biological theories about gender propose that "masculine" females and "feminine" males may be a natural evolutionary response to a society plagued by overpopulation. However intriguing this concept is, in that it brings attention to transgenderists and the environment, it is basically flawed. As feminists long ago observed, putting people on pedestals or making them the "other" negates their real existence. Moreover, socio-biological theories that do not differentiate between sex and gender confuse transgenderists and transsexuals with gays and lesbians and erroneously assume that gays and lesbians do not reproduce. This idea is contradicted by the current baby boom (aided by advances in reproductive technologies) among some gays and lesbians. Sociobiology, by not allowing for individual differences among transgenderists, transsexuals, gays and lesbians, pigeonholes them into categories having little to do with reality. Perhaps more as a wish than reality, masking their homophobia, some sociobiologists portray gays and lesbians as self-sacrificing altruists willing to give up their reproductive rights to enrich the lives of their siblings' children (see Wilson).

This type of logic regards transgenderists and transsexuals as "aliens" and encourages their objectification and isolation. In a society where technology has aided in the objectification of the body and people are increasingly treated like robots and *reduced to their hormonal secretions*, Dorner's socio-biological and genocidal vision becomes a distinct possibility.

The predominance of such endocrinological theories about gender has vast implications. The devaluation and treatment of "femininity" in males is a blatant enactment of cultural sexism and misogyny. In an article on technology, Riane Eisler observed that societies with "correspondingly rigid stereotypes of 'masculinity' and 'femininity' are typically violent societies characterized by the abuse of women." In such societies, Eisler argues, all things associated with males are valued and all traits associated with women are devalued.

Such hierarchical thinking is implicit in endocrinological theories which assign cultural values to sex hormones. Testosterone, thought of as being predominantly a male hormone, supposedly makes you strong, while estrogen, thought of as being predominately a female hormone, is thought to make you weak and over-emotional. These clinical stereotypes do not take into account that at a certain level, testosterone converts into estrogen. The danger of stressing endocrinological differences based on cultural assumptions can be seen when females are denied access to certain jobs, based on unproven hormonal theories maintaining that during menstruation women are dangerously unstable.

Returning again to the question of what being born in the "wrong" body means, perhaps there is a clue in the way cultural critic and psychoanalyst Robert Romanyshyn regards the body. In his impressive 1989 book, *Technology as Symptom and Dream*, Romanyshyn suggests the body is a "cultural invention" that suits the world in which we live and that our diseases are really "symptoms of cultural denials." He suggests that "symptoms as a sign of illness" also provide a guide to health. If Romanyshyn is correct, the transsexual's distress at being born in the "wrong" body may be extended to mean being born in the "wrong" culture.

A culture that denies social space and existence to those who do not adhere to rigid cultural gender maps and insists on treating them as "diseased" is not only a culture intolerant of variation or change, but a hostile environment. If we adopt Romanyshyn's advice and follow the "symptom" as a guide, then we must give voice to the growing numbers of self-defined transgenderists and transsexuals. It is essential that researchers become acquainted with the transgender community, not to exploit, but to better understand how gender is negotiated. It is equally imperative that researchers realize and accept responsibility for the effect their theories and "treatments" have already had on the transgender subculture and the rest of American society. One of the areas that transmits clinical transsexual ideology is contemporary American popular culture. Although it is saturated with traditional transsexual ideology, popular culture has the potential to change public attitudes about transgender persons.

Chapter Four

Images of Transsexuals and Transgenderists
in American Popular Culture

The great democratic U.S. American dream of equality, as Alexis de
Tocqueville long ago observed, does not extend to everyone. Like other
minority groups in American culture, transgenderists and cross-dressers are all
too often victimized by negative stereotyping and are heirs to a nightmare of
inequality.[1] The abundance of demeaning images and stereotypes of
transgenderists, transsexuals and cross-dressers found in contemporary
American popular culture reinforces their social and personal stigmatization
and inequality. Since most of these images are media generated and reach large
audiences, they have the power not only to reflect culturally biased beliefs
about gender but also the potential to shape them. In most cases,
sensationalized media portrayals of transgenderists have little to do with the
day to day reality of most transgenderists and everything to do with the ratings
and sales of popular cultural products featuring transgenderists.

This chapter will examine popular cultural depictions of transgenderists,
transsexuals and cross-dressers, as well as the persons frequently confused
with them. The major focus will be on what cultural ideologies are being
conveyed through these representations as well as an analysis of audience
reactions to them as a measure of contemporary gender attitudes in America.
As we head toward the twenty-first century, television continues to be the
dominant conveyer of popular culture in America. Due to TV's widespread
accessibility and its power to enculturate and to rapidly disseminate
information, I will largely focus upon television broadcasts of transgenderists,
transsexuals and cross-dressers from the early 1980s through the present. This
analysis will also include films, popular books, entertainment programs,

103

documentaries, rock stars, music videos, commercials, film reviews, news, tabloids and, most specifically, television talk shows. But first, a brief discussion of popular culture and our relation to it provide the framework of this study.

Popular culture, simply defined as "mainstream culture," includes the everyday world of television, films, music, fads, celluloid heroes, advertising, entertainment, consumer products and the mass media. What we do, where we go, as well as personal and corporate definitions of who we are or should be, what we believe or should believe, and what we desire or should desire constitute some of the basic components of popular culture. Popular culture reflects personal and cultural values, beliefs, hopes and fears of both the creators and the consumers of popular culture. Analysts of popular culture Christopher Geist and Jack Nachbar, sum up popular culture as

a two-way relationship with our lives—both affecting the values we construct for ourselves and reflecting values we have already constructed—that popular culture taken as a whole is the most common part of our cultural heritage and our present living environment. (3)

Our relationship to popular culture is complex and, as new research into audience interaction with television reveals, continually negotiated. Much of that negotiation has historical antecedents in events that transformed the relationship between people and products, creating new identities. The early nineteenth-century "new consumer democracy" fueled by mass production and the idea that products could be available on a mass scale "gave rise to a notion of class, defined almost exclusively by patterns of consumption," according to cultural analyst Stuart Ewen (61).

Ewen suggests "consumer democracy" laid the foundation for a major shift in personal identity. Skilled workers, no longer responsible for the creation of whole products due to mass manufacturing, were no longer defined by what they did but now by what they had. The transformation from craftsperson to "consumer" helped advance the industry of advertising, in which the selling of goods was accomplished by linking them to cultural ideologies. Within the last decade, electronic media, traveling at the unprecedented "speed of light" and circulating the media spectacle everywhere, have made us not only consumers but consumer-spectators, hungrily gobbling up mass manufactured images (Baudrillard 193). Critics of popular culture argue that the shift from skilled worker to consumer has affected our very ideas and practice of democracy. For contemporary American consumers, the cherished democratic idea of "freedom" is less likely to translate into personal and political freedom, and more likely to mean consumer "freedom" to choose between products. This new "freedom of choice," as a red, green, white and orange flag draped across 7-Eleven "convenience" stores, read in the early 1990s, influences the ways in which we construct our own identities. In our consumer-spectator society, identities are shaped not only through social relations but also from the products we buy.

With the rise of television as the single most important social force in America, personal identity largely became synonymous with that of the consumer-spectator. The importance of television as a dominant social force is demonstrated in cultural anthropologist Conrad Kottak's statement:

Television is stigmatized as trivial by many people (particularly orthodox intellectuals). However, it is hardly trivial that the average American household has more television sets (2.2. per home) than bathrooms. Given the level of television's penetration of the modern home, we should hardly ignore its effects on socialization and enculturation. (7-8)

The marriage of mass manufacturing and technologically transmitted information created an unparalleled world of advertising and "hype" where multinational corporations have become "masters of our desire" and major conveyers of cultural ideology. Prior to the early 1980s consumer-spectators of popular culture were often thought of as "zombies," mesmerized by pop culture's dazzling technology. However, current research reveals that audiences' interaction with popular culture plays an important role in the construction of identities. For example, media analyst Larry Gross's research, based on audience responses to the mass media, concludes that because sexual minorities have been negatively stereotyped or completely left out of most media depictions, they have been forced to create their identities in "opposition" to mainstream media. Gross's observation can be used as a starting point to examine the way transgenderists as gender minorities have been forced to construct themselves in "opposition" to mainstream media.

Oppositional Viewing for Gender Minorities

Remote Control, an exciting book derived from international American Studies symposia on television, proposes that for minority groups "the pleasure of television viewing is often oppositional" (Seiter, Borcher, et al. 4). Because most mass media contain a dominant ideology that ignores "any presumed threat to the 'natural'...order of things," gender minorities, like other minorities, are either "symbolically annihilated" by their invisibility or "kept in their places" by often inaccurate portrayals in the mass media (Gross 130-33). Larry Gross, in a poignant article on visual media and sexual minorities, "Out of the Mainstream," articulates: "Minority positions and interests which present radical challenges to the established order will not only be ignored, they will be discredited" (134).

Drawing on Vito Russo's work on the roles of gays in popular films, Gross cites patterns that can be used as a launching point to critique the roles of transgenderists, transsexuals and cross-dressers in contemporary film and media. Russo argues that most popular film and TV portrayals with gay characters were not made for gays or by gays, but rather for mainstream audiences to consume images of gays within the context of dominant ideology. The result, Russo maintains, is demeaning and discrediting to gays. Russo's research revealed that until recently "out of 32 films with major homosexual characters...13 feature gays who commit suicide and 18 have the homosexual murdered by another character" (Russo 32).

While mainstream depictions of transgenderists and cross-dressers are often confused with gay characters, due to the director's ignorance or intent to confuse sex and gender, gender minorities, like sexual minorities, are routinely demeaned and negatively stereotyped in the mass media. Russo's findings that a disproportionate amount of gay characters either committed suicide or were murdered in films directly reflects the cultural climate toward lesbians and gays, particularly evident in the late 1970s and early 1980s. In the same vein, films like *Psycho, Dressed to Kill, Murder by Moonlight* and *The Silence of the Lambs* disproportionately portray transgenderists and cross-dressers as "berserk murderers" on a rampage. This demeaning and inaccurate stereotype of the male-to-woman transgenderist "dressed to kill" reflects the cultural fear that the "dressed to kill" transgenderist will annihilate the bipolar gender system. For this "transgression," the cross-dressed protagonist is almost always punished. Most films accomplish this by sentencing the "dressed to kill" protagonist to an insane asylum or death. This symbolic gesture serves to restore and reinforce rigid sex and gender roles and reject gender variations. On a personal and social level the repeated portrayal of transgenderists and cross-dressers as dangerous in mainstream media functions to stigmatize, discredit and isolate them.

Gross observes that due to the increased political pressure by gays and lesbians opposed to demeaning stereotypes in mainstream productions, stereotypical themes and plots of loneliness, insanity and suicide are being challenged. As a result there has been a small movement in the media to depict gays and lesbians as "normal." Transsexuals, transgenderists and cross-dressers now politically defining and organizing against their oppression are posing challenges to negative and demeaning media-generated stereotypes (Lynn, "My Workshop,..." and "What's Happening,..."; Parker). Failure to debunk harmful media stereotypes rests on the fact that until recently most transsexuals bought into "medical solutions" and clinical definitions which enforced their blending into, rather than challenging, dominant ideology. As a result, even non-surgical transsexuals have been isolated from other gender minorities because of their forced assimilation and duplication of bipolar gender roles. Ultimately, mainstream media themes of transsexuals and transgenderists as sick, deviant, dangerous and in need of medical treatment are used to arouse audience responses of "shock," confusion, outrage, feelings of betrayal and titillation. Consequently, these highly propagandized images of transgenderists, cross-dressers, and transsexuals in popular culture function to get audiences emotionally riled up. The ultimate goal of this and other propaganda is to present information in an emotionally charged way, so the listener or viewer will accept the message unconditionally and without analysis. In the patriarchal and capitalist U.S.A. the maintenance and enforcement of a dual gender system is highly profitable to multinational corporations, who are the major advertisers and owners of commercial TV.

Transgenderists as Popular American Icons

Larry Gross observes that in the entertainment industry not only are we treated to mass manufactured images of persons, but also to "showbiz gossip" about these persons. Television entertainment programs based on showbiz gossip provide a prime example of how commercial television acts as a conveyor of specific gender ideologies. Because of the preponderance of demeaning stereotypes linked to transgenderists and cross-dressers, the standard showbiz gossip program provides an opportunity for actors to distance themselves from the transgendered characters they play or interact with. This is usually accomplished by actors asserting, in front of a live TV audience, their sex and gender "normalcy." This was demonstrated in a July 1989 airing of "Entertainment Tonight," when actor Tony Randall strolled on to the cozy-looking living room set, purposely designed to get popular celebrities to reveal bits of "personal" information for public consumption. At the time, Randall was starring as the lover of a male-to-woman "transvestite" in the Tony award winning Broadway play, *M. Butterfly*. The purpose of his appearance was two-fold. To elicit publicity for the play, and assert his gender and sex "normalcy." He managed to state, during the interview, that he was not, nor had he ever been a cross-dresser or a homosexual. Randall further asserted his sex and gender "normalcy" by assuring the audience he was definitely not attracted to cross-dressers or homosexuals. His statements were punctuated with frequent references to his "wonderful wife," whom, he added, he simply adored. While his remarks drew audience applause, they also did a disservice to gender and sexual minorities by stereotyping them as sexually undesirable and deviant.

The fact that most mainstream film and TV programs featuring transsexuals and transgenderists reinforce the dominant bipolar gender code at the expense of gender minorities should come as no surprise, since, like members of other minorities, transgenderists have little control of mainstream media. However, recently some transgenderists and transsexuals involved with the International Foundation for Gender Education, headquartered in Wayland, Massachusetts, have begun to produce videos and literature which challenge demeaning mainstream depictions of them. The production of written and visual documents created by gender minorities is a hopeful step towards presenting a more realistic view of transgenderists, an essential task not only in countering media propaganda, but also in gaining civil rights and equality. At this stage, these productions, consisting of videotaped documentaries, interviews and comedic routines designed to raise gender awareness, are available primarily to members of the cross-gender subculture and a few gender researchers. However, activists are attempting to disseminate them to a more mainstream audience.[2] For the most part, though, gender minorities are still forced to create themselves in opposition to a mainstream media that continues to generate harmful and exploitative stereotypes.

For our purposes, an important question to address is why negative portrayals of transsexuals and transgenderists have become so popular. What do these depictions tell us about transsexuals and transgenderists, as well as about ourselves and our culture? The study of how images can overpower and obscure content, an important concern in popular culture theory, suggests that as consumer-spectators our desire to consume images has reached the point where we are starting to ignore the substance and meaning behind the images, relying instead on whether we like or dislike a particular image.

An example of this is the way presidential politics in America have been reduced to spectator events. In the 1988 presidential campaign we were flooded with televised images of presidential candidates wrapping themselves in the

American flag to indicate patriotism and driving tanks to signify military might. The 1992 presidential campaigns bombarded us with images of Clinton's similarity to J.F. Kennedy, Clinton as a family man, and a champion of the people. Bush's media consultants portrayed him as very presidential and ready to defend America against international threat. Sadly, these images had little to do with issues and everything to do with creating good pictures that the public, as spectator-consumers, would buy (see Jameison, *Dirty Politics and Packaging the Presidency*).

Because of the media's growing ability to manipulate images and our ever increasing role as hungry spectator-consumers, we must not only ask what images we are consuming, but what cultural ideologies are embodied in those images. Because of the increased media attention given to transsexuals during the last decade, transsexualism has become a household word. This does not mean that everyone hearing the term or consuming the image of transsexuals understands what it means. Since the image of the transsexual and transgenderist in popular culture is always presented in the context of mainstream ideology, generally these images tell us little if anything about the reality of being a transsexual or transgenderist in contemporary America. However, they do reveal a great deal about the dominant culture's gender attitudes and practices.

As suggested earlier, many Americans exposed to media representations of transgenderists and transsexuals confuse them with other groups of cross-dressers and report feeling overwhelmed and intimidated by their images. This was demonstrated in a 1986 American Studies undergraduate course I taught on "Sex and Gender in America." When I announced to the class that a male-to-woman transsexual was going to be a future guest speaker, a male football player blurted out, "I will have to hit her." As we explored his reaction during class, it became apparent that he was worried he might be sexually attracted to the speaker. Since this student's identity was based on traditional notions about masculinity and heterosexuality, he feared his sexual identity would be threatened if he were attracted to the speaker. When the 65-year-old male-to-woman pre-operative transsexual spoke to the class, the student, admittedly more comfortable with himself, participated fully in the class discussion.

After analyzing over 40 American TV talk shows and documentaries aired from 1985 to 1992 that featured transsexuals, transgenderists, cross-dressers, transvestites and female impersonators, it became apparent that my student's anxious response upon hearing about the transsexual speaker's impending visit paralleled televised audience reactions to transgenderists and transsexuals and those frequently confused with them. The majority of televised audience members, like my student, exhibited varying degrees of discomfort and anxiety. Without exception, each program featured at least one audience member or call-in viewer who responded as if their personal identity were under severe attack.

Mitroff and Bennis maintain that for contemporary Americans faced with the daily threats of mounting sociopolitical, economic and environmental problems, compounded by the threat of nuclear war, the need for entertainment and "unreality" has become insatiable. As global and national problems become more complex and more Americans feel a loss of control over the "real" world, they escape to the "unreal" world of TV which at least provides an illusion of control. In our fast-paced society, where individuals increasingly report feeling alienated and isolated from others, mainstream TV talk shows have become among the most watched and imitated programs on commercial television. TV talk shows, seeking to involve studio and home audiences in the pseudo-interviews with featured guests, provide the illusion of an open forum, a bastion of democracy, where all opinions are heard. Yet in reality, live TV broadcasts are carefully manipulated to reinforce mainstream ideologies.

Much of the entertainment value of the TV talk show format for mainstream consumer-spectators is that it reinforces dominant ideology. During the early 1980s, TV talk shows featuring transsexuals, transgenderists and cross-dressers began to appear with greater frequency, making them popular television icons. Because of the enormous success of these programs during rating wars, transgenderists and transsexuals are routinely paraded across the TV talk show stages of America. As popular icons, one of their major functions on the talk show circuit has been to get both studio and home audiences so emotionally involved in the program that they will keep tuning in. Because of the strong emotional responses transgenderists and cross-dressers are able to elicit in mainstream audiences, most talk show hosts are barraged by an overwhelming audience response which, of course, *boosts their ratings.*

Safe on Stage

The presentation of transsexuals and transgenderists on popular television programs has both historical precedents and contemporary drag antecedents. Males and females in drag, a major feature of Vaudeville, debuted early in American TV broadcasting history. Milton Berle first appeared in a dress on a 1947 broadcast. By 1951, American audiences were watching Jonathan Winters in a dress, wig and make-up. From the early 1950s to the present, cross-dressed comediennes like Flip Wilson and Bill Cosby were joined by popular TV cross-dressed and transgendered characters like Jody on *Soap*, Klinger on *MASH*, Church Lady on *Saturday Night Live* and the cross-dressed FBI agent Denise/Dennis on *Twin Peaks* and the wildly popular RuPaul on MTV. Lily Tomlin and Judy Tenuta's male impersonation performances no doubt were inspired by Lucille Ball and Judy Garland's drag routines on early TV. Today, almost all contemporary TV serials and sitcoms employ cross-dressing themes in at least one episode. However, the stage performance of female and male impersonators differs vastly from that of the day-to-day reality of transgenderists, transsexuals and cross-dressers. The standard audience expectation for drag performances is that at the end of the show the performer will return to "normal" dress and the appropriate bipolar gender role and behavior, as in the popular 1982 film *Tootsie*, the inspiration for the 1993 *Mrs. Doubtfire*, featuring the cross-dressed Robin Williams. In the case of transgenderists or cross-dressers, when this does not occur, audiences are left uneasy. In post-World War II America, televised drag routines based on the idea that a male in a dress or a female dressed like a man is ridiculous and hilariously funny worked to reinforce a highly gender-stratified society.

There is a crucial difference between comediennes and performers who cross-dress to evoke laughter and transgenderists and cross-dressers who appear on TV talk shows in order to validate and defend their lives. In the case of most comediennes and performers, after the performance is over, the costume and make-up come off. In the case of the transsexual or full-time transgenderist, there are no costumes or make-up to remove. After the show the entertainer disappears into dichotomized and socially sanctioned gender roles. After the show, transsexual and transgenderist guests are stigmatized as "abnormal" by a bipolar social order. For example, Linda Phillips, a male-to-woman transgenderist and her wife, Cynthia Phillips, are gender activists seen frequently on the national and local talk show circuit. They reported that after appearing on the *Sally Jesse Raphael* show they were not allowed to pick up their purses in the waiting room, for fear they would somehow "contaminate" a famous guest with transgenderism (pers. comm. 1991).

The stage is one of the few socially sanctioned safe spaces for transgenderists and cross-dressers in America. In 1953, American TV audiences, used to laughing at drag routines in which the real sex of the entertainer is always revealed at the end of the show, were shocked and confused by the appearance of transsexual Christine Jorgenson on the *Hy*

Gardner Calling TV talk show. While Cubans were celebrating Christine's "sex change" with "Christine of Denmark," the number one song on the Cuban hit parade, American police were threatening to arrest Jorgenson if she used the women's public toilets in Washington (Jorgenson 26). According to Jorgenson, a professional entertainer, not only was she banned from performing for the military, but also a recording she made about her "transformation" was pulled from distribution.

Images of Transgenderists on TV Talk Shows

While TV talk show presentations of transgenderists and cross-dressers vary depending on the different talk show hosts, most share similar traits. The initial telecast images of the show almost mandatorily expose audience reactions of bewildered amusement and titillation in response to transgender and cross-dresser guests. After the guests are introduced, TV viewers are shown images of audience members lapsing into uncomfortable laughter which gives way to disgust as gender minority guests discuss living in the "opposite" gender role. By far, the most common audience response of "shock" that TV talk shows thrive on, appears when members of the audience attempt to distance themselves from the guests. Most of the programs featuring cross-dressers and/or transgendered guests concentrate mainly on audience attempts to reconcile and reaffirm their own sex and gender roles.

"Transsexual Regrets: Who's Sorry Now?" (*Geraldo*), "Mistaken Identity" (*The Reporters*), "The Man Who Became a Woman and Changed Back" (*Joan Rivers*), "Sexual Minorities" (*Donahue*) and "Changing Sex for Success" (*Sally Jesse Raphael*) are just a few of the titles of popular TV talk shows broadcast from mid-1989 to early-1990s that featured transsexual and cross-dressers as guests. Although the titles are suggestive of the way transgenderists, cross-dressers and transsexuals are regarded by mainstream media, televised mainstream audience reactions almost always include anger, aggression and hostility toward transgender and cross-dressing guests, which is indicative of socio-cultural attitudes towards gender minorities. A sample of common questions transgender guests are usually asked by audiences include:

How can you do that to your children?
How would you feel if everyone knew your father walked around in a dress?
What makes you think you can play God with your body?
What bathroom do you use?
Do you scare off a lot of people? (*Donahue*)

The nature of the questions asked reflect the audience's attitude toward transsexuals and cross-dressers. Clearly, the construction of the questions suggests that often broadcast mainstream audiences view gender minorities as "monstrous perverts," "condemned by God" and "harmful to children." Transsexuals are invariably asked questions about the appearance and reproductive function of their sex organs. Audience concerns about whether they might be "tricked" into bed by a transsexual and not know it reflect a deeply ingrained cultural homophobia and transgenderphobia.

As products of their own culture, televised transsexuals often inadvertently stigmatize other transsexuals. Ms. Terry, a surgical male-to-woman transsexual, mayoral candidate and a frequent guest on the talk show circuit, spread the cultural gospel of gender and sex bipolarity. A profound believer in the medical model, she left audiences with the misconception that transsexualism was a hormonal medical problem. Ms. Terry was highly critical of transsexuals that deviated from her idea of what a transsexual is. This was demonstrated when Ms. Terry, in an appearance on *The Sally Jesse Raphael Show*, blasted a non-surgical male-to-woman transsexual for wanting to stay with her wife.

I don't understand it...I never dated a girl...I don't know what a sexual relationship with a woman would be like, I like men, I'm confused... My god, here you are two women in the same bed. (*Sally Jesse Raphael*)

To punctuate her homophobic and misogynist remark, Ms. Terry shook her large breasts and winked at the audience, who reinforced her with wild applause. Jerry Sousa, a former female-to-man transsexual and born again Christian, another frequent guest on talk shows, also provokes intense audience response. On one *Geraldo* program Jerry, promoting her new book, *Bailing Out of Homosexuality* tearfully confided to the audience how, through prayer, "God opened my eyes...and I saw for the first time...and I couldn't believe what I had done to myself...and said God help me" (*Geraldo*). If transsexuals assimilate into socially sanctioned dual gender roles, or if they repent and confess the errors of their ways, audiences appear to be more accepting. However, if they transgress the Western sex and gender code, audiences and talk show hosts are anything but accepting. The exception is Joan Rivers' occasional endorsement, delight and acceptance of gender non-conformists.[3]

In his introduction of a lesbian transsexual, Geraldo Rivera on an April 2, 1989, broadcast shook his head in disbelief, while laughing and gasping under his breath as he announced to his audience, "Kate Ornstein changed from a male to a female, but this former fellow still prefers sex with women. Kate is a lesbian transsexual who prefers to be a woman as well as love a woman." Of course, the audience reacted with shock to Geraldo's statement. Mimicking their reactions, Kate dropped her jaw and opened her mouth and eyes, wide with horror. Because she challenges traditional sex and gender beliefs, Kate became an object of scorn for mainstream American audiences of the late 1980s through the early 1990s. Televised audiences, brainwashed by sex and gender dualism, seem most disturbed by Kate's assertion that she is a lesbian. Kate is repeatedly asked why, if she loves females, did she become a woman. Kate offers an explanation that makes the crucial distinction between sex and gender. Defining what she believes the difference is, Kate observes:

In this society we are told that if you're a woman you love men and we are told that if you're a man you love women. Well, there I was wanting to become a woman...I broke up the difference. My gender identity was woman. It answered the question who I am. My sexual orientation was woman. It answered the question of who I wanted to be romantically involved with. (*Geraldo*)

Although televised audience responses give the impression that they are confused by Kate's statement, observing the difference between sex and gender is fundamental if one is to understand the political repression of gender minorities.

While Kate's response may be helpful to individuals struggling with their gender identity, negative audience responses, as well as Geraldo's exaggerated gesture of scratching his head and looking perplexed, work to undermine, trivialize and discredit her. Unfortunately, Kate's endorsement of surgical solutions to transsexualism on the *Geraldo* show reinforces the erroneous belief that transsexualism is a personal illness requiring surgical solutions. The insistence on the deeply rooted belief in the medicalization of cross-gendered persons obscures my contention that transsexualism is a symptom of the cultural illness brought on by a rigid bipolar gender system, whose cure may only be effected by the radical transformation of the current gender system.

For the most part however, talk show programs using transgenderists and cross-dressers to provide audience entertainment and boost ratings are reminiscent of carnival freak shows featuring pickled "two headed babies" and "bearded ladies." As audience members are invited to "share their views" on the "democratic" talk show, where all voices are supposedly encouraged, it becomes clear that transgenderists and cross-dressers are regarded more like "aliens" than as part of U.S.A. culture. This widespread televised audience attitude toward gender minorities contradicts the myth of America as a democracy that tolerates and values cultural diversity and pluralism.

In the late 1980s through the early 1990s, the *Donahue* TV talk show exposed how treating gender minorities in a demeaning stereotypical manner that reinforced bipolar gender attitudes is a ploy that satisfies most audiences. Regarded as the champion of the "underdog," Donahue went so far as to wear a skirt during one sweeps week. But did the skirt represent his solidarity with gender minorities or serve as an attention-getting device to boost his show's ratings? Donahue's gesture provoked a great deal of publicity. Tabloids across the U.S.A. predictably questioned whether he was gay. Is Phil Donahue merely interested in ratings? Or is he an advocate for gender minorities? Finally does *Donahue* do more than merely *capitalize* on harmful and demeaning stereotypes about gender minorities?

In a subsequent *Donahue* program featuring British transsexual actress and model Catherine Cossey, also known as Tula, Donahue openly encouraged bipolarism and sexism by concentrating more on Tula's attractiveness as a woman rather than her important pending case for civil rights. In his introduction of Tula, Donahue made light of her quest for civil rights by emphasizing instead her possible appearance in *Playboy* magazine:

one of the most talked about transsexual profiles in recent years...she did get married but not legally. And she is taking her case to the European courts and is here in America to talk to *Playboy* about doing a layout. (*Donahue*)

After his introductory remarks, Donahue informed the audience that English law prohibits transsexuals from marrying anyone of their "former" sex, as determined by the sex recorded on their birth certificates. Tula's argument was that this law deprived transsexuals of their civil rights by denying them the right to marriage. At the time of the broadcast, she had petitioned the European courts to change the sex on birth certificates for transsexuals who had undergone sex reassignment surgery. One of her major arguments rests on the fact that the British government recognizes the need for sex reassignment surgery by funding the procedure in many cases. Since the broadcast her request has been denied. However, the issue raised is an important one. Unfortunately, on the *Donahue* show it was reduced to little more than a few sound bites. Donahue's only lip service to the issue was noting that in America, depending on state laws, transsexuals are allowed to marry. Of interest here is that in most states permission is based on the transsexual's ability to sexually consummate the marriage which, of course, was not addressed.

Instead, the major focus of his program, like most TV talk shows, becomes the exploitation of transsexuals for maximum "shock" value. Visually, this was accomplished by bombarding the audience with before and after images of Cossey as a male and as a "gorgeous" woman model. This juxtaposition of images not only created the desired audience tension, but also evoked the standard responses of shock and bewilderment. In the process, the civil rights issue was abandoned as the focus became the sensationalist issue of whether audiences would buy an issue of *Playboy* if Tula were the center-fold.

Like other transgenderists, transsexuals and cross-dressers who are products of their bipolar culture, Tula's statements reinforced the stereotypical medical formula that transsexualism is a personal illness. She maintained that her "problem" and "illness," based on a "chromosomal disorder," was a "mistake of nature" that resulted in a growth (penis) that had to be surgically removed because "God turned his back on me" (*Donahue*). Once again, transsexualism is presented as an individual "illness," not as a cultural symptom of a sex and gender segregated society. Predictably, one of the audience's major concerns centered on whether Tula was capable of "sexual intimacy" with a man. A true actress, Tula offered to prove her "womanhood" by inviting Phil to come by her dressing room later so she could "show him." Her response may have titillated the audience and boosted ratings, but it also reduced the definition of woman to genital appearance and heterosexual function. Such a definition has implications not only for transgenderists, but all women in a patriarchal culture.

In contemporary American society, it is not acceptable merely to feel like a man or a woman; rather, social conventions insist that one must prove it by submitting to extensive surgical reconstruction of the genitals. Donahue's program, like many others, reinforces homophobia and the belief that gender, like sex, is inborn. A Marine in the audience offered the homophobic comment that "knowing she used to be a guy...I wouldn't want to touch her" (*Donahue*). A similar view expressed by another Marine in the audience helped reinforce dominant ideology at the expense of gender minorities. After noting that he regularly read *Playboy* magazine, he asserted loudly, inspiring much audience applause, that if Cossey were the centerfold, "I would not buy that *Playboy* magazine" (*Donahue*). With traditional sex and gender roles reaffirmed, Donahue seized the opportunity to fan the flames by asking the audience to imagine the "shock" it could cause in a guy, if he found out after they had been intimate, that she was once a male.

Do Americans prefer unreality? The *Donahue* show demonstrates how the important and real issue of civil rights for gender minorities has been obscured by conjecture over whether or not audience members would buy an issue of *Playboy* magazine featuring Cossey as the centerfold. Apparently *Playboy* editors are aware of U.S. gender phobias. Tula did appear on several pages of the U.S. *Playboy*, but not as the centerfold. In the French and Israeli *Playboy*, she was featured on the cover and in a more extensive layout. Although talk shows pretend to be informative by using an interview format, they are still part of commercial TV, dependent on advertising revenues for survival. Since mainstream ideology is purposefully reinforced in commercial TV advertising, any minority challenge to that ideology in the programming is trivialized and dismissed.

What have we really learned about transsexuals? Tula, herself, reinforced the idea that transsexuals need medical "treatment." Audience response to Cossey as a transsexual suggests that many people still believe that gender is inseparable from sex. Both attitudes reinforce the differences between the sexes, homophobia and the cultural belief in bipolar sex and gender roles.

In sum, we learn very little about transsexuals and transgenderists from TV talk shows. The information audiences are provided with usually coincides with dominant gender ideology and suggests that people like this must be cured. We learned a lot more about how Americans defend their rigid gender beliefs. Out of nearly 35 comments from the audience, only three were supportive of Tula. Yet of these three, none suggested transsexuals should be treated as equals. In late 1992 to early 1993, audience responses towards Tula seem to be shifting. She has emerged as somewhat of a transsexual superstar, not only appearing on numerous TV talk shows, but also hosting specials on drag artists for show-biz talk shows like *Entertainment Tonight* (November 1992). However, most programs still focus on how well she passes, how beautiful she is and her new marriage!

Gender minorities regularly tune into TV talk shows featuring transgenderists and cross-dressers, even though most broadcasts foster negative and demeaning stereotypes. Like racial, ethnic, sexual and socioeconomic minorities, transgenderists and cross-dressers in mainstream TV are almost always "marginalized, trivialized, and insulted" (Gross 138). Like gays and lesbians in the mainstream media, gender minorities remain largely defined by their "problem." So why do large numbers of transgenderists and cross-dressers watch these TV talk shows? Overall, it may be because for now TV talk shows provide the most media representation they have. A local male-to-woman transgenderist's remark that a TV talk show "had us on again" is typical (pers. comm. December 1989). Many transgenderists and cross-dressers have suggested that programs featuring gender minorities help the American public to become deconditioned to the "shock" and thereby more accepting. From this perspective, even though most mainstream talk shows generate misinformation and negative stereotypes and continue to exploit and treat transgenderists and cross-dressers as a joke, they at least, on one level, *acknowledge their existence.*

A member of the local cross-dressers' support group observed that seeing a transgenderist on the mainstream media can be an "empowering experience." This attitude recalls Larry Gross's theory that people do not feel validated unless they are represented on TV. Perhaps the most frequently voiced response of transgenderists and cross-dressers, viewing those with similar gender identities on TV talk shows, was expressed by Linda Phillips, a frequent guest on the talk-show circuit; she voiced that "It removed the burden of thinking I was the only person in the world who felt this way" (pers. comm. March 1991).

At this historical juncture, mainstream TV talk shows, dependent on viewer ratings, encourage prejudice toward gender minorities in the quest of eliciting strong audience involvement to boost program ratings and increase advertising dollars. Does it matter that in the process transgenderists and cross-dressers are stripped of their individuality and reduced to stereotypes? The talk show presentation of transgenderists provides consumer-spectators with a situation in which they are able to objectify gender minority guests as "the other," setting up a "safe" psychological distance between themselves and the guests. The rare positive or affirming responses voiced by audience members supporting gender minorities seem to backfire when the majority of the audience members heckle and boo, attempting to invalidate any pro-gender minority speaker. What is at stake here is creating a product that consumers will buy. Perhaps the ultimate commercial value of having transgender and cross-dresser guests on the TV talk shows is that it lets consumers "purchase" again and again their bipolar gender identity.

Exploitation for Shock Value

"Ken in Barbie's Clothing a Shocker" reads the bold headline of a popular national news story. This blurb highlights the repetitive formulaic media representation of transgenderists and cross-dressers in contemporary America (*Albuquerque Journal*). Once again, these stereotypes reveal little, if anything, about transgenderists and cross-dressers themselves, and more about contemporary gender attitudes in America. A Ken doll in drag could only elicit shock in a sex-segregated culture. Here, clothing as a sartorial symbol is used to signal and reinforce culturally biased essentialist beliefs in the "innate differences" between the sexes based on genital assignment at birth. This article really plays up the "shock" element by informing us that the woman and her 12-year-old daughter who purchased

a one-of-kind—a Ken doll dressed in Barbie's clothing...were *shocked* to find a "My First Ken" doll clad in a purple tank top and lace apron over a turquoise and purple skirt... 'When I looked at this one, I said, "Oh my God, now we have a crossed-dressed Ken."' (*Albuquerque Journal*)

Semiotically decoded, the story functions to both alarm and reassure readers about traditional gender roles. By implying this is the one and only cross-dressed Ken doll, consumers are given the assurance it won't happen again. This sentiment also expresses the cultural desire to stop cross-dressers through medical prohibitions. On a semiotic level "My first Ken doll" translates as "my first boyfriend" and signifies the growing cultural awareness that boyfriends may be cross-dressers. The Mattel corporation that manufactures Ken immediately offered to replace the doll, implying that a cross-dressed Ken was not only a "defective product," but a threat to the bipolar gender system (*Albuquerque Journal*). This attitude parodies contemporary medical theories. One psychological "authority" on transsexuals and cross-dressers, Richard Docter, in a lecture to wives and partners of cross-dressers, stated that they would always be "damaged goods." Whether Ken's "femme" attire was a result of industrial sabotage or an attempt to symbolize gender minorities remains unknown at this time. But the fact that it happened calls attention to a disenfranchised segment of the population and repeats popular culture themes and formulas commonly attributed to gender minorities in contemporary America. Dolls are used to enculturate children into mainstream values. What if cross-dressed Ken dolls were routinely manufactured and sold? Would America become more tolerant of gender diversity?

Standard themes of *shock* related to transsexuals or transgenderists can also be found in contemporary tabloids, newspapers, magazines, television and film. Traditionally, these depictions, whether dealing with manufactured images that suggest transsexualism or "real" transsexuals, capitalize on their shock value to sell products. Again, much of the shock response results from the disorientation audience members experience upon seeing or hearing about a woman who used to be a male, or a woman who is really a male, or varying degrees of gender blending that suggest "sex reversal." A sample of popular headlines and stories from contemporary tabloids, newspapers and magazines that combine transgender, cross-dressing, and transsexual images with the theme of shock include:

> It's a guy, it's a girl—IT'S BOY GEORGE! Joke, freak or pop genius. (*People Magazine* 1984)

> Polluted Water Turns Woman, 36, Into a Man. (*Sun* 1987)‘

> Sex Change Shocker! Can You Guess Which One's Daddy? The Answer's Inside. (headline *Weekly World News* 1989)

> Texas Polls Get a Shock: Transsexual Candidate with a Colorful Past Forces a Runoff. (*The Advocate* 1991)

> Band Members Devastated: New Kids Sex Change Shocker! Jordan Wants to Become A Girl. (headline *News Extra* 1991)

> Elvis Lives—As a Woman. (*News Extra* 1992)

Besides using the shock value of transgender, transsexual and cross-dressing images and persons to sell print media, most mainstream articles, like TV talk shows, incorporate negative stereotypes commonly associated with transgenderists.

Transgender Images in Rock and Roll

The use of transgender images in rock and roll has a long history. Most recently these images have been incorporated into music videos by such rock and pop artists as Arrowsmith, Alice Cooper, Jane's Addiction's and Madonna. While their messages may vary, until recently most employed negative and shocking stereotypes. For example, Jane's Addiction "Been Caught Stealing" music video (1991) features cross-dressers strapping on huge grotesque foam models of female breasts and pregnant stomachs. The image of the cross-dresser here is horrible and nightmarish. In contrast, Madonna's controversial music video "Justify My Love" (1990) celebrated erotic and gender variability. This is most evident as Madonna sings "I want to know you...No not like that," during which her male lover switches to a woman.

Before the advent of music videos, rock and roll artists often incorporated transgender images into their performances by using a "femme" name or persona. What is notable about these performers is that they attracted huge audiences and profits, observes rock and roll gender historian, Steve Simels. This tradition in America can be traced back to the 1950s when "Gorgeous George," a male wrestler with Jean Harlow hair "threw gold plated bobby pins to his fans" and singers like Little Richard appeared in "lipstick, wild hairstyles, and the heaviest of eye makeup" (19). Popular rock stars and performers of the last decade known for their adoption of cross-gender names or appearances while performing include: David Bowie, Annie Lennox, Boy George, Grace Jones, Twisted Sister, The Cramps, The Plasmatics, early Mötley Crue, Alice Cooper, Prince, Wayne Jayne Country (who has since had SRS), Michael Jackson, Jane's Addiction, Guns n' Roses, Nirvana, Arrowsmith, and k.d. laing.

According to popular press accounts, the U.S. was under an "invasion of the gender blenders," from the early to mid 1980s (Dilberto). Popular magazines and newspapers of the time were filled with photographs, show-biz gossip and pop theories on the phenomenon. Linda Yellen, the producer of *The Second Serve*, a biographical film about transsexual tennis star Renee Richards, thought the popularity of transgender images reflected "adolescent desires for sexually non-threatening idols." David Bowie's ex-wife Angela Barnett, once known for her gender blended appearance, suggested gender blending is "a political statement...having to do with sort of a role confusion...I wore three-piece suits years ago as a social reminder that a person's brain is what counts, not her legs" (Dilberto). Designer Calvin Klein, whose line of women's lingerie "modeled after men's undershirts and jockey shorts" became a great commercial success, observed that "there's something incredibly sexy" about gender blending (*Dilberto*). Rock and roll transgender images which were once a "revolutionary rejection" of middle-class values, Simels laments, have become just another image commodity

adapted for purely commercial purpose—no more, no less. Like rock-and-roll itself, once the spontaneous, beautiful spectacle of both geniuses and fools expressing their innermost selves without the slightest regard for what scorn it might bring on them, it is now just another tool in the all-American process of moving merchandise, as devoid of substance and insignificant as a empty can of Diet Coke. (Simels 108)

In spite of their complexity, most mass-manufactured transgender images in popular culture fail to address the personal and socio-political needs and reality of transgenderists, cross-dressers and transsexuals. As a result, most transgender images in popular culture function to reinforce and maintain the idea that the sexes and genders are separate and "opposite," thereby reinforcing the dual sex and gender system.

An article in *RIP*, a popular heavy metal fan magazine, demonstrates how transgender images, combined with rock and roll, can create shock, profit and negative stereotypes of transgenderists that reinforce social myths about gender. "Lizzy Borden, Electroshock Therapy" shouts the provocative headline the article opens with. The first "shock" volt delivered to the readers is that Lizzy is a 27-year-old male, lead singer of the heavy metal band "Lizzy Borden." The entire article is written in the style of a psychological case study. The interviewer, pretending to be a psychiatrist interviewing a patient, purposely reinforces the stereotypical media myth that transgenderists are dangerously insane.

We now take you to a psychiatrist's office. It is 1987. A 27-year-old man, who will give no name except Lizzy Borden, lies on the psychiatrist's couch. According to his case history, he is a rock musician. Four years ago he formed a rock group using the name of his alter ego, Lizzy Borden...The patient, who is lying here, his foot long red frizz becoming matted on the pillow, has been known to deal with bouts of schizophrenia. (Summers)

The interview with Lizzy incorporates a number of themes illustrative of popular culture's formulaic treatment of transgenderists and transsexuals or people presenting a transsexual or transgender illusion. As popular icons, even manufactured images of transgenderists (like Lizzy) are medically stigmatized as mentally unstable or insane. In the case of Lizzy this is accomplished, in part, by pretending the interview takes place in a psychiatrist's office. The use of pop-psychological terms like "case history...alter ego" and "schizophrenia" helps forge the link between transgenderists and insanity, mirroring medical transsexual ideology and celluloid images of transgenderists and cross-dressers.

Celluloid Myths of Homicidal Maniacs "Dressed to Kill"

Popular cultural portrayals of transgenderists as crazed homicidal maniacs, while echoing early sexological theories, have been transformed into cultural archetypes by two popular films, Alfred Hitchcock's *Psycho* (1960) and Brian DePalma's *Dressed to Kill* (1980). Both suspense thrillers feature "gender dysphoric" males dressed as women, who savagely murder females. Numerous pop-psychoanalytic film reviewers, by failing to distinguish between a manufactured movie stereotype of a male-to-woman transgenderist as a homicidal maniac and the reality of the male-to-woman transgenderist in contemporary society, have helped perpetrate the dangerous and inaccurate social myth that all male-to-women cross-dressers are highly disturbed and dangerous. These pop-psychoanalytic film reviews, like the movies, convey to audiences the idea that the male-to-woman transsexual or transgenderist is not only insane but highly lethal to women. A popular review of the 1990 cable-TV movie *Psycho IV: The Beginning* by author Bill Cosford repeats misconceptions about transgenderists. Cosford argues that the film *Psycho IV* is essential to our understanding of the character of Norman Bates, the cross-dressed, woman-murdering star of *Psycho*, because it is the "oedipal epic" which tells us not only "how Norman got that way" but also "Creepy things. Things about Mother, and how she went from mom to mummy. That's why you need *Psycho IV The Beginning*" (Cosford).

Such portrayals and psychoanalytic film criticism mirror contemporary psychoanalytic theories about the etiology of transsexualism (see Chapter Three), which maintain that the "feminine" boy must separate from his mother in order to develop a "normal" gender identity. As such, the brutal murder of females by the cross-dresser becomes rationalized in popular films as the symbolic slaying of his "wicked" mother, the cause of his "gender dysphoria." In a society that still blames mothers for causing femininity in their sons, matricide, at least on the symbolic level, is often encouraged as a healthy act, a step toward individuation. These demeaning stereotypes of cross-dressers, transgenderists and transsexuals as dangerous psychopathic murderers, reflected in films, fiction, TV, rock concerts and pop therapy, reinforce harmful gender attitudes that are both anti-woman and anti-transgenderist.

The stereotypical image of a feminine male as a pathetic, mother-abused psychopath driven to murder in order to escape the pain inflicted on him by his mother is a popular formula found repeatedly in both the electronic and print media. One of the more recent manifestations of this formula can be found in best-selling author Robert Bly's advice to his followers. He calls on the "soft young men," who, he argues, as a result of the Women's Movement, have become dominated by "older, harsh" feminists, to call up "Iron John," the wild man within, to slay the Medusa. This call for symbolic "femicide" is a gross enactment of cultural misogyny and recalls "treatments" for "feminine" boys that require getting rid of the "feminine" and the female.

Returning to the interview with Lizzy Borden, we can see how Borden's formulaic performance of a transgendered homicidal maniac "dressed to kill" elicits "shock" from his audiences in a grizzly drama that recalls negative transgender stereotypes found in Hitchcock, DePalma, and Jonathan Demme's chilling film *The Silence of the Lambs*. In the interview Borden establishes:

I realized that what I'm into is the initial shock. That's what Lizzy Borden is all about—...From the premiere performance we were doing weird things, like beheading a mannequin and the reaction was great...When I cut the head off it went, "Whippppp!" and flew across the stage, popped up on the monitor and fell into this girl's lap. In her mind, when it rolled across the stage, it became real, and she screamed! It was the highlight of my life. (Summers)

While Borden admits he is into the "initial shock," he maintains that after the shocking "surprises" he not only directs but enacts, he wants the audience to "go home and laugh." Clearly Borden, like many of his predecessors in rock and roll, uses the transgender "psycho killer" image to make money. After the performance, the character supposedly disappears. Borden's transgender persona constructed for shock and consumption, again, has little to do with the day-to-day reality of transsexual or transgender persons who statistically are much more likely to be the victims of homicide, rather than the perpetrators.

Utilizing formulaic transgender and cross-dresser images to evoke shock in a rock performance can leave a lasting emotional imprint on many audience members. The stereotype of the transgenderist as psychotic and dressed to kill, particularly when this is the only information the person has about transgenderists, may result in generalizing this negative view to all transsexuals, transgenderists, and cross-dressers.

Evidence that audience responses of shock and fear to popular cultural representations of transgenderists and cross-dressers become internalized and carry over to real life is demonstrated by personal reactions to real transgenderists and cross-dressers. A 1986 documentary about cross-dressers and transsexuals, "What Sex Am I?" includes an interview with a longtime co-worker of a surgically reassigned male-to-woman transsexual who confided that, "I was really scared of him...everybody was afraid of him." Because of such culturally sanctioned, deeply ingrained negative stereotypes associated with transgenderists, transsexuals and cross-dressers, her response is typical.

Additionally, the airing of "What Sex Am I?" as a feature of "America Undercover," an HBO cable TV special that focuses on such topics as criminals, wife abusers, drug addicts, prostitutes, prisoners, "incurable" schizophrenics and other topics "of interest," indicates the cultural space transsexuals, transgenderists and cross-dressers are so often relegated to in contemporary American culture. That these images can reinforce negative social myths is demonstrated by a personal incident. In the last six years, as co-founder and facilitator of the local cross-dressers' support group, many professional associates, friends and family members have demonstrated their belief in popular social myths about transgenderists and cross-dressers by repeatedly inquiring if I was afraid that one of my group members "might murder me!"

As long as there is no opposition to negative presentations of transgenderists and cross-dressers, these harmful stereotypes will continue, further stigmatizing those who dare to exist outside socially sanctioned definitions of gender.[5] At the present time there is a growing movement to delete transsexualism, transvestism and other cross gender categories from the *DSM IV*. Hopefully, this much-needed action will decrease negative stereotypes about gender minorities in pop culture and also cast doubt on sensationalistic articles that find their way into the medical literature and reinforce these popular culture stereotypes.

An article published in the *Canadian Journal of Psychiatry*, entitled "Homicidal Transsexuals," erroneously reinforces celluloid images of transsexuals as homicidal maniacs (Millken). There is no evidence to back up this assumption. That such an article was published suggests how pervasive damning images of transgenderists of popular culture have become. The formulaic pattern of linking transsexuals to homicide is routinely exploited in countless newspaper articles. We are far more likely to read about the rare instance of a murderer who happens to be a transgenderist, than a well-adjusted transgenderist like Phyllis Frye, who has an engineering degree, law degree, manages several businesses and contributes greatly to the transgender community. Evidence that the "shocking" images generated by films such as DePalma's *Dressed to Kill* have made a lasting impression on the American psyche is demonstrated in numerous popular mainstream and alternative press cartoons, articles and advertisements that employ such captions as "Dressed to Thrill," which not only plays on the stereotype of transgenderists and cross-dressers as fetishistic and homicidal maniacs, but also puns on the most popular image of transgenderists and cross-dressers as "dressed to kill." These recurring clusters of images attest to pop culture's recyclability, as well as the impact the mass manufactured image of the transsexual or transgenderist as a berserk homicidal maniac has had on contemporary consciousness.

Gender researcher Holly Devor suggests that the reason the images of cross-dressers and transgenderists elicit such profound emotional reactions may in part be due to the fact that:

Most societies use sex and gender as a major cognitive schema for understanding the world around them. People, objects and abstract ideas are commonly classified as inherently female or male...Gender then becomes a nearly universally accepted early cognitive tool used by most children to help them understand the world. (*Gender Blending* 46)

Devor's accurate perception that we project gender categories upon the world around us must be extended to include the socio-political ramifications of accepting a dual gender world. Historically, gender categories have been used to exclude, control and suppress whole groups of individuals who do not fit neatly into socially designated gender categories based on the shape of one's genitals. Transgender and cross-dresser challenges to culturally prescribed gender roles continue to be perceived as direct threats to personal and cultural existence. Depicting transgenderists and cross-dressers as marginal, unattractive, dangerous, lunatics, unfortunate accidents, or jokes, works to maintain a social order whose most basic social organization and deepest rooted problems are gender based.

In contemporary American culture where gender is the social by-product of a sex-segregated society, transgenderism and cross-dressing, when not in the service of entertainment, are social taboos. Even in the context of popular entertainment, a message against transgender behavior is almost always reinforced in the end. This message is often preceded by a period of "titillation," during which audience members vicariously break social taboos through identification with the transgender protagonist. In the dark movie theatre, or before the blue glow of the TV screen, mesmerized audience members are allowed for a brief moment to vicariously live outside the bipolar gender code, momentarily escaping the bored fragmented, violent and suppressed condition of the postmodern self.

One of the most popular and highest grossing films of all times, *Tootsie*, provides such a vehicle of escape by titillating audiences with the fantasy of living in the role of the "opposite" gender, which provides the ultimate escape from the detested self. In *Tootsie*, Dustin Hoffman portrays an out-of-work male actor, forced to dress and act like a woman in order to get an acting job. The film uses the formulaic elements of shock, titillation and escapism to capture audience attention. However, in order to construct a "happy ending" and return the audience to a "normal" social order, the dual sex and gender system must be restored. As I noted earlier, this occurs when Tootsie sheds the cross-dressing facade, returns to his male role and wins a girlfriend in the process.

Although the use of transgender images in the film provides audience titillation by allowing audiences to vicariously break cultural gender taboos, the final message mainstream audiences are left with is that transgender images are acceptable for entertainment but not "real life." Transgender audiences often construct a different meaning from *Tootsie*. A common response to the film by gender minorities is "if Dustin Hoffman could pass as a woman, I knew I could too." Negative stereotypes of transgenderists generated in the film undoubtedly still resonate on an unconscious level. Still on the conscious level, by concentrating on Hoffman's ability to pass, gender minorities resisted and subverted mainstream meaning.

Most popular culture images are received unconsciously. For consumer-spectators in a media saturated society, some of the most satisfying images are those that move quickly. As Ehrlich and Ornstein suggest, many of them work directly on the central nervous system mobilizing our fight/flight responses. They argue what once was a necessary response to actual physical danger, for example, the shadow of a bear passing the opening of a cave, has in contemporary times been transferred to TV commercials and programs that mobilize our responses with fast-moving colorful images and loud noises. In a spectator-consumer society, we voraciously consume these fragmented images without thinking about what we have ingested. Researchers of subliminal advertising note that this is the best way for specific ideologies, embedded in these images, to lodge in our unconscious mind. The use of transgender images in TV commercials and music videos, media known for compressing colorful, fragmented images into short time frames in order to sell products, reach deep into our cultural imagination and in most cases reinforce bipolar gender and sex roles.

A series of fast movements, loud noises, and "bizarre" imagery combined in the long-running "Almond Joy" and "Mounds" candy commercial (late 1980s to early 1990s) to capture audience attention. The commercial features an actor made up as a half-woman and half-man. The woman-side of the actor appears on the screen first, carrying a huge Almond Joy candy bar like a package. Her head is thrust back, revealing a smile as she waltzes among huge Greek-style columns. Suddenly the actor turns, revealing the man-side, dressed in a tuxedo, eyes staring straight ahead, carrying a huge Mounds candy bar like a weapon.

As he moves determinedly through the columns and black walls decorated with abstract pastel drawings of men and women dancing together, the scene switches to a house painter in a room with a black and white tile floor and a porthole. He begins to draw an outline for a door when suddenly the half-man/half-woman breaks through the door, waltzing across the room. As the figure leaves, the camera focuses on the bewildered and shocked face of the painter.

The accompanying jingle, "sometimes you feel like a nut...sometimes you don't" puns on the word *nut*, which refers to both the male genitals and insanity. Both the painter's reaction to the titillating image and the stereotypical gender roles enacted by the actor posing as a man and a woman work to reinforce the dual gender and sex code. Note that her bar contains the nuts, "male genitals," the socially conditioned focus of female and male-to-woman transsexual desire in a gender and sex divided society. In a transgenderphobic and homophobic culture it is no surprise that his candy bar, a consumer product, promising to fulfill personal and cultural desires, does not contain "nuts." The word "nut" also refers to the half-man/half-woman, reflecting pop culture depictions, as well as contemporary gender attitudes of transgender and cross-dressers as insane, but oh so titillating!

By contrast, the half-man/half-woman in some Native American, Siberian, Polynesian, Hawaiian, Yemen, and other societies are regarded as having special talents and are often given preferred social status. Half-men/half-women also appear in folklore and mythological traditions throughout the world. A significant point of difference in cultural attitudes toward gender can be distinguished by observing the image of the American candy icon, split down the middle, one side man, one side woman, separate and apart. By contrast, societies that provide an institutionalized role for individuals who transcend bipolar gender roles, emphasize the intermingling of gender, rather than gender differences. As Walter Williams observes, American gender attitudes rest on the "material" genital basis for gender, while more tolerant cultures emphasize the "spiritual" or psychological dimensions of gender.

A popular music video that incorporates transgender images is Alice Cooper's "Poison." Again working with fast-moving fragmented images set to music, the audience is presented with a series of images suggesting singer Alice Cooper is trying to resist the woman within. In scene after scene, a woman is shown superimposed over his body, disappearing into him. At one point in the video her hand becomes his hand. These scenes are juxtaposed to images of Cooper chained up, attempting to resist the call of his inner siren. Finally, in the last scene, we see an image of Cooper, his head bent forward, hair covering his face. As his head slowly rises, a woman's hand throws off the Alice Cooper wig, revealing a woman beneath it, she laughs and takes a sip of wine from a glass. The camera pans to Alice Cooper holding a bottle with a skull and cross bones label. The woman dressed like Cooper clutches her throat and gasps. The dual gender system has been saved. The woman within has been "poisoned." The heavy metal music in the background pays homage to gender dualism:

I don't want to break these chains...I hear you calling, it's needles and pins...I don't want to touch you, but you're under my skin...your poison is running through my veins... I don't want to break these chains...I hear you calling...but I better not touch...You're Poison. (Cooper)

A 1993 "Paul Mitchell" commercial, selling hair care products, broadcast on the major networks, uses similar transgender images. Paul Mitchell really does have a woman "under his skin," as we see a "feminine" female peeling off a life-like mask of Mitchell, exposing her long hair. A voice-over states you don't always get what you think you do.

While most popular culture images of transgenderism and cross-dressing titillate, shock and ultimately reinforce a dual gender system, Carl Jung and some neo-psychoanalysts have advocated incorporating unconscious archetypes, like the anima, the woman within the male and the animus, the man within the female, into consciousness as a means of attaining a state of "wholeness" and good mental health. Jung's theories, heavily influenced by images drawn from mythology and alchemy, advocated the psychological blending of the androgynous and bisexual god Mercury in order to transform consciousness. Of note here is that in the alchemical process of the transformation of base metal into gold, a metaphor for the transformation of consciousness, the metal mercury is the essential ingredient. Jung's ideas are in direct conflict with most popular cultural representations of "mercurial" images, which are regarded as cultural "poison."

There have been a few attempts at a more sympathetic representation of transsexuals, transgenderists and cross-dressers in film. However, most of these depictions incorporate negative formulaic stereotypes of gender minorities as well. The inability to sustain a positive image throughout the film may be because protagonists are still culturally defined as having a "problem." Roberta, the feminist transsexual protagonist in *The World According to Garp* provides both positive and negative messages about transsexualism in contemporary culture. Roberta functions as a breakthrough character, one of the few portrayals of a transgender person that debunks the stereotype of a homicidal maniac "dressed to kill." She is portrayed as compassionate and concerned for others. As she tries to patch up the relationship between Garp and his wife, Helen, her role is reminiscent of the Native American "berdache," acting as the "go-between" for male and female relationships.

However, throughout the film we are reminded that her personal life is lonely. Her relationships with men are doomed to failure and she laments throughout the film her inability to have or adopt children. The war between the genders and the sexes and the medicalization of transsexuals is reinforced throughout the film. Perhaps one of the most hopeful messages of the film is the fight for feminism, a demand for equality. The struggle for equality and acceptance, modeled on the contemporary Women's Movement and Lesbian and Gay Liberation, is the one cross-dressers and transgenderists are just beginning.

The film that anticipated a gender revolution, Richard O'Brien's ingenious 1975 *The Rocky Horror Picture Show* is the longest running midnight cult film. *Rocky Horror* not only challenges culturally sanctioned stereotypes of sex and gender but also provides a "safe social space" for sex and gender minorities. Every weekend for the last 18 years, gender and sexual minorities have joined disenfranchised individuals in dressing up, cross-dressing and putting on their own show during the showing of *Rocky Horror*. After the film, the "cast" get-togethers, inspired by the film, provide an occasion for the acceptance and celebration of human diversity. Unfortunately, in some cities the film event has also inspired gay and transgender bashings.

The basic message in the film, "don't dream it, be it," is advocated by the film's protagonist, Dr. Frank N. Furter, "a sweet transvestite from Transsexual, Transylvania." Frank N. Furter, a dazzling spectacle in his high heels, fishnet stockings and sequined corset, portrays a brilliant scientist who not only has created life, but also transforms the bipolar consciousness of the American dream couple, Brad and Janet. After freeing them from the sex and gender prison enforced by a dual sex and gender culture, Frank, an alien, is killed for his "transgressions."

In a scene punning on King Kong, his gay object of desire, Rocky, climbs the RKO tower with Frank's body slung over his shoulder. The tower falls into the pool. Rocky is electrocuted. Riff-Raff, Frank's butler and assassin, and his sister Magenta return to their planet Transsexual in the galaxy Transylvania. The only survivors are the American dream couple Brad and Janet and their science teacher, Dr. Scott. Gender bipolarity is restored. Challenges of "don't dream it, be it," to the gender system are dead. The U.S.A. is once again "safe"; or is it? Hopefully not.

The first made-for-TV biography of a male-to-woman transsexual, *The Second Serve*, documents Dr. Renee Richards' life from childhood through her struggles to play tennis in the women's national competitions. The airing of this special in 1986 announced the existence of transsexuals and transgenderists in contemporary society. While the film is useful in depicting transsexuals as real people deserving of equal treatment, it resorts to simplistic and inaccurate textbook stereotypes. Too many scenes are spent blaming an overbearing mother, a weak father and reinforcing the myth that all transsexuals are heterosexual. The wrap up scenes in the film show Renee's life turned into a media spectacle, her privacy violated. Yet amid the confusion, her father and super masculine male friend are shown standing by her. This movie portrayal contradicts reports by transgenderists of how women, for the most part, are more likely to stand by them. This reversal of reality, so common in pop cultural depictions of transgenderists, works to support psycho-social myths that blame women for creating feminine men.

Though more research is necessary before definite conclusions can be reached, it is likely that the more probable female acceptance and male rejection of male-to-women transgenderists is the result of the highly punitive gender system which regards women as second-class citizens and forces men to internalize homophobia. The message imparted by *The Second Serve*, as well as most contemporary biographies and documentaries on transsexualism, is that surgery is the "only solution" to the "problem" of transsexualism.[6] Ultimately, the movie paints transsexuals as peripheral persons, defined and permanently "scarred" by their "problem."

Madonna's popular music video, "Justify My Love," did challenge negative depictions of transgenderists and cross-dressers. The video, banned from MTV and blasted by the mainstream media for showing "blatant homosexuality, bisexuality, and transvestism," pushes beyond the borders of the dual sex and gender system and reinforces human diversity. In one scene Madonna announces to her male lover "I want to know you." As he comes down on her, she pushes him away saying, "no not like that." In the next scene his gender has changed to a woman. Madonna sings, "I just want to be your lover, kiss me." As they give in to their passion, in the background, images of alternative sexualities and gender abound. Between scenes in the video, a male in a tight body suit emphasizing the outline of his penis, dances, waving his arms and hands, revealing extremely long fingernails and a heavily made-up feminine face. Other scenes include a female and a male applying make-up and drawn-on mustaches to each other in order to look more alike. Traditional roles are reversed. A masculine female fondles a passive male wearing a harness. In the background, two males and a female erotically embrace on a couch. In a quick film cut, Madonna, while making love to a male, briefly transforms into a man wearing lingerie. Depicting males dressed like women and females dressed like men and people combining gender "as objects of desire" represents a shift from the standard iconic representations of transgenderists and cross-dressers as "objects of hate." Imagistically, the video rejects a mainstream bipolar sex and gender system coded in dualistic opposites which exclude all genders and sexualities that do not conform. The stereotypical image of the transgenderist and cross-dresser as either inflicting or deserving of pain, forced to enact only the role of victim or killer, is shattered in this video. In "Justify My Love," transgenderists are finally liberated from the stereotype of pain and allowed the most basic right of loving and being loved and giving and receiving pleasure.

Unfortunately, sympathetic and challenging portrayals of transsexuals, transgenderists and cross-dressers in the mass media remain in the minority. Madonna's 1992 commercial endeavor, *Sex,* a $50 book of "erotic" photos and sexual fantasies, contains photos of female cross-dressers, a few young "feminine" males and a male with one male breast and one female breast under a magnifying glass. Male-to-women transgenderists and cross-dressers are noticeably absent in Madonna's exploitive gallery of desire, unless we count Madonna, who alleges in her book that "I think I have a dick in my brain, I don't need to have one between my legs" (Madonna). Most popular films and TV broadcasts continue to leave mainstream audiences with contradictory messages. These negative depictions of transgenderists emphasize their marginality and deviance, as opposed to more positive representations which indicate the existence of transgenderists in contemporary society and signal socio-historical changes in gender, slowly taking place as worn-out traditional gender roles are collapsing.

Film analyst Pauline Kael observed that movies are like "samples, swatches of cloth—of the period they were made" (Kael 16). Examined collectively, movies can "yield insights that other historical methods cannot" (Walsh 57). Although most prime-time TV pokes fun at gender minorities, a few weekly series in the early 1990s such as *L.A. Law, Twin Peaks, Good Grief* and *Picket Fences* have demonstrated an understanding of gender minorities as real people. While these productions almost mandatorily incorporate formulaic stereotypes of shock, titillation, humor and anger, they also show an acceptance, rather than a rejection, of gender minorities. This was demonstrated in a 1990 episode of *Good Grief*, a Fox network sitcom (no longer broadcast) that revolved around a family-owned funeral parlor. This particular episode focused on the problems encountered by the mortuary in honoring the last wish of a male-to-woman cross-dresser who left instructions to be buried as a woman. Opening scenes featured cross-dressed male staff members, for comic relief. However, the end of the program took a surprising twist, compared to most prime-time depictions of cross-dressers, when the widow of the cross-dresser announced to the shocked group of mourners that her deceased husband was a "good, kind, and loving" person; to which she added, "so what if he cross-dressed" (*Good Grief* 1990).

In a like manner, the cross-dressed FBI agent Denise/Dennis, who appeared in the now defunct ABC's *Twin Peaks* also challenged the formulaic portrayal of transgenderists. Denise was portrayed as a highly competent, intelligent, attractive and stable individual. CBS's new toned-down version of *Twin Peaks, Picket Fences*, aired its Christmas special about the town's favorite teacher, Louise, a male-to-woman transsexual who was fired from her job because she was discovered to be a transsexual. Although she wins a court case and is reinstated, Louise is pressured by parents, fearful of her influence on their children, to withdraw from the school's Christmas pageant she has organized. During the pageant in the midst of a nativity enactment the children stop and deliver a scathing critique of the transgenderphobic adults. They proclaim

The children are not happy and do not like the world of grown-ups...the children of Rome reject the prejudice of our parents...reject your fear...and embrace the theory of tolerance and individual freedom. (*Picket Fences*)

After their bold speech they ask Louise to join them on the stage. The conclusion gives the impression that the TV town of Rome has worked through its gender prejudice.

Although these positive pop cultural depictions hold out the hope that gender minorities will one day be depicted as regular people, the best-selling book and award-winning film, *The Silence of the Lambs*, reinvoked all the negative and demeaning stereotypes associated with transgenderists. The transgender and gay protagonist, Jame Gumb, is a contemporary reincarnation of Norman Bates. In the story, Gumb, abandoned by his mother, becomes a psychopathic, homicidal maniac "dressed to kill." In the Thomas Harris book the film was based on we are told that his character, nicknamed Buffalo Bill, is not a "true transsexual." However, both the film and the book create Gumb's character according to formulaic stereotypes of transgenderists. The book informs us that

Buffalo Bill kidnaps young women and rips their skin off. He puts on these skins...Buffalo Bill thinks he is a transsexual and has been rejected for surgery by the gender clinics. (Harris 183)

The image of Gumb skinning his female victims so he can become a woman by capering around in their torsos and scalps, can't help but conjure the shocking image of cross-dressers and transgenderists as homicidal psychopaths "dressed to kill" women. True to the formulaic code that blames mothers for transgender sons who kill, Bill's mother is implicated as the real abuser in the film. Commenting on the abuse subplot, film director Jonathan Demme maintains he was taking a poke at patriarchy.

I wanted to get in the meaning of child abuse. Behind every serial killer is a profoundly abused and neglected child. (Taubin)

Is blaming the mother for her son's action really taking a jab at patriarchy? Naming the mother as the abuser of the child never addresses that Gumb's beauty queen mother, unable to make it as an actress, is driven to alcoholism and forced to give up her child to her parents. Blaming the mother obscures that she, too, can be viewed as a victim of a rigid patriarchal hierarchy that values one sex and gender over the other.

Film critic Meredith Berkman calls Bill the personification of evil. But we must ask if he is considered "evil" because he is a murderer or because he has "violated" the bipolar sex and gender code? Hannibal Lecter, the film's real star is also a serial killer who eats his victims' internal organs, and engages in some skinning of his own, such as biting off a nurse's face. Yet across America, Lecter, who helps FBI agent trainee Clarice Starling solve the "Buffalo Bill" case was widely heroized.

Lecter's face appeared on numerous magazine covers. So popular was Lecter that the 1992 Academy Awards were carried out with a Hannibal Lecter theme. Host Billy Crystal was wheeled out as the strait-jacketed and masked Lecter, much to the audience's delight. The film won awards for Anthony Hopkins' portrayal of Lecter, Jody Foster's portrayal of Agent Starling and Jonathan Demme's direction. Audiences couldn't get enough. Most film audiences across the U.S.A. detested Gumb so much that many hurled verbal abuses at the screen when he was on. In the audience I was in, many people shouted "kill the queer" at Gumb's cross-dressed screen image. No such insults were hurled at the gender "normal" and presumed heterosexual Lecter. One pop article on Lecter reveals that psychologists across America reported patients "so impressed" with Dr. Lecter's intelligence that some even asked where they could "find a therapist as brilliant as Lecter" (Berkman).

Remember, both Lecter and Gumb are serial killers that have committed heinous crimes. However, Lecter is heroized while Gumb is villainized. The film reproduces the cultural sex/gender hierarchy, where transgenderists are always placed at the bottom along with such sex criminals, as pedophiliacs. This hierarchical distinction between the two serial killers forces us to ask if Gumb's worst crime is wanting to be a woman. In a *Village Voice* interview with Amy Taubin, Director Demme claims his film is about a man who doesn't want to be a man, instead he wants to become as different from himself as he can by trying to become a woman. Like earlier films, *The Silence of the Lambs* reinforces sex and gender differentiation and stigmatizes transgenderists as sick and dangerous to women.

That popular portrayals inform reality was once again demonstrated in a *USA Today* interview with FBI agent John Douglas, who served as the model for agent Jack Crawford, Starling's boss in *The Silence of the Lambs*. The interview revealed that Douglas loves to

joke about the two chiffon dresses hanging in the outer office. They were a gift to him because he's always saying that someday he'll go nuts from 20 years of tracking criminals...The man who has probably spoken with more serial killers than anyone says he'll either retire in four years...or he'll be found in his office wearing a blue chiffon dress. (Trebbe)

Clearly, the interview, like the film and book, plays off the mainstream stereotypical link between cross-dressing, transgenderism and insanity.

Once known for its scathing critiques of mainstream society, *Saturday Night Live* introduced "Pat," a new character of ambiguous sex and gender whose skits often contribute to demeaning stereotypes of transgenderists. As *Village Voice* columnist Michael Musto, who covers the drag scene, observes, each skit focuses on the "amorphously creepy...character...this indeterminate blob...drooling all over...whose gender everyone struggles to figure out to no avail." The majority of Pat's skits concentrate on the discomfort individuals around her feel, because they don't know if Pat is a man or a woman. In one such skit, a male co-worker tries to discover what sex or gender Pat is by asking questions that commonly elicit gender-specific responses. He asks Pat whether he is going to watch "a big Giant/49er game" or "Murphy Brown?" Pat replies that she isn't going to watch either because she has rented the movie *Tootsie*. On the way to lunch a curious co-worker pretends to be short on cash and asks Pat "well why don't you just get your wallet or purse, or wal-purse." Again, Pat foils his attempts at discovering whether Pat is a female or male by stating I don't "carry a wallet or a purse but a sports sack" (*Saturday Night Live*).

Another skit with guest host Roseanne Barr centers on trying to find out the sex and gender of Pat. Roseanne's treatment of Pat is harsh. She fires question after question about monthly cramps, ladies' rest room keys, and what the name Pat is short for, hoping to find clues as to Pat's sex and gender. Each time Pat skillfully responds with gender neutral responses. Highly frustrated, Roseanne states:

Well, I'm glad you're here, Pat, because as a woman, I sometimes feel vulnerable late at night. That's why it's good for us—humans, us—people—us—mammals to stick together, Right? (*Saturday Night Live*)

Predictably, Roseanne's desperate attempts to find out Pat's sex or gender fail. In response to the idea of women sticking together, Pat notes that as a student of martial arts, "I feel safe wherever I am." Highly frustrated, Roseanne hopes meeting Pat's partner Chris will at long last reveal what gender and/or sex Pat is. Of course this attempt also fails as Roseanne discovers an equally ambiguous Chris. While the basic concept behind the character of Pat hopefully challenges viewers to think about the flaws in a bipolar gender system, Pat's visual presentation works against this. Pat is depicted as a gross, drooling, open-mouthed, fidgeting, scratching, overweight, acne-scarred, spastic and deranged individual. Utterly disgusted, Roseanne sums up mainstream audience response when she screeches to Pat and Chris, "Gee you guys give me the creeps. Get out of here."

Barr's response to Pat is disturbing. In 1990, Roseanne presented a cross-dressing theme on her popular weekly series. The program focused on her young son wanting to dress as a witch for Halloween, which greatly upset Roseanne's husband. In this episode, Roseanne also cross-dressed as a man to highlight the different ways males and females are treated (*Roseanne*). Her disgust at a gender ambiguous person carries a double punch. As an outspoken and anti-establishment hero and an avowed feminist, Roseanne's oppression of a gender minority is disappointing and works to trivialize, marginalize and stigmatize anyone who does not conform to socially sanctioned sex and gender roles. Further, Pat's remark of feeling safe anywhere is a reversal of reality, since Pat has become an object of the audience's fear and hate.

Like *Silence of the Lambs*, *Psycho* and *Dressed to Kill*, the *Saturday Night Live* skit reinforces the idea that transgenderists or gender ambiguous people are weird, disgusting, undesirable, irritating, isolated, sick and potentially dangerous. The implication here is that gender minorities are undeserving of love or compassion and only someone equally "deranged" like "Chris" could care for such a person. Unlike Madonna's "Justify my Love" video and the few hopeful TV and film portrayals, most popular culture portrayals of transgenderists continue to be both negative and demeaning, used for exploitation and to reinforce dominant ideologies. Even Neil Jordan's *The Crying Game*, a low-budget Irish film that became the most-talked about film in 1992, while progressive on some levels, still reinforces dominant gender ideology. The film gained notoriety when the movie industry launched a massive campaign urging audiences to keep the film's "secret." It worked. In movie houses across the country movie goers in on the secret anxiously waited to see if their friends and relatives would be shocked during the crucial moment of the film when Dill, the love object of the male lead, Fergus, is revealed to be a male who passed as a woman.

Predictably, Fergus's on-screen reaction is of shock, disgust and subsequent throwing-up when he sees Dill naked, a woman with a penis. His response reminds me of the cultural anxiety and fear homophobics have surrounding gays and lesbians in the military. When Fergus loses his dinner in the sink he also loses his sexual desire for Dill. Such a dramatic act reinforces the media myth that transgenderists are unworthy of love and destined to be alone. True to the formulaic stereotype of transgenderists as homocidal maniacs dressed to kill, Dill shoots a female IRA terrorist. However, in a twist on the formula, Fergus takes the blame. The final scene shows Dill visiting Fergus in prison. He still rebuffs her advances. Members of the gender community observe that this may be one of the few films in which a transgenderist actually plays a transgenderist. This hope was reinforced when Academy Award nominee for best supporting "actor" Jaye Davidson who played Dill arrived at the 1993 Award's ceremony looking very feminine. Noting the historical significance of such an act for the gender community, Linda Phillips invited us to imagine what if Davidson had been nominated for best supporting "actress." Such an act would certainly force us to collapse current gender categories.

We can no longer afford to keep the secret of *The Crying Game*. As the film's theme song sung by Boy George warns, "first there is sorrow then there is pain." Keeping a secret of this magnitude keeps transgenderists suffocating in the closet and culturally invisible. Doing so supports the dominant gender ideology, which encourages the infliction of pain, suffering, and the extermination of transgender persons.

It is no coincidence that some of the most visible cross-dressers and transgenderists at this historical juncture are African-Americans like Dill, RuPaul and much of the cast of Jennie Livingston's *Paris is Burning*. As critics have observed, the black transgenderist is in double or triple jeopardy, where race interplays with gender and class serving to stigmatize her more. RuPaul sings about the black male being at the bottom of the social heap in "House of Love." In her essay "Is Paris Burning" bell hooks questions why white audiences derive such pleasure from a film in which transgenderists, cross-dressers, and drag queens mimic the white ruling class that colonizes them. Historically, the black male has been castrated by a dominant white patriarchy that resists equality, by subordinating or "feminizing" males of color. Remember, the first "official" sex reassignment surgery was performed on an African-American male-to-woman transsexual. On one level popular images of black transgenderists and drag-queens function to ghettoize cross-gender persons. However, on another level the African-American transgenderist who is two or three times oppressed calls attention to race, class and gender oppression and conveys an urgency for activism.

Overall, most popular culture portrayals of trangenderists, cross-dressers and transsexuals relegate them to being shadow figures, the embodiment of our fears in a racist bipolar gender culture, people who may leap out of the dark to slay us. This unfair stigmatization of transgender individuals as sick, deviant, and dangerous in mainstream productions encourages the continued infliction of pain and punishment upon them. In reality this is a blatant reversal.

Rarely in real life do transgenderists and other gender minorities act as perpetrators of pain and punishment. Quite the opposite is true. We are far more likely to hear tragic stories like the brutal murder of male-to-woman transsexual Venus Extravaganza, who was featured in Jennie Livingston's film on the Harlem drag balls, *Paris is Burning*.[7] In contemporary American society, transgenderists, denied their civil rights and their right to pleasure, are frequently the victims of violence and murder. The homicidal maniac who targets gender minorities is almost always a white heterosexual "masculine" male, a living emblem of America's highly dichotomized sex and gender code.

What most popular cultural representations fail to address is that transgenderists in the real world do not "dress to kill," but because they dress, they are killed.

Phyllis Randolph Frye is a transgender activist. She is an engineer and a lawyer and was instrumental in organizing the first and second International Transgender Law and Employment Conferences in Houston. An advocate for transgender civil rights, she was the transgender spokesperson for the 1993 Lesbian, Gay, and Bisexual March in Washington.

Merissa Sherril Lynn, editor of *Tapestry*, founder of IFGE and International Gender Education Foundation, and gender activist.

Merissa Sherril Lynn.

Donna Mobley—Gender Activist, former President of "FIESTA" (cross-dressing organization). Involved in *Creating Archives* video, documentaries of cross-dressers and transgenderists for I.F.G.E. Also does comedy to raise gender awareness.

Colleen and Phil (Phyllis!) Hurd on
their wedding day, October 7, 1989.
Zilker Park Rose Gardens Austin,
Texas.

Phyllis and wife Colleen, July 1992.
Newcomers to gender community.

Gender activists Jim (Linda) Phillips and Cynthia Phillips. Linda and Jim married 35 years. Linda is a male-to-woman transgenderist.

Linda and Cynthia Phillips, 1992—gender activists and writers—have been on most of the major TV talk shows. Responsible for changing the public image of transgenderists. Organizers of the Texas "T" Party, the largest international transgender gathering for transgenderists and their partners and friends of the community. Cynthia and Linda own the "Transvestite Castle," the home to many transgender organizations.

Dr. Virginia Prince, Pioneer Trans-genderist. She coined the term trans-genderist and has contributed greatly to the transgender and cross-dressing community. Dr. Prince is the founder of the first cross-dressing organi-zation Tri-Ess and the first cross-dressing journal "Transvestia," and is widely regarded as the "Grand Dame" of transgenderism.

Chapter Five

The Gender Movement

During the last decade in America there has been a dramatic shift in consciousness among individual transgenderists and transsexuals. Much of this change in consciousness has been inspired by social and support groups that provide a safe social space in which transgenderists, transsexuals and cross-dressers can "come out." As a result, the gender community has grown, become more political and visible. Realizing that they lack civil rights and suffer from severe discrimination and social ostracism, members of the gender minority are actively forming a social movement to end this discrimination.

This new social movement, the Gender Movement of the 1990s, takes its inspiration from the Civil Rights Movement, the contemporary Women's Movement and the Gay and Lesbian Liberation Movement. Like their predecessors, members of the American Gender Movement have been victims of severe social, economic, historical and political repression and discrimination. This chapter examines the social-historical and political events that have led up to the Gender Movement, along with the new scholarship that is encouraging the rethinking of current gender theories. Questions addressed throughout this chapter include: What kind of impact can the Gender Movement have on contemporary American culture? Is transsexualism moving from a psychological "disorder" complete with "symptoms" and "cures" to a grass roots civil rights movement? If we examine transsexuals' and transgenderists' relation to the postmodern state it appears to be one of submission to power. Current court and congressional rulings encourage discrimination against transsexuals and transgenderists. A majority of the Supreme Court have refused to hear cases involving transsexual and transgender discrimination. The transsexual challenge to gender bipolarity has, to this point, been controlled through surgery. Surgery becomes the means through which transsexuals are promised cultural "acceptance."

146

Leslie Savon notes in an article on advertising that "acceptance leads to assimilation. Assimilation leads to bliss" (136). Transsexuals receive the very same message encouraging assimilation in surgical propaganda. For transsexuals, the ticket to "acceptance" in a bipolar gender culture carries the price of surgical castration and genital reconstruction. Getting a cosmetically altered body is supposed to allow the transsexual to "assimilate" into the "blissful" world of "real men and women," a frightening proposition if one abides by the dominant S&M gender code. How can disappearing through the looking glass of "assimilation," which for most transsexuals entails denying their entire personal history, ever lead to bliss?

Catherine Millot writes in *Horsexe* that "Transsexuality is now a social phenomenon, and may even constitute a symptom of our civilization" (Millot 16). Using the Lacanian thesis of desire, Millot asserts that because of their recent dependence during the last 40 years on medical technology for sex-reassignment surgery, transsexuals have replaced their desire with the desire of the "other," meaning the desires of a bipolar culture achieved through medical science. According to this logic, sex-reassignment surgery fulfills the cultural dream of maintaining the bipolar gender order. Herein lies a fundamental problem. By subordinating personal "desire" to cultural "desire," do surgical transsexuals become incapable of experiencing true pleasure or *jouissance*? Robbed of their desire by cultural bipolarism, can surgical transsexuals resist the false lure of assimilation? In contemporary American culture, assimilation into bipolar gender roles can have grave consequences.

The Gender Wars

As long as contemporary culture remains organized on the principles of a strict bipolar gender system, the prospect of full equality for gender minorities remains grim. In the U.S.A., masculine cultural stereotypes like authority, power, aggression, violence, competition and domination not only are prized over feminine cultural stereotypes like compassion, sensitivity and intuition, but they also provide the foundation for a capitalistic, corporate and militaristic society. As Bem observes, most people are unaware that "their perceptions are (but need not be) organized on the basis of gender" (Bem 309). According to Bem's gender schema theory, males and females behave differently, not because they are inherently different, but because cultural gender myths have "become self-fulfilling prophecies" (Bem 308). These bipolar gender myths are used as ammunition in the battle for social control. Such ammunition fuels the gender war of dominance and submission in which "real men" and "real women" (those who live according to cultural gender creeds) are pitted against one another. In this warfare, found at the root of all wars, "masculinity" is glorified and "femininity" is devalued and terrorized.

Fueled by the populist fervor of patriotism and nationalism that swept America in the aftermath of the Persian Gulf War, the gap between the sexes and the genders became magnified. Nearly all of the media imagery associated with the war—before, during and after—stressed not only traditional gender roles, but a hyper-masculinity that associated maleness with murderous (though socially sanctioned) violence and the conquest of their "enemies." For example, in a story on the mood of the troops just prior to the onset of the war, *Newsweek* magazine reported that: The sign at a U.S. airfield in Saudi Arabia says it all: "SEND US IN TO KICK SOME OR SEND US HOME TO GET SOME" (*Newsweek* 1/21/91). Such a statement, equating dropping bombs on the enemy with "fucking" women, betrays not only a harmful misogyny but also reflects a hypermasculinity which must continually reconstitute itself through (eroticized) "victories" over (fuckings of) others.

Because learning how to be "masculine" involves a denial of all that is female or "feminine," "masculine" identified males are conditioned to perceive "femininity" as the enemy and therefore all enemies are characterized as "feminine." Significantly, after the "liberation" of Kuwait, a '"feminized" image of the allegedly defeated Saddam Hussein was repeatedly broadcast on network and cable news. Someone had drawn a "feminine" hairstyle and make-up on his large portrait displayed on a wall in Kuwait. Within moments of seeing this image of Hussein "in drag," TV viewers witnessed the "feminized" image destroyed by an angry, mostly male, mob. They were surrounded by a cheering crowd including American male soldiers. Symbolically, the destruction of the "feminized" Iraqi leader accomplished two purposes. First, feminizing the image rendered it powerless. Second, such imagery communicated the essential dynamic of the gender hierarchy, the triumph of "masculinity" over "femininity."

Throughout the "Crisis in the Gulf," hyperfemininity on the home front was encouraged to match the hyper-masculinity being inculcated in male soldiers. A nationwide network of support groups for wives and partners of the male troops was created within the military, groups specifically designed to issue advice to "women" on how to behave in a complementary gender manner toward their partners. These groups instructed "women" to downplay their "independence" gained while the males were at war and to allow the males to "take charge of the family" when they returned. At this time I am not aware of any analogous support group that issued the same advice to the male partners of female troop members. Most support networks for males at home were geared toward helping males "temporarily" cope with "women's work."

Of course, the fact that the largest number of female soldiers ever deployed was present in the Middle East throughout the Gulf crisis suggests that females and males may be more similar than different. However, working against any appreciation of the similarity between the sexes are the military's ban on females in combat as well as the media war propaganda that reinforced gender bipolarity. Even with a large number of female war correspondents, most media coverage on females in the gulf focused on stories which reinforced traditional roles, including the female's assumed greater need for hygiene and the question of whether females should be taken from their families.

Spurred on by wartime propaganda, essentialist arguments stressing innate differences between the sexes and genders were resurrected. Such vociferous and insidious sex and gender propaganda was followed by the Hill-Thomas hearings (10/91) which dramatized in an unprecedented manner the real inequities of gender under patriarchy. In a society that so overtly prizes hyper-masculine behavior, the true casualties are "femininity" and those who embody it or by nature of their sex are expected to embody it. Since "femininity" is viewed as compatible with females, females as well as "feminine" men become casualties. Object relations theorist Nancy Chodorow maintains that gender differences do not exist as things in themselves but are created relationally. Because of this, she argues, we cannot understand difference apart from these relational constructs. According to this theory, the development of masculinity requires a repudiation and a strict separation by men of all that is female or "feminine"; therefore, not only females, but also male-to-women transgenderists pose a threat to the maintenance of "masculinity."

The covert mission of the Gulf War, as in any war, was to dominate and destroy the enemy, which, when defeated, becomes "feminized." However, we must question the need to feminize the enemy. The greatest threat to masculinity may well be the inner "femininity" that males are conditioned to fear lurking in themselves. According to popular belief, George Bush became president in 1988 by overcoming his "wimp" factor, that is, by ridding himself of weakness, which is conventionally associated with "femininity" and females. One wonders if Bush's continued quest to dissociate from the feminine was a factor in his hard-line, aggressive decision not only to wage war against Iraq, but to also stomp around in Grenada and Panama. Rather than acknowledging the "femininity" within, "real men" project it on to the "other" whom they then must symbolically and literally annihilate.

Although they are devalued as women, female-to-men transgenderists represent a potentially lethal threat to "masculinity." The very existence of a "feminine" male suggests that gender may not be a fixed construct, bound and inextricably tied to the genitals. Because of the repressed fear the "feminine" male is capable of arousing in a hyper-masculine male, the former is frequently the target of that male's violent attacks. The cultural scapegoating of femininity encourages a war of domination and control over females and male-to-women transgenderists by "real men." Gulf War propaganda aided in legitimating and reproducing "real men." That war may be over for now, but any survey of contemporary hate crimes against women and transgenderists shows that the war against the "feminine" on the home front is in full swing.

Recent statistics (Caputi; Caputi and Russell) reveal that rape, assault and murder of females by males is at an all-time high. Studies confirm that 1/3 to over 1/2 of all females seen in hospital emergency rooms are there as a result of being attacked by their husbands or boyfriends. A recent senate committee analysis confirmed that violent crimes against women have risen over 50 percent during the last 15 years. Again, implicit in the dualistic gender paradigm is the idea that in order to maintain power, or be "real men," you must wage war against anyone that challenges the "absolute power of masculinity," which usually means against the "feminine." As I mentioned earlier, in a bipolar society where "masculinity" can only be cultivated by the personal rebuking of anything "feminine" the routine torture and murder of women and transgenderists is tolerated, if not quietly socially sanctioned. An article entitled "Self Protection and Self Defense for the Genetic Male While in the Female Role" addresses the reality of masculine violence against females and male-to-women transgenderists and observes,

Becoming a woman means adopting the principles of "learned fear"...women learn very early in life they must live under the constant threat of being a target...that they are vulnerable to attack and physical abuse. (Kelley 39)

Further, the authors warn male-to-women transgenderists and cross-dressers that if they are ever abducted by a male attacker "when the attacker discovers that you are not physically a woman, he will likely become extremely enraged and may try to mutilate or even kill you" (Kelley 40).

Several media-reported cases of violence against male-to-women transgenderists illustrate this point. Two cases occurring a couple of days apart were featured items on the front pages of two newspapers, *The San Antonio Light* and the California *Marin Independent Journal*. In the early 1990s, *The San Antonio Light* reported that a transvestite was found "bludgeoned to death" and when an attempt to burn "his" (sic) body in a furnace for tempering steel failed, "some kind of flammable chemical was poured over his (sic) body." The reporter added the investigator's observation that "There's so much stuff in there, you can't even tell if there is blood or grease on him (sic)" (Lopez). Such a lingering emphasis on how the body was mutilated serves as a warning for transgenderists and cross-dressers who "violate" bipolar sex and gender codes. The article proceeds to reinforce gender bipolarity with unnecessary details that serve to undermine the victim, and cast "him" as a possible criminal "prostitute":

...a shop employee...happened upon the burned body of a slightly built man in his 20's. The identity of the victim, clad in women's clothing and jewelry, had not been released late Friday...The victim might have been a prostitute. "One of the hazards of female impersonators who offer themselves as prostitutes is that a lot of time they hide it from their customers...When the customer finds out they get very angry"...homicide Lt. Albert Ortiz said. (Lopez)

Two days later (4/1/91) The *Marin Independent Journal's* headline states "Danny Partridge jailed in beating of transvestite." The article informs us that

Former child television star Danny Bonaduce, best known as Danny Partridge of "The Partridge Family" was arrested on charges of robbing and beating a transvestite prostitute...dressed as a woman. (*Marin Independent*)

Referring to the victim as a "transvestite prostitute...dressed as a woman" reveals a subtext that medicalizes, criminalizes and stigmatizes males who cross-dress. Doing so not only objectifies and marginalizes these individuals, but also passes a moral judgment that places males in dresses at the bottom of the gender hierarchy. The article on Partridge's arrest includes a picture of him as he appeared in the 1970 television series *The Partridge Family*. The photograph conveys the image of the "all American boy" on the proper path to "masculinity" and heterosexuality. Reinforcing his role as "Danny Partridge" on the "family oriented" prime time TV series also operates as a subtext to villainize the "transvestite" as a corrupter of "family values." Since this incident Bonaduce's career has been revitalized. He is currently a popular radio disk jockey and frequent guest on talk shows.

These same tactics are employed by the New Right and the radical Christian Right who were reinforced during the Reagan-Bush era. The major focus of these groups is enforcing the dominant bipolar gender ideology on everyone, particularly those perceived as deviating from "traditional family values" including lesbians, gays, transgenderists and feminists. Dan Quayle, Pat Buchanan and Pat Robertson spread their hate mongering and intolerance of others at the 1992 Republican convention where they shared with the Christian Coalition (who made major contributions to the Republican campaign) the belief that they must "wage warfare against those who would destroy our...families" by their "sexual perversions" (LaHaye). One zealot from Roswell, New Mexico, involved in censoring books about "non-Christian" lifestyles, summed up the radical Christian attitude:

We are only trying to put into everyday life the word of God as we interpret it. If people would only do the things we ask and live the way we tell them to, there would be no trouble at all. (*Out Magazine*)

She is not alone in her thinking. Each night popular radio and talk show host Rush Limbaugh, known for his views against such groups as transgenderists, gays, lesbians, feminists, people of color and the homeless etc., brings his gospel of hate and intolerance into the homes of millions of North Americans. In 1993 Limbaugh called Atlanta the "transsexual capital" of the U.S. or the world and indicated it would be wise to stay away from there.

This widespread intolerance is accompanied by new legislation like Colorado's Amendment #2, which is currently being appealed to the Colorado Supreme Court for being unconstitutional, that allows for discrimination against anyone thought to be lesbian or gay, which, in the public mind, always includes males who appear "too feminine" and females who appear "too masculine." Such legislation and the narrowly defeated Measure #9 (which supporters threaten will be on the ballot again) in Oregon have publicly declared open season on gays, lesbians, transsexuals, and transgenderists. The results are predictable. Two weeks after the 1992 Republican National Convention, people perceived to be lesbian, gay or transgender were reportedly thrown on subway tracks, slashed, sprayed with battery acid in the face and harassed by police. Reports of violence against gender and sexual minorities has shot up. Conservative estimates say violence in New York alone is up more than ten percent from last year. "The message from the Republican convention," "some biased police officers" and the board of education (often comprised of members of the Christian Coalition, the group responsible for passage of Amendment #2) is "that people have permission to bash us" (Minkowitz).

In late 1992, another "Death in Drag" occurred as "a body surfaced in the Hudson River...it looked like the body of woman," but "these were the remains of a genetic male with a large hole in the head" (Goldstein). Friends and witnesses observe that Marsha P. Johnson, as she was known, was yet another victim of gender-bias crime. The night she disappeared, a witness reported seeing Marsha, an African-American, Stonewall veteran and streetwalker, being violently attacked and thrown to the ground by four men. Yet police have called her death a suicide and are reluctant to reopen the case (Goldstein). How many career choices does an African-American male-to-woman transgenderist have in this culture? Recall the hateful words of warning uttered by Right Extremists: "If only...they would...live the way we tell them to, there would be no trouble."

Even some devout Leftists are guilty of summoning images of cross-dressers to symbolize sleaze, deception and depravity. For they, too, have been brainwashed by a rigid gender code that condemns gender non-conformists to hell on earth. Why is a male who dresses, acts and/or lives as a woman or a female who dresses, acts and/or lives as a man the target of personal and cultural melt-downs? This displacement of fear and enforcement of gender conformity is not only frightening but dangerous as well. On the Right, Jerry Falwell, Pat Robertson, Jesse Helms, Phyllis Schlafly, Dan and Marilyn Quayle, Pat Buchanan, William Dannemeyer, Robert Dornan and Rush Limbaugh comprise but a few of the gender bashers of our time. In their "righteous" demands for a strict division between the genders and the sexes, they have been responsible for halting civil rights legislation for transgender persons, females, bisexuals, lesbians and gays. Their battle cry of a return to "traditional family values" is a cowardly and reactionary act in response to the civil rights and the sex and gender movements of the late 1960s through the early 1970s that posed a radical challenge to traditional patriarchal and hierarchical arrangements of race, class, sex and gender. Such reactions reinforced by the neo-conservative and radical Christian Right's dream for the social reorganization of America have had a two-fold impact on the gender community. First, by denying gender minorities equal rights, they have actually politicized the gender community; and secondly, they have planted the seeds for the Gender Movement that is gaining in momentum.

The Gender Community

The modern politicization and mobilization of members of the gender community began when one male-to-woman transgenderist stepped forward to found the first transgender organization. Virginia Prince, the pioneer transgenderist who had the courage and the means to "come-out" and cross-live as a full-time transgenderist in 1968, is the person most responsible for the establishment of national and international gender communities and networks for transgenderists, transsexuals and cross-dressers. Through the publication of her cross-dresser/transvestite magazine *Transvestia*, Prince established national and international networks of support. A former biochemist researcher at a university with a doctorate in biochemistry, Prince began to make public appearances in 1963 and recalls: "I exposed myself like that so others could find me because I had no means of finding them" (Prince, "Yesterday" 50).

Through her magazine, Prince located numerous other transgenderists and cross-dressers. In 1962, the first weekend gathering for transvestites and cross-dressers took place at a resort in the Catskills. Prince remembers the weekend as one in which the girls "were busy...having fun" and the researchers learned there was more to cross-dressing than the erotic component. Prince reports that Wardell Pomeroy, one of the original Kinsey researchers who attended the gathering, called it "the most asexual weekend he had ever spent" (Prince, "Yesterday" 51). The following year the event was repeated and Prince took the opportunity to announce the formation of the first official organization for cross-dressers:

It was called FPE which stood for Phi Pi Epsilon as a sorority which in turn stood for Full Personality Expression. The idea being to provide a safe location where the CD could dress and meet others of the same persuasion thus relieving the loneliness which is the common lot of all CDs until they discover there...are actually others in the world that feel just as they do. (Prince, unpublished manuscript 140)

In 1980, the group joined with another organization and was renamed "Tri-Ess," which means "The Society for the Second Self." Because of Tri-Ess policy, transsexuals, defined by Prince as cross-dressers seeking surgery, were not allowed membership. However, as researchers and transgenderists have observed, sometimes transvestites and cross-dressers decide to have sex-reassignment surgery. So the line between transsexuals and cross-dressers is not always clear. Because of this, some Tri-Ess organizations do not strictly enforce discriminatory national policies.

Prince observes that, like many transgenderists of her time, she, too, was influenced by the publicity surrounding Jorgenson's "sex-change" and at one point seriously considered having sex reassignment surgery. "Thankfully," Prince states, she was unable to afford it when she desired it. She subsequently changed her mind, preferring to cross-live as a "transgenderist" for the last 24 years. Prince has remained a strong opponent of sex reassignment surgery, maintaining that the only reason transsexuals undergo reassignment surgery is so they can have intercourse with members of their same sex.

Open Wounds and Cultural Scabs

At the first International Foundation for Gender Education (IFGE) Conference in 1987, Prince was honored as the person who has made the greatest lifelong contributions to the cross-dressing community. The founder of IFGE and editor of *Tapestry* (currently the most widely distributed journal for cross-dressers), Merissa Sheril Lynn noted that seeing Virginia Prince on a talk-show not only changed her life, but gave her purpose. Lynn, a transsexual, was caught cross-dressed at age 13 by her parents and severely beaten. Over 30 years later, the scars on her back are still visible. But, Lynn asserts, the biggest scars were not on her back, but "on my very soul." She states:

that beating taught me three powerful lessons: (1) It taught me bitterness towards my parents. (2) It taught the fear of social reprisal. If my parents could hurt me for no reason, then so could anyone and everyone. (3) It also taught me resentment for having been born male. ("Virginia" 5)

After the incident Lynn began to think of herself as a misfit and a social outcast. Fearful of others, she avoided people for the next 13 years. Lynn says that the experience of seeing Prince on television took away the isolation she felt. She remarks:

Even though I had only watched her for a few moments, I can justifiably credit Virginia with keeping me sane...keeping me whole and perhaps even saving my life. ("Virginia" 6)

Lynn's history of abuse, fear and loneliness is an all too common theme in the lives of many transgenderists. "Sheila," a 27-year-old local transgenderist, recalls that when she was a teenager, her father, "a truck driver," tried to "scare the femininity out of me by dangling me over a cliff." Sheila reports that afterwards he called her a "sissy" for screaming and beat her with his fists. Even though "he broke my nose and ribs countless times, he couldn't beat the woman out of me," Sheila added. It is the rare transgenderist, transsexual or cross-dresser who can emerge from childhood unscathed. The important function the gender community can serve is replacing years of self-hate and social stigmatization with acceptance. Lynn is not the only person whose life was changed by coming in contact with another transgenderist, transsexual or cross-dresser.

In 1987 I was called to the burn and trauma center at the University of New Mexico Hospital to see a 17-year-old male-to-woman nonsurgical transsexual, "Rita," who had burned most of her penis off with liquid nitrogen. Rita lived with her Christian fundamentalist grandparents in rural New Mexico. A constant source of conflict and anger between Rita and her grandparents was her insistence that she felt like a girl. Besides condemning her to "the fires of hell," her grandparents demanded that she act like a "man" at all times. Any display of "feminine" behavior was brutally punished. Rita explained she could no longer live masquerading as a man. In desperation, she attempted to rid herself of her maleness. She dipped her penis in liquid nitrogen, burning over 80 percent of it off, an act she hoped would result in sex-reassignment surgery. It did not.

Most of Rita's "knowledge" of transsexuals came from the tabloids and TV. She begged to talk to someone who felt as she did. After she left the hospital, Rita began correspondence with "Lorie," an older male-to-woman transsexual, who took an interest in Rita, encouraging her against further self-mutilation and toward attending the University of New Mexico. When Rita's grandmother learned of her plans to leave, she ended the correspondence. Rita became severely depressed. One evening I received a call from her informing me she was attempting to remove her testicles with a razor blade. Corresponding with Lorie, who understood and accepted her, had opened up a world of possibilities for Rita. Deprived of this, her self-hatred resurfaced. For Rita, her penis and testicles represented the maleness she learned to hate and resent. Isolated, alone and forced to hide her feelings, removing the symbols of maleness was a desperate act to validate who she was.

Because they are gender non-conformists, Rita and other transsexuals and transgenderists are often relegated to a life of suffering and torture under a dichotomous sex and gender system. The suicide rate among gay and lesbian teenagers is reportedly "two to three times the rate of other teens." It has been estimated that the suicide rate for cross-gender teenagers is even higher (Lynn et al. 55). This alone provides an important reason for outreach in the gender community. There is a need for positive role models as well. But before transgender individuals can safely step forward in the public, prejudice and discrimination against gender minorities must stop.

The struggle for civil rights is a long and complex process. It involves overcoming irrational prejudices and "linguistic tags of rejection" gender minorities have suffered for years (Allport 304). This means overcoming social taboos that ban males from expressing their "femininity." A society that did not discriminate against gender minorities and neutralized bipolar "linguistic tags of rejection" like *sissy, pussy,* and *wimp,* which demean women as well, would be a far more equal society.

As Wendi Pierce, chairperson of IFGE and a surgical transsexual observes, gender is a multifaceted process.

Gender perception begins with the processing of general sensory signals such as appearance, speech, content, scent, mannerisms, etc. ("The Mechanics" 10)

Pierce uses the analogy of "templates" to discuss how gender affects our everyday interactions. She suggests that in our bipolar society we use gender cues to make up "masculine" and "feminine" templates. According to her, in day-to-day interactions with others, the first thing we do unconsciously is to make judgments about what gender one is. When the "masculine" or "feminine" side of the "template" is filled with enough cues, we decide if a person is a woman or a man. Then we relate to them in stereotypical ways, based on gender bipolarity. In a society where gender variations are taboo, mixed gender messages often trigger negative responses such as "you're sick."

Gender prejudice starts at an early age. Studies reveal that gender discrimination starts before first grade. Even so, reports indicate most first graders still play with "opposite" gender children at least one quarter of the time. By fourth grade only a few students choose "opposite" gender playmates. By the time eighth grade is reached, some "opposite" gender friendships re-emerge, but for only a small percent of the population. These results suggest that the older we get, the more prejudiced we get toward the "opposite" gender. No doubt this is influenced by years of bipolar conditioning and acting out. Allport observes prejudiced people demonstrate a need to think in dualistic ways that emphasize differences rather than similarities. For such individuals, it becomes an "us against them" mindset, making it impossible to appreciate differences. This use of imagined and exaggerated differences is also a factor in the formation of racial prejudice, which, in these bigoted times, is unfortunately making a come-back. Gender prejudice follows the same patterns. As Allport observes:

For some people—misogynists among them—the sex-grouping remains important throughout their lives. Women are viewed as a wholly different species from men, usually an inferior species. (33)

A belief in false gender "opposites" encourages "opposite" gender prejudice and discrimination as well as transgender discrimination by exaggerating the differences. In a society where children are socialized to discriminate against the "opposite" gender, the transgender child who does not fit rigid gender stereotypes is discriminated against by both genders. I am unaware of any studies done on prejudice toward transgender children. However, based on the memories of tortured childhoods voiced by adult transgenderists, the prejudice suffered seems severe and practiced by members of "both" genders. Based on the recall by adult transgenderists, it is evident that the social stigmatization and hatred toward gender nonconformists who exist apart from dominant ideology become internalized as self-stigmatization and hatred. Self acceptance is a major prerequisite for social acceptance.

"Be All You Can Be," or "Don't Dream It, Be It"

The process of replacing self hatred and stigmatization with self acceptance and pride began when Virginia Prince founded a local cross-dressers support group, followed by a national cross-dressers magazine. Besides appearing on radio, television, doing public speaking tours and research projects, Virginia started "Chevalier Publications." Her publishing company began to print "non-erotic" books and pamphlets for cross-dressers and their wives. This was a groundbreaking venture at the time, since almost all publications for cross-dressers were limited to the "cock 'n' frock trade" and could only be purchased in adult bookstores (Lynn, "Virginia" 7). As Lynn observes, these sex magazines focused only on erotic interests and were "aimed at the wallet and the groin." The person from the neck up was forgotten. But the existence of these publications did indicate that there was a large audience out there. A study conducted by Prince and Bentler in the late 1960s found that the cross-dressing community constituted approximately five percent of the entire population, which means millions of people and millions more associated with them. Although a new large-scale study is essential to the Gender Movement, Prince's conservative estimates reveal a significant population of cross-dressers in America. On a sociocultural level, these numbers reflect a challenge to dominant gender ideology.

Although Prince's influence and her prolific writings dominated the transgender and cross-dressing community of the 1960s and the 1970s, by the 1980s it was time for a change. With a shift to the political Right during the Reagan years, in order for the gender community to survive it needed to update. As Merissa Sherril Lynn observes, Virginia is a "woman of her times."

Prince's organization came into being in the aftermath of McCarthyism. During this time the homosexual was the feared American bogeyman. This, no doubt, combined with personal harassment and threats to Prince by the postal authorities, helped determine to some extent Tri-Ess's membership being limited to heterosexual cross-dressers and their spouses. While the group fills a necessary need in the community, it also excludes gays and transsexuals and downplays erotic motives for cross-dressing. As a result, some members of the gender community argue it does not meet the needs of a diverse gender community and fosters homophobia and isolationism. However, as Lynn points out, Prince has also long been a "catalyst" for the formation of new groups. She observes that almost every cross-dresser and transsexual organization has in some way been influenced by Prince. Usually the founders of the organizations have disagreed with Virginia or been excommunicated by her. The important point here is, as a catalyst, Prince inspires the creation of new groups and stimulates change, which is vital and essential if the gender community is to survive (Lynn, "Virginia" 8).

Perhaps the most dramatic and important change has been the transfer of leadership in the gender community from Virginia Prince to the "philosopher" Merissa Sherril Lynn. In the 1980s Lynn decided to follow Virginia's lead. Like Virginia, she started a local support group, began publishing *Tapestry*, and then founded the International Foundation for Gender Education (IFGE). Unlike Prince, who catered primarily to heterosexual cross-dressers and their spouses, Lynn's influence has been to try and unite the diverse members in the gender community to work together. *Tapestry* and IFGE provide an outreach to transsexuals, transgenderists, cross-dressers, androgynous persons and their significant others. As chief editor of *Tapestry*, Lynn maintains a neutral policy of not condemning any group that helps the gender community.

With more transgenderists coming out in the 1990s, a new kind of gender politics is emerging. The act of coming out signals self-acceptance, crucial to a group that has been seriously stigmatized. Because of their lack of civil rights and the persistence of negative stereotypes that encourage violence, not all cross-dressers and transgenderists can come out publicly at this time. For most the process takes years. However, based on the new political awareness and the availability of groups and national networks, indications are that transgenderists and cross-dressers may be coming out earlier. In the past, most transgenderists and cross-dressers usually came out in their 30s by first telling a significant other or members of a support group. Later, some may come out to friends, family and employers.

If the transgender person plans to cross-live, the process of coming out depends on whether or not one plans to "assimilate" into cultural bipolarism, which means "staying in" instead of "coming out." This is a highly important concern for the gender community. Unfortunately at this time, many transsexuals, even if once active in the gender community, gradually disappear from the community and assimilate into bipolarism. In doing so, they also abandon the terms with which they have self-defined. Merissa Sheril Lynn's decision to have sex-reassignment surgery created fear among some members of the gender community that she, too, would desire to assimilate, and abandon the community she helped propel into political activism. Lynn's choice to remain active after her surgery signals a new hope as well as a new role for surgical transsexuals which may heal the historical mistrust that has existed between some transgenderists, cross-dressers and transsexuals due to the fact that in the past the majority of transsexuals assimilated. In spite of this, members of the gender community have been trying to concentrate on shared similarities while respecting differences. This also means terms like *cross-dresser* and *transgenderist* that stress similarities, rather than differences, are being used more frequently.

Coming Together

The 1990s marks a radical shift in attitudes among gender minorities, not only towards themselves and each other, but also the dominant culture. Just six years ago, our local support group saw many transgenderists, conditioned by dominant ideology (as we all are), to think something was wrong with them. Most of the time they thought of themselves in the language of the oppressor, as "deviant" and perverted. At the time, the medical model dominated most of our thinking about transgenderism. As such, many support groups, including the one I co-founded, were structured around eliciting case histories and searching for "causes" of cross-dressing, transgenderism, or transsexualism. As gender awareness increased, the self stigmatization decreased and the groups changed for the better. Hopeful books from the social sciences like Walter Williams' *The Spirit and the Flesh* impress that not all cultures have a disdain for transgenderists. Works like Williams' and, more recently, Will Roscoe's *The Zuni Man-Woman* provide important historical and cross-cultural evidence of transgenderists and attitudes toward them that will hopefully increase awareness about gender minorities. The value of publishing non-medical books and articles about transgenderists indicates that they are an important group to study because, like the "berdache," they have something to tell us about ourselves and our culture. New research focusing attention on transgenderists and cross-dressers, although not all of it is positive, has reportedly been empowering for members of the gender community. One break-through work is Marietta Pathy-Allen's *Transformations*, a collection of photo-essays which present transgenderists and cross-dressers in "normal" situations with friends and family. However, Pathy-Allen's struggle to get published was difficult because of gender biases against the gender minority and those that present them in a positive, non-exploitive manner. She was criticized for even attempting her project in a headline story in the *New York Post* which charged, "Tax Dollars Paying for Men in Drag." Her finished book is testimony to the diversity of the gender community.

With this new empowerment, bolstered by writings in *Tapestry* by transsexuals, transgenderists and cross-dressers, attitudes have begun to change drastically. Support groups in the 1990s seem to have moved from pseudo-therapy groups to more informal political rap groups. The personal is becoming political. This change in consciousness is reflected in external appearances as well. In many cases, gone are the super stiff wigs, the hyper-feminine clothes and tons of make-up. Local support group members, more comfortable with themselves and more critical of social stereotypes, appear more relaxed. Hardly anyone, excepting some newcomers, wears full wigs. Most wear small hairpieces if balding. The relaxation of outer signs of gender like clothes and hair is a reflection of new inner attitudes of self-acceptance. The once chauvinistic attitude of the male-to-woman transgenderist toward the female-to-man transgenderist is also starting to change. The tendency to rigidly categorize the self and others is eroding. With self-acceptance comes the acceptance of others. The founding and former editor of the local Tri-Ess newsletter *Fiesta*, gender activist Jessa "B." expresses a hopeful view of the dissolution of gender categories. After attending one of the largest annual transgender conventions, "The Texas 'T' Party," a social and educational get together, she made the important observation that the gathering was not a convention of crossdressvestites or transgendersexualists, but people. Sweet and gorgeous people to talk about anything, plus everything you can't talk about with anyone else! As I've said before—we've got community and it works...We can get together and get along quite well. Thank-you. (Jessa B. 2)

Donna Mobley, a former president of the New Mexico chapter of Tri-Ess and IFGE board member who is in the process of creating historically significant video archives for the community, echoes the new openness happening in the gender community. At the 1990 IFGE convention in Boston, she had the opportunity to get to know some of the female-to-men transgenderists. As Donna was watching one of their video-taped interviews, she reported something "deep and profound happened" which made her aware of "how similar our stories and childhood experiences were" (Mobley 5). Donna describes the experience that changed her attitudes:

Suddenly it was as though all the lights in the room were turned on!...There were one or two who seemed to have gone a little too far...at what our culture considers masculine...It somehow seemed almost a parody of men. I recall being a little amused by this, but as I watched that video I suddenly felt very ashamed of myself for feeling that way. When I looked around at the young men in that room, I was seeing a mirror image of myself. (Mobley)

Donna's new awareness of the similarity between gender minorities plus the realization that "masculinity" and "femininity" are constructed is an awakening process many members of the gender community are experiencing.

Recently, "Rhea," a member of the local Albuquerque Cross-Dressers Support Group who has been reading *The Spirit and the Flesh*, asked other group members: If gender roles were not so polarized, would they still try and "pass" as women? Most members agreed they would be more comfortable somewhere in between the cultural gender roles of men and women. Rhea, whose dress and make-up resemble that of a professional model, stated she wished she could wear women's clothing, but not have to bother with wigs, make-up or even shaving. Sadly, she lamented, she felt she could never do this in public without evoking threats and/or violence. A new group member sitting next to her suggested that "we will have to change society."

The Cry for Civil Rights

Title VII of the Civil Rights Act of 1964, as amended by the Equal Opportunity Act of 1972 prohibits discrimination in employment in Federal, state, and local government, and in the private sector on the basis of race, color, religion, sex, or national origin. Unfortunately, recent court decisions at both the District and Appellate Court levels have ruled that Title VII does not include transsexuals or transgenderists. (Elizabeth 4-5)

Although a lower court ruled in favor of transsexual Karen Ulane, fired after sex-reassignment surgery in *Ulane v. Eastern Airlines Inc.*, the hope that transsexuals might be covered under the term "sex" in Title VII was dashed by the U.S. Court of Appeals' reversal of the lower court's judgments. Subsequent rulings reveal that not only transsexuals, but also transgenderists, cross-dressers, lesbians, gays and bisexuals are not covered by the Civil Rights Act. An exception is the 1993 Minnesota gay Civil Rights law, which for the first time in the U.S. history prohibits discrimination against people "having or being perceived as having a self image or identity not traditionally associated with one's biological maleness or femaleness." Blatant discrimination, such as loss of employment based on gender preference, has been upheld by the high courts. As the Appellate Court confirmed: "the Civil Rights Act prohibiting discrimination on the basis of sex should be given a narrow traditional interpretation which would exclude transsexuals" (Benedict 50). With no recourse for protection against employment discrimination, at one point, members of the gender community hoped the handicap amendment to Title VII, which included mental and physical handicaps, might protect them from unwarranted discrimination. If this had worked, it would have reinforced negative stereotypes of transsexualism as a psychological "disorder," but it might also have aided in their economic survival. The definitions of handicap include "having a handicap which limits...walking, talking, hearing, seeing, and working." It was thought that possibly transsexuals might qualify under this section since their ability to work was limited due to being fired for being transsexuals or transgenderists (Benedict 49).

However, before one of several test cases even reached the courts, Senator Armstrong from Colorado tacked on an amendment that excluded transvestites, transsexuals and homosexuals from protection under the Americans with Disabilities Act. To add insult to injury, Armstrong lumped sex and gender minorities with criminally excluded groups including child molesters, drug addicts and sex offenders. With absolutely no discussion on the Senate floor, the bill passed 76-20. Even though the House was lobbied, the bill also passed the House 35-0.

With the stark realization that the high courts and Congress encourage discrimination by such rulings, the Gender Movement is mobilizing to fight discrimination. The motto of the movement of the 1990s is drawn from Benjamin Franklin's statement: "We can all hang together, but surely, we *will* hang alone if we don't unify and work together" (Parker 54).

Goals of the Contemporary Gender Movement

Working together involves networking with other sex and gender minorities. Networking and political activism began on a large scale in 1990 at the "Coming Together—Working Together" convention sponsored by IFGE. Speakers from the Gay and Lesbian Coalition of Massachusetts, the Lesbian Rights Committee and the National Organization of Women joined with the American Civil Liberties Union, the Transsexual Rights Committee and members of IFGE to fight discrimination. Merissa Sherril Lynn opened the convention with a speech calling for unity:

We are, in effect, in a war. What war? It is the war for equality and justice, and for *all* people to live happier and more successful lives. When I say *all* people I mean members of our community, the gay community, and women....We must fight for our ideals...The first fact...is we exist...And, we have a *right* to exist. The second fact is *we are all vulnerable to and victims of discrimination.* (Lynn, "My Workshop," The Tri-Ess Issue 52)

Members of IFGE implored the gender community to develop an attitude that "transcends ourselves and goes beyond our special interests." David LaFontaine of the Gay and Lesbian Coalition observed that gender minorities like gays and lesbians are in "an emergency situation" and the goal must be to save people's lives. It was agreed that this could best be accomplished by changing people's attitudes about gender minorities. LaFontaine, drawing on his experience organizing gays and lesbians, advised gender minorities to start with the realization that "There's nothing wrong with us—there's something wrong with the world that doesn't allow people to be themselves" (Lynn, LaFontaine, et al. 56).

Following this line of thinking, the Gender Movement, inspired by the Gay and Lesbian Movement's success in having "homosexuality" as a disorder deleted from *DSM III*, have called for the removal of "transsexualism" and "transvestism" from the *Diagnostic and Statistical Manual of Mental Disorders*. Clinical supporters of the proposal observe it won't happen by the time the fourth edition comes out but hopefully by *DSM V*. George Brown, a psychiatrist who has worked and learned from the gender community for the last 11 years, suggests transforming "disorders" into definitions that no longer personally stigmatize, but reflect socio-cultural factors, like bipolarism. Brown, using Thomas Szasz's thesis in *The Myth of Mental Illness*, maintains that defiance and disagreement with societal norms "do not qualify as criteria by which psychiatrists should be making diagnoses" (Brown, manuscript 1992 prepub.). Last May due to transgender activists protesting outside the APA convention, the American Psychiatric Association advised that "well adjusted transsexuals not automatically be diagnosed as having a mental disorder" (Clark).

A recent report given at the "First International Conference on Transgender Law and Employment Policy" organized by Phyllis Frye (August 1992), aware that one of the effects of de-medicalizing transsexualism is that insurance-funded sex-reassignment surgery might disappear, advises:

The solution of continued medicalization of transgender behavior works a greater harm on more people. Continued medicalization of transgenderism sets up a tier of psychologists as the gatekeepers of what we do with our own bodies, unfairly paints the entire transgender community with a brush of mental illness and maintains the pernicious fiction of separate male and female classes of people with associated separate gender roles, a fiction which has been especially unfair to women from time immemorial. (First International Trangender Conference)

So complete has the medicalization of transgenderists been that even their partners are stigmatized. Attempting to dispel the myth that partners of trangenderists suffer from mental illness, Brown and Cynthia Phillips conducted a study on the partners of cross-dressers. Their results presented at the 1993 Texas "T" Party contradict clinical stereotypes that branded wives of transvestites as "moral masochists" suffering from "low self esteem." Unfortunately, a number of contemporary studies continue to reinforce the low self-esteem myth for wives and partners of transgenderists. Such assumptions perpetrate negative stereotypes about transgenderists. Annie Woodhouse's work on transvestites' wives refers to them as the "forgotten women." She argues that genetic males can never be women. Such assumptions, steeped in medical myths and gender bipolarism are usually based on too few subjects and interviews and contradict observations by those who have long been associated with the gender community.

My own observations, as well as Phillips' and Brown's, refute Woodhouse's and others' accusations that partners of transgenderists are frequently driven to drug abuse, insanity and/or alcoholism simply because their partners are transgenderists or cross-dressers. Donna Mobley's "Couples" video documentary featuring transgenderists and their partners will hopefully counter such negative stereotypes. Mobley's video features transgenderists and their partners discussing their relationship and how transgenderism affects it. The interview with Linda and Cynthia Phillips is particularly encouraging as they discuss being together for over 35 years and what it was like when male-to-woman Linda went full time. This is not to imply that all transgenderists' relationships are problem free. Many of the problems they face, however, are a direct result of social stigmatization and rigid categorizations of sex and gender. Currently, members of the gender community are attempting to come to terms with their own homophobia; that mindset still holds sway as some partners of male-to-women transgenderists and cross-dressers worry that they might be lesbians. As the transgender activists advise, cultural bigotry such as sex and gender bipolarism must be challenged and refuted. To do so, one must not assimilate or replicate the roles of the oppressors, but revolt.

Conclusion

As this work has progressed to an examination of the Gender Movement, my emphasis on stressing the differences among gender minorities has become less important. This is not in any way meant to negate the diversity that makes up the gender community. At this time however, leaders of the Gender Movement have wisely advised that gender minorities must also group together to fight gender oppression. As I mentioned earlier, gender appears to be on a continuum. It is not fixed. When I asked members of the local support group if they could live without discrimination full-time as women, without surgery, would they do it? Every hand shot up,[1] regardless of whether individuals self-defined as cross-dressers, transgenderists or transsexuals. This might indicate that among self-defined transsexuals, the decision for surgery might not always be a personal decision, but a decision rooted in cultural fear and anxiety and reinforced by gender bipolarism.

With the increased use of terms like "transgenderist" and "cross-dresser" among gender minorities, stigmatization is reduced. Even so, because of increasing social pressures and anxieties, transsexual surgery seems to be on the increase. Unfortunately, it seems easier to "fix" individuals than the culture. On a sociocultural level, uncritically accepting clinical transsexual ideology means assimilating into the dominant culture. The Gender Movement is challenging such assimilation. An encouraging event is taking place as transsexuals who once disappeared after surgery seem to be finding their way back to gender communities.

The examination of transsexualism as a social phenomenon in contemporary America has numerous implications. Early categorizations of cross-gender people, which formed the basis of later categories of transgender psychological "disorders," reveal not only severe gender prejudice against gender minorities, but also against gays, lesbians and women. Leaders in the Gender Movement have pointed out how discrimination against males who want to exist as women is discrimination against females in this culture at the same time as well. In a plea for more females to join the Gender Movement, Wendy Parker asked, "Is a man who does what a woman does mentally ill?"

Freedom for transgenderists and cross-dressers is a step toward freedom and justice for all those oppressed by gender bipolarism.

This can only be accomplished if gender minorities join with other groups affected by sex and gender oppression. This is starting to happen. The radical group Queer Nation includes gay, lesbian, bisexual, transgender, transsexual and cross-dressed people. The battle against sex and gender oppression is also being waged by politicized drag queens, like the Sisters of Perpetual Indulgence, who use artifices of gender to challenge gender roles and to encourage tolerance for people who are different. A member of the Sisters of Perpetual Indulgence observed drag was a way to "make political points, do outrageous things and change society." RuPaul furthers the point observing "Everytime I bat my eyelashes it's a political act." Political drag concentrating on gender diversity shares the goals and fears of the Gender Movement. The message of this drag has taken the "Silence=Death" motto from Act Up, an AIDs activist group.

For gender minorities, "Silence=Death" is a growing reality. At this point in time, most transgenderists fired from their jobs despite excellent work records, or denied housing, have no protection against gender discrimination. During these economically depressed times, they are usually the first to be dismissed. In addition, many are subjected to unfair and humiliating treatment. For example, a male-to-woman transsexual who worked at Boeing was informed that she could wear "only unisex clothing" and was forbidden to use the women's rest room. Despite petitions of support and an excellent work record, she was fired for being a transsexual. At this time, her court case is pending.

As a rule, discrimination usually has more serious consequences than prejudice. Prejudice tends to escalate as negative attitudes about disliked groups increase. Congress's recent lumping of gender minorities with child molesters and sex offenders and Colorado's passage of Amendment #2 reinforce negative attitudes toward gender minorities. In 1954, Gordon Allport delineated five stages in which the escalation of negative attitudes and prejudices can become lethal. The first stage, *antilocution*, involves people with prejudices talking about them with like-minded friends. Stage two, *avoidance*, occurs when individuals avoid members of the disliked group, but do not inflict physical harm. *Discrimination*, the third stage, occurs when prejudiced persons strive to exclude members of the disliked group from "employment, housing, political rights, educational, recreational opportunities, churches, hospitals, or other social privileges." By stage four, heightened emotion fueled by prejudice leads to *severe threats and violence*. Stage five involves *extermination* of members of disliked groups (Allport 4-15).

Prejudice in its initial stages can be modified. Merissa Lynn gives an example of how negative attitudes can be changed through personal contact and education. Lynn reported that when a young girl was reported missing in Boston, police stormed the IFGE headquarters, operating under the erroneous assumption that transgenderists and cross-dressers are child molesters. Outraged, Lynn took the opportunity to educate them about gender minorities. As a result, members of the gender community joined police and other citizens in the search for the missing girl (Lynn, "My Workshop"). Frye's International Transgender Conferences educate judges and lawyers as well as draft legislation. Although theses events provide the chance to change attitudes through education, if discrimination has escalated to stage four or five, that of violence, it can be too late. A year ago a news item in *Tapestry* reported that an Irish minister, Pastor Douce, dedicated to founding international organizations for gender minorities, was found murdered. His assassins had been to his gender center in Ireland several times. They identified themselves as police inspectors and proceeded to insult and attack gender minorities. They returned late at night and demanded entry. When the police came they fled. Later, two men returned, taking Pastor Douce with them. His body was found three weeks later in the woods. No suspects have been apprehended.

Negative actions against the community have already reached stage five. Lynn maintains that the Gender Movement is 30 years behind the Women's Movement and the Gay and Lesbian Movement in organizing and fighting for rights. However, because of increasing discrimination, if the Gender Movement is to survive, its activists must catch up quickly. Gender minorities working to support feminist, gay and lesbian legislation are learning valuable political lessons, as well as networking with other oppressed groups. Because of combined efforts, gay rights bills passed in Seattle and Minnesota also forbid discrimination in housing for cross-gender people.

In 1980, attorney and transgender activist Phyllis Frye forced the Houston city council to repeal a code that made it illegal to dress in the clothing of the opposite sex. Frye recalls:

I was never arrested. But each and every day for four years I left the house in the morning not knowing if I'd be back that night or in jail. And each and every day for four years my spouse left the house to go to her work not knowing whether I'd be back at night or in jail. I've always felt that was very cruel. ("On Actvism")

Frye reports she went downtown "several days each week and wrote a myriad of letters and made numerous phone calls. I lobbied the Municipal judges and council members and anyone who would listen." Frye became active in the feminist movement and the League of Women Voters who Frye felt were influential enough to "convince many people of the fact that I was serious and deserved their attention" ("On Activism"). One of the council members felt she was a joke, to which Frye responded by explaining "this was not a game...but a real life situation" ("On Activism"). At last her efforts paid off. Activist Frye advises:

Once again I say this to you my sisters and brothers, "If I can do that in the late 70s-early 80s, what is your excuse for staying scared and staying closeted and not being the true person you are? This is our decade: Make it happen for you Now!" ("On Activism")

In August of 1992, Frye organized the First International Conference on Transgender Law and Employment Policy in Houston. Items on the agenda included the Health Law Committee Report that recommended changing the current view of transgenderism from a psychological illness deserving of medical treatment to recognizing it as "a lifestyle choice" that should be protected by the "right of privacy" and "freedom of expression."[2] This would "include redefining transgenderal behaviors as part of 'sexual orientation and gender identification suspect class' consisting of gay, lesbian and transgenderal behaviors" (First International Transgender Conference: Draft Report of the Health Law Committee August 1992). The factors used to determine a *suspect class* include groups that have "suffered a history of purposeful discrimination," been "burdened with prejudices unrelated to performance" and "lack political power." The intention here is to provide protection against discrimination to "suspect classes" including lesbians, gays, bisexuals and transgendered persons *under which transsexuals are categorized* by amending Title VII of the Civil Rights act of 1964 to include "sexual orientation and gender identification." The report summarizes that

the most progressive direction for health law is toward a declassification of sex and a de-medicalization of transgenderism. This is tantamount to a celebration and protection of sexual and gender diversity in human life.

Due to current severe economic, social and environmental problems, public anxieties have risen, evidenced by Colorado's passage of Amendment #2 which denies lesbians and gays minority status and wipes out laws in Aspen,

Boulder and Denver designed to protect sexual minorities (under which transgenderists are classified) from discrimination.

As Allport warns, when anxieties rise, people look for scapegoats. This was the case in Oregon as many out-of-work loggers and others were susceptible to right wing propaganda spreading the lie that if gays and lesbians were thought of as minorities they would get "special treatment" in hiring procedures. If passed, Oregon Amendment #9 would have denied gays, lesbians and transgenderists (classified among them) their civil rights. This piece of legislation drafted and funded by the Christian Coalition was just narrowly defeated. Proponents of Measure #9 vow it will be back on the ballot again.

Transgenderists can no longer afford to be politically unaware. In order to avoid becoming scapegoats, members of the gender community must be united and courageous. We are all suppressed by a rigid dual gender system. To not fight gender discrimination means supporting a fascist bipolarity which enforces gender conformity. Under this reign of terror, nonconforming males and females who are not transgenderists or cross-dressers are becoming increasingly suspect. There is an increase in incidents nationwide of genetic males and females being expelled from restrooms because they don't conform to gender stereotypes. Albuquerque's 1991 Fiesta newsletter reports that masculine appearing females and feminine appearing males are being pulled out of public restrooms and asked to prove what sex they are. The *gender police are everywhere*, limiting individual freedom of expression and the pursuit of happiness.

Social scientists can facilitate the Gender Movement's struggle against gender oppression by contributing scholarship on bipolar gender roles and non-medicalized profiles of the gender community. A nationwide survey on transgenderists should be launched to yield new numbers, reflective of the large population of gender minorities. Articles dealing with civil rights and gender minorities as well as the history of gender minorities must be encouraged. It is crucial that books and anthologies *authored by transgenderists*, particularly those who do not assimilate, be published and it is essential that these writings reach mainstream America.

Walter Williams urges the development of a new all-encompassing gender scholarship reflecting the revolutionary changes occurring in gender. He writes:

gender and sexuality are among the most controversial topics with which modern humanity must grapple...It is time for a new Gender Studies to emerge, incorporating into its core topics that have previously been marginalized...Only by taking this larger view can we begin to understand the incredible changes occurring all around us, and appreciate the benefits that come with the acceptance and celebration of human diversity. ("Women, Men, and Others" 141)

If we keep focusing on heterosexual/homosexual dichotomies, as Williams astutely warns, we are in danger of missing some of the most important trends of our times. Perhaps a more radical way to categorize people, Williams suggests, may be based on their gender identity and gender role. By breaking up past genitally-based associations, we can see a great diversity which heretofore has been completely ignored. Such a schema would define as *heterogender* those relationships that contain: a masculine male with a feminine female, a masculine female with a feminine male, a feminine male and masculine male, as well as a feminine female and masculine female. *Homogender* relationships would be: a masculine male and masculine female, a feminine male and feminine female, two masculine females, two feminine females, two masculine males and two feminine males. Although Williams' system is not the final solution, it does detach erotic attraction from the genitals and reattach it to gender. As such, it might alleviate some of the baseline S&M horrors that the requirements of strict psychological and anatomical gender alignment have wrought. This is a vital step toward creating a gender-transcendence theory in which gender categories are no longer linked to biological sex. And a step toward realizing a "certain percentage of society is being forced into an unwanted gender role" (First International Transgender Conference: Health Law Committee Draft Report August 1992). Therefore, we must struggle to dismantle the current one-nation-under-gender-divided-and-unequal and recognize the transgender nation. Only when this becomes a possibility, can there occur a true Gender Revolution.

Notes

Introduction

[1]A good example is Queercore, a spin-off group of Queer Nation, comprised of radical sex and gender minorities who disdain the assimilationist politics of the more "traditional" sex and gender organizations.

[2]The term "gender community" refers to individuals as well as events in the cross-gender subculture. Individuals who provide support or services to cross-dressers and transgenderists are also often considered to be part of the gender community and are almost always welcome to attend the gender community's social, educational and political gatherings.

The term "Gender Movement" refers to the social movement dedicated to fighting for civil rights for cross-dressers and transgenderists.

Chapter One

[1]The pronoun "she" reflects the gender Sondra feels she is. Throughout the work, the use of such pronouns as "he" and "she," "her" and "him" will refer to the gender individuals feel themselves to be and not to their genital assignment at birth.

Although Sondra is able to "pass" extremely well as a woman, her co-workers in the federal office who knew her as Sam refuse to refer to Sondra as "she," even though she has had sex-reassignment surgery and has been living as a woman for the last seven years.

[2]Rena Swifthawk, a Native American transsexual, argues that the term "berdache" is not a Native American term, but a derogatory word. "Berdache" came from the Persian "bardaj" and was spread through the Arabic, Italian, Spanish and French languages. It was commonly used to refer to "a boy who was shamefully abused" (Williams 1986). Later it was used by European colonizers to describe male homosexuals. Although contemporary researchers generally use the term to describe genetic males who live in the role of the "opposite" gender, Swifthawk suggests that the native words like "nadle," the Navajo term for transgender males, be used instead (pers. comm. Merissa Sherril Lynn 1992).

[3]This is particularly evident in right wing TV and radio talk show host Rush Limbaugh's conservative rhetoric. In the spring of 1993 Limbaugh poked fun at transgenderists by showing people on the street being asked what transgenderists were. The responses aired revealed confusion and disgust toward transgenderists.

173

Chapter Two

[1]Sexual perversion seems to include anything deviating from monogamous, heterosexual, reproducing couples.

[2]For more information on LaVey's theories see "The Way We Wear Out Genes: Could a Cluster of Brain Cells Be the Cause of Homosexuality" by Robert Massa in *The Village Voice*, Dec. 24, 1991.

[3]This is most evident in Phyllis Frye's definition of *transgendered* community which she noted includes transvestites, passing women, female and male impersonators pre-, non and post-operative transsexuals and "females-to-male." See transcript of speech given by Frye for March on Washington April 25, 1993. Recently Richard Docter has attempted to medicalize Prince's term "transgenderist" (see Docter 1988). Most recently, Prince has suggested the term "bigenderist" as a more accurate term to describe transgenderists and cross-dressers. Prince's new label has at this point not caught on in the gender community.

[4]For an enlightened and different perspective see Jessa Bryan's "Hermaphrodite's Love" in which she rewrites Ovid's myth of Hermaphrodite so it becomes "A coming together of male and female," a positive transformation. In *Chrysalis Quarterly* no. 6, 1993.

[5]There is no supporting evidence that nadles were actual hermaphrodites.

[6]For further discussion of Native American female-to-man transgenderist, see Evelyn Blackwood "Sexuality and Gender in Certain Native American Tribes: The Case of Cross-Gender Females" in *Signs* 10, #1, 1984 and Yudkin 1978, Williams 1986 and Roscoe 1991.

[7]For more details on this see Joan Nestle 1992 and Keith Clark 1993.

Chapter Three

[1]While acknowledging other acquired statuses, such as race, class and age, sex forms the basic social division, in which we are divided according to gender.

[2]This was first called to my attention by Annie Esturoy 1990. It seems to be the case in S. America and Germany as well (pers. comm. 1992).

[3]Walker made this comment in Lee Grant's documentary, "What Sex Am I?" The documentary first aired on HBO in 1986. However, because of pressure in May 1993 the APA argued well adjusted transsexuals should not automatically be diagnosed as "mentally ill." This advice has yet to be adopted for *DSM-IV*.

[4]This is Money's description of himself! (see Holder's interview with him, 1988).

[5]Roger Gorski is allegedly a mentor to Simon LaVey, the gay researcher who has popularized the idea that gays' brains are structurally different from heterosexuals' brains.

Chapter Four

[1]Under other minority groups I am specifically including: racial, ethnic, sexual and socio-economic minorities.

[2]Some of the videos are available through IFGE Inc., P.O. Box 367, Wayland Mass., 01778. IFGE board member Donna Mobley has created some excellent and highly educational tapes.

[3]A recent *Joan Rivers* (Fall 1993) broadcast was revolutionary in television history as guest Leslie Feinberg, author of *Stone Butch Blues*, a female-to-man cross-dresser, took the "experts" to task. Eloquently, Feinberg asked that the cross-dressers and transsexual guests be allowed to *speak for themselves*, thus quieting counselor Roger Peo. Joan was a little uneasy.

[4]This headline may in fact have anticipated a story run in *The New York Times* (1990) indicating that polluted water caused by chemicals in the Great Lakes was causing waterfowl and other wildlife to mix and reverse their gender roles. The story also warned that high concentrations of PCBs, lead and dioxins were found in human residents in the area!!

[5]Here I am in no way advocating that these images be censored but rather calling for an analysis of what they reveal culturally. Additionally, self-produced videos and films by gender minorities can help counter false images by showing gender minorities as "real" people.

[6]Other documentaries that demonstrate this include: Lee Grant's "What Sex Am I?," first broadcast on HBO 1986 and Lisa Leeman's "Metamorphosis: Man into Woman," broadcast on PBS in July of 1990.

[7]See Jesse Green's "Film, Fame, Then Fade Out" where he details how five principal actors in *Paris Is Burning* died tragic and violent deaths (*New York Times*, April 19, 1993).

Chapter Five

[1]The first subheading is taken from the name of a national event sponsored by the gender community. It reinforces self-empowerment as a means to combat negative cultural stereotypes. The second subheading is from the *Rocky Horror Picture Show*; it reinforces taking action.

Conclusion

[1]Only male-to-women transgenderists were present when the question was asked. However, I later asked several female-to-men transgenderists the same question and received the same response.

[2]A step toward this would be if the draft revision for *DSM-IV* becomes official. If it does, persons identified as transsexual can no longer be assumed to have a mental disorder. See Draft 2nd report of the Transsexual and Transgender Health Law Project by Martine A. Rothblatt (August 1993).

Works Cited

Abel, Gene. "What to Do When Non Transsexuals Seek Sex Reassignment Surgery." *Journal of Sex and Marital Therapy* 5.4 (Winter 1979): 374-76.

Abramowitz, Stephen. "Psychosocial Outcomes of Sex Reassignment Surgery." *Journal of Consulting and Clinical Psychology* 54.2 (1986): 183-89.

Ackroyd, Peter. *Dressing Up. Transvestism and Drag: The History of an Obsession.* New York: Simon and Schuster, 1979.

Adkins, Elizabeth Kocher. "Genes, Hormones, Sex and Gender." *Sociobiology: Beyond Nature/Nurture?: Reports, Definitions and Debate.* Eds. George Barlow and James Silverberg. New York: Westview P, 1980. 385-415.

Albuquerque Journal. "Ken in Barbie's Clothing a Shocker." 21 July 1990.

Albuquerque Tribune. "My Bundle Baby." 23 May 1992.

Allport, Gordon, W. *The Nature of Prejudice.* Reading, MA: Addison-Wesley, 1954 and 1979.

Alper, Joseph. "Sex Differences in Brain Assymmetry: A Critical Analysis." *Feminist Studies* 11.1 (Spring 1985): 7-39.

American Psychiatric Association (APA). *Diagnostic and Statistical Manual of Mental Disorders,* Third ed. (*DSM III*). Washington, D.C.: APA, 1980.

American Psychiatric Association (APA). *Diagnostic and Statistical Manual of Mental Disorders.* Third ed. Rev. (*DSM III-R*). Washington, D.C.: APA, 1987.

Archer, John, and Barbara Lloyd. *Sex and Gender.* New York: Penguin Books, 1982.

Armstrong, C.N. "Transsexualism a Medical Perspective." *Journal of Medical Ethics* 5 (1980): 90-91.

Associated Press. "Doctor Wants Another Sex Change." *San Francisco Chronicle* 13 Oct. 1989.

_____. "Sex Change Operation: Transsexual Wins Lawsuit." *Albuquerque Tribune* 3 June 1983.

"B." Jessa. "Affiliation and Delight." *Fiesta Chapter Newsletter* Apr. 1991.

_____. Personal communication, 1991.

"B." Jessa (Bryan, Jessa). "Hermaphrodites Love." *Chrysalis* 6. AEGIF Service, 1993.

Barker-Benfield. *The Horrors of the Half-Known Life: Male Attitudes Toward Women and Sexuality in 19th Century America.* New York: Harper & Row, 1976.

Baudrillard, Jean. *Fatal Strategies.* Translated by Phillip Beitman & W.G.J. Niesluchowski. New York: Semiotexte, 1990.

_____. *The Transparency of Evil: Essays of Extreme Phenomena*. New York: Verso P, 1993.

Belli, Melvin. "Transsexual Surgery: A New Tort?" *Journal of the American Medical Association* 239.20 (May 1978): 2143-48.

Bem, Lipsitz Sandra. "Masculinity and Femininity Exist Only in the Mind of the Perceiver." *Masculinity and Femininity, Basic Perspectives*. Eds. June M. Reinish, Leonard Rosenblum, Stephanie A. Sanders. New York: Oxford UP, 1987. 304-15.

Benedict, Jill. "Title VII: Who is Actually Covered? Prohibition of Discrimination in Employment on the Basis of Sex." *Information Book Revised*. Denver, CO: Gender Identity Center, 1990. 49-51.

Benjamin, Harry. *The Transsexual Phenomena*. New York: Julian P, 1966.

Benjamin, Harry; Paul Walker; Jack Berger; Richard Green; et al. "Standards of Care: The Hormonal and Surgical Sex Reassignment of Gender Dysphoric Persons." *Archives of Sexual Behavior* 14.1 (1985): 79-90.

Berkman, Meredith. "Review on *The Silence of the Lambs*." *Entertainment Weekly* 29 Mar. 1991: 17-23.

Biber, Stanley. Interviewed on ABC's *Prime Time News* (repeat). Aired Summer 1993.

Blanchard, Ray. "Classification and Labeling of Nonhomosexual Gender Dysphorias." *Archives of Sexual Behavior* 13.4 (1989): 315-33.

Blanchard, Ray, Suzanne Legault, and William Lindsay. "Vaginoplasty Outcome in Male to Female Transsexuals." *Journal of Sex and Marital Therapy* 13.4 (Winter 1987): 265-75.

Blackwood, Evelyn. "Sexuality and Gender in Certain Native American Tribes: The Case of Cross-gender Females." *Signs* 10.1 (1984): 27-42.

Bly, Robert. *Iron John. A Book about Men*. New York: Addison-Wesley, 1990.

Bogdan, Robert, ed. and compiler. *Being Different: The Biography of Jane Fry*. New York: Wiley-Interscience, John Wiley & Sons, 1974.

Bolin, Anne. "Transsexualism and the Limits of Traditional Analysis." *American Behavioral Scientist* 31.1 (Sept.-Oct. 1987): 41-65.

_____. *In Search of Eve. Transsexual Rites of Passage*. South Hadley, MA: Bergin & Garvey, 1988.

Brown, George. "Counseling the Wife of a Transvestite." Pre-publication manuscript for primary care physicians, U of Texas Health Science Center, San Antonio, TX, 1992.

Brown, Veronica. "On the Road to Brussels." *Transsexualism: A Collection of Articles, Editorials, and Letters*. Wayland, MA: IFGE, 1988. 47-52.

Bulliet, C.J. *Venus Castina. Famous Female Impersonators, Celestial and Human*. 1928. New York: Bonanza Books, 1956.

Bullough, Vern. "A Nineteenth Century Transsexual." *Archives of Sexual Behavior* 16.1 (1987): 81-83.

Butler, Judith. *Gender Trouble: Feminism and the Subversion of Identity*. New York: Routledge, 1990.

Califia, Pat. "Playing with Roles and Reversals: Gender-Bending." *The Advocate* 15 Sept. 1983.

Caputi, Jane. *The Age of Sex Crime*. Bowling Green, OH: Bowling Green State University Popular Press, 1987.

Caputi, Jane, and Diane Russell. "Femicide: Speaking the Unspeakable." *Ms.* 1.2 (Sept./Oct. 1990): 34-37.

Cauldwell D. "Psychopathia Transsexuals." *Sexology* 16 (1949): 274-80.

Caulfield, Mina Davis. "Sexuality in Human Evolution: What is 'Natural' in Sex?" *Feminist Studies* 11.2 (Summer 1985): 343, 365.

Chodorow, Nancy. "Feminism and Difference: Gender, Relation and Difference in Psycho-analytic Perspective." *The Scholar and the Feminist, Volume One: The Future of Difference*. Eds. Hester Einstein and Alice Jardine. Boston: G.K. Hall, 1980.

_____. "Oedipal Asymmetries and Heterosexual Knots." *Female Psychology: The Emerging Self*. 2nd ed. Ed. Sue Cox. New York: St. Martin's, 1981.

_____. *The Reproduction of Mothering: Psychoanlysis and the Sociology of Gender*. California: U of California P, 1978.

Clare, Dorothy, and Bryan Tully. "Transhomosexuality, or the Dissociation of Sexual Orientation and Sex Object Choice." *Archives of Sexual Behavior* 18.6 (1989): 531-36.

Clark, Keith. "What a Drag Crossdressing Crosses Over." *OUT: New Mexico's Gay, Lesbian and Bisexual News Magazine* July 1993.

Cooper, Alice. *Poison*. Music video. Aired on MTV 1989.

Cooper, Marc. "Enter Measure 9." *Village Voice* 13 Oct. 1992: 10-13.

Cosford, Bill. "Psycho Goes Suburban." *Entertainment Weekly* 26 Oct. 1990.

Crocker, Catherine. "Pregnancy Doll Proving to Be Best Seller." *Albuquerque Tribune* 9 (May 1992): C-8.

Daly, Mary. *Gynecology: The Metaethics of Radical Feminism*. Boston: Beacon, 1978.

"Danny Partridge Jailed in Beating of Transvestite." *Marin Independent Journal* 1 Apr. 1991.

Degler, Carl. *At Odds: Women in the Family in America from the Revolution to the Present*. New York: Oxford UP, 1980.

Devor, Holly. *Gender Blending: Confronting the Limits of Duality*. Bloomington, IN: Indiana UP, 1989.

_____. "Gender Blending Females. Women and Sometimes Men." *American Behavioral Scientist* 31.1 (Sept.-Oct. 1987): 12-20.

Dilberto, Gloria. "Invasion of The Gender Blenders." *People Magazine* 23 Oct. 1984: 97-99.

Dinnerstein, Dorothy. *The Mermaid and the Minotaur: Sexual Arrangements and Human Malaise*. New York: Harper & Row, 1976.

Dixen, Jean, Heather Maddever, Judy Van Maasdam, and Patrick Edwards. "Psychosocial Characteristics of Applicants Evaluated for Surgical Gender Reassignment." *Archives of Sexual Behavior* 13.3 (1984): 269-77.

Docter, Richard. *Transvestites and Transsexuals. Toward a Theory of Cross-Gender Behavior.* New York: Plenum P, 1988.

Dolan, Jeremiah. "Transsexualism: Syndrome or Symptom?" *Canadian Journal of Psychiatry* 32 (Nov. 1987): 666-72.

Donahue. "Sexual Minorities." CBS. Aired 4 July 1989.

_____. "Tula." CBS. Aired 2 July 1990.

Dorner, Gunter. "Neuroendocrine Response to Estrogen and Brain Differentiation in Heterosexuals, Homosexuals, and Transsexuals." *Archives of Sexual Behavior* 1-1.1 (1988): 57-75.

Edgarton, Milton. "The Role of Surgery in the Treatment of Transsexualism." *Annals of Plastic Surgery* 13.6 (Dec. 1984) 473-76.

Edgarton, Milton; Richard Edlich; and U. Turner. "Male Transsexualism—A Review of Genital Surgical Reconstruction." *American Journal of Obstetrics and Gynecology* 132.2 (15 Sept. 1978): 119-33.

Edgren, Gretchen. "The Transformation of Tula: The Extraordinary Story of a Beautiful Woman Who Was Born a Boy!" *Playboy Magazine* Sept. 1991: 103-05.

Eicher, W. "Genital Transformation by Inverted Penis Skin Implantation Technique." *Emerging Dimensions of Sexology: Selected Papers from the 6th World Congress: Sexual Medicine* Vol. II. Eds. R. Seagrave and E. Haebull. New York: Praeger Scientific, 1984. 207-09.

Eicher, W., M. Spoljar, et al. "H-Y Antigen in Transsexuality." *Emerging Dimensions of Sexology: Selected Papers from the 6th World Congress: Sexual Medicine.* Vol. II. New York: Praeger Scientific, 1984. 161-66.

Eichler, Margrit. *The Double Standard: A Feminist Critique of Feminist Social Science.* New York: St. Martin's, 1980.

Eisler, Riane. *The Chalice and the Blade.* New York: Harper & Row, 1987.

_____. "Rediscovering a Partnership Society." *Utne Reader* Mar./Apr. 1990.

Eliade, Mircea. *The Forge and the Crucible: The Origins & Structures of Alchemy.* New York: Harper & Row, 1962.

Ellis, Havelock. *Studies in the Psychology of Sex.* 1906. 2 Part 2. New York: Random House: 1937.

Elizabeth, Sr. Mary. "Transsexual Civil Rights." *Transsexualism: A Collection of Articles, Editorials, and Letters.* Wayland, MA: IFGE, 1988. 4-6.

Escoffier, Jeffery. "The Politics of Gay Identity." *Radical History Review* 20 (Spring/Summer 1979): 119-53.

Ewen, Stuart. *All Consuming Images: The Politics of Style in Contemporary Culture.* New York: Basic Books, 1988.

Feinbloom, Deborah Heller. *Transvestites & Transsexuals.* New York: Delta, 1976.

180 Trangender Nation

Feinbloom, Deborah Heller, Michael Fleming, Valerie Kijewski, and Jan Schulter. "Lesbian/Feminist Orientation among Male-to-Female Transsexuals." *Journal of Homosexuality* 2(1) (Fall 1976): 59-71.

Ferguson, Ann; Philipson, Ilene; et al. "Forum: The Feminist Sexuality Debates." *Signs: Journal of Women's Culture and Society* 10.11 (1984): 106-35.

First International Conference on Transgender Law and Employment Policy. Draft Report of The Health Law Committee, Houston, TX: Aug. 1992.

Fisk, Norman. "Gender Dysphoria Syndrome-The Conceptualization that Liberalizes Indications for Total Gender Reorientation and Implies a Broadly Based Multi-Dimensional Rehabilitative Regimen." *The Western Journal of Medicine* (May 1974): 386-91.

Foucault, Michel. *The History of Sexuality: An Introduction.* Vol.1 Trans. Robert Hurly. New York: Vintage Books, 1980.

Fredrickson, Tere. "Red Alert Your Civil Rights Are in Danger." *Gender Euphoria.* Oct. 1992.

Freedman, Estelle, and Barrie Thorne. "Introduction to The Feminist Sexuality Debates." *Signs: Journal of Women in Culture and Society* 10.11 (1984): 102-06.

Freud, Sigmund. "The Differentiation Between Men and Women." *Three Essays on the Theory of Sexuality.* By James Strachey. New York: Basic Books, 1962.

_____. *Sexuality and the Psychology of Love.* New York: Collier Books, 1963.

Freund, Kurt, Betty Steiner, and Samuel Chan. "Two Types of Cross-Gender Identity." *Archives of Sexual Behavior* 11.1 (1982): 49-63.

Frye, Phyllis Randolph. "On Activism." *Gender Euphoria.* Nov. 1992.

_____. "Transcript of Actual Speech." Given at Gay, and Lesbian and Bisexual Equal Rights March in Washington, 25 Apr. 1993.

Futterweit, Walter, Richard Weiss, and Richard Fagerstrom. "Endocrine Evaluation of Forty Female-to-Male Transsexuals: Increased Frequency of Polycystic Ovarian Disease in Female Transsexualism." *Archives of Sexual Behavior* 15.1 (1986): 69-79.

Futuyma, Douglas, and Stephen Risch. "Sexual Orientation, Sociobiology, and Evolution." *Journal of Homosexuality* 9.2-3 (1983-84): 157-67.

Garber, Marjorie. *Vested Interest: Cross-Dressing & Cultural Anxiety.* New York: Routledge, 1992.

Gender Euphoria Monthly Newsletter. Ed. Tere Fredrickson. San Antonio, TX: Boulton & Park, 1991-93.

Geist, Christopher, and Jack Nachbar, eds. *The Popular Culture Reader.* 3rd ed. Bowling Green, OH: Bowling Green State University Popular Press, 1983.

Geraldo. "Transsexual Regrets: Who's Sorry Now." ABC. Aired 2 Apr. 1989.

Goffman, Erving. "On Fieldwork." Ed. and trans. Lyn H. Lofland. *Journal of Contemporary Ethnography* 18.2 (July 1989): 123-33.

Goldstein, Richard. "Death in Drag." *Village Voice* 10 Nov. 1992.

Goodwin, Joseph P. *More Man Than You'll Ever Be: Gay Folklore and Acculturation in Middle America.* Bloomington, IN: Indiana UP, 1989.

Gooren, Louis. "Letter to the Editor." *Archives of Sexual Behavior* 18.6 (1989): 537-38.

Green, Richard. *The "Sissy Boy Syndrome" and the Development of Homosexuality.* New Haven: Yale UP, 1987.

Green, Richard, ed. *Sexual Identity Conflict in Children and Adults.* New York: Basic Books, 1974.

Green, Richard, Stanley Biber, and Stephen Wachtel. *Human Sexuality: A Health Practioner's Text.* 2nd ed. Baltimore: Williams & Wilkins, 1976.

_____. "On the Expression of H-Y Antigen in Transsexuals." *Archives of Sexual Behavior* 15.1 (1986): 51-67.

Green, Richard, and John Money, eds. *Transsexualism and Sex Reassignment.* Baltimore: Johns Hopkins P, 1969.

Grimm, David. "Toward a Theory of Gender: Transsexualism, Gender, Sexuality, and Relationships." *American Behavioral Scientist* 31.1 (Sept-Oct. 1987): 66-85.

Gross, Larry. "Out of the Mainstream: Sexual Minorities and the Mass Media." *Remote Control: Television, Audiences, and Cultural Power.* Eds. E. Seiter, H. Borcher, G. Kreutzner, and E. Warth. New York: Routledge, 1989. 130-50.

Haeberle, Edwin. "A Movement of Inverts: An Early Plan for a Homosexual Organization in the United States." *Journal of Homosexuality* 10.1-2 (Fall 1984).

Hamburger, C., G.K. Sturup, and I. Dahl-Iverson. "Transvestism, Hormonal, Psychiatric and Surgical Treatment." *Journal of the American Medical Association* 152 (1953): 391-96.

Haraway, Donna. "The Biological Enterprise: Sex, Mind, and Profit from Human Engineering to Sociobiology." *Radical History Review* 20 (Spring/Summer 1979): 206-37.

Harris, Thomas. *The Silence of the Lambs.* New York: St. Martins, 1988.

Hart, John. "Therapeutic Implications of Viewing Sexual Identity in Terms of Essentialist and Constructionist Theories." *Gay Personality and Labeling.* Ed. John De Cecco. New York: Harrington Park, 1985. 39-53.

Heilbrun, Carolyn G. "Androgyny and the Psychology of Sex Differences." *The Future of Difference.* Eds. Hester Einstein and Alice Jardine. New York: Rutgers UP, 1988.

Henley, Nancy. "Psychology and Gender." *Signs: Journal of Women in Culture and Society* 11.1 (1985): 101-19.

Hilbert, Jeffrey. "The Politics of Drag." *The Advocate* 23 Apr. 1991.

Hirschfeld, Magnus. *Sexual Anamolies and Perversions.* 1938. New York: Encyclopedia P, 1946.

Hockenberry, Stewart Robert Billingham. "Sexual Orientation and Boyhood Gender Conformity Scale (BGCS)." *Archives of Sexual Behavior* 16.6 (1987).

Holden, Constance. "Doctor of Sexology." *Psychology Today* May 1988.

Hoyer, N. *Man into Woman: An Authentic Record of a Change of Sex.* New York: E.P. Dutton & Co., 1933.

Huxford, Susan. "Phalloplasty." *Gender Review* 3.5 (Summer 1985).

Ihlenfeld, Charles. "A Memorial for Harry Benjamin." *Archives of Sexual Behavior* 17.1 (Feb. 1988): 1-33.

International Foundation for Gender Education (IFGE). *Transsexualism: A Collection of Articles, Editorials, and Letters.* Wayland: 1988.

Jameison, Kathleen H. *Dirty Politics: Deception, Distraction and Democracy.* New York: Oxford UP, 1992.

_____. *Packaging the Presidency.* New York: Oxford UP, 1984.

Janus Information Facility (JIF). *Guidelines for Transsexuals.* San Francisco, CA: JIF, 1980.

_____. *Information for the Family of the Transsexual and of Children with Gender Identity Disturbances.* San Francisco: JIF, 1977.

Joan Rivers. "The Man Who became a Woman and Changed Back." ABC. Aired 10 July 1990.

Johanes, V.K., and Peggy Cohen-Kettenis. "Effects of the Pure Antiandrogen RU 23.903 (Anandron) on Sexuality, Aggression, and Mood in Male-to-Female Transsexuals." *Archives of Sexual Behavior* 18.3 (1989): 217-27.

Jorgenson, Christine. *A Personal Autobiography.* New York: Paul S. Erikson, 1967.

Jung, Carl. *Mysterium Coniunctionis: An Inquiry into the Separation and Synthesis of Psychic Opposites in Alchemy.* 2d ed. *14 Collected Works of C.G. Jung.* Bollingen Series 20. Princeton: Princeton UP, 1970.

Jung, Emma. *Animus & Anima.* Dallas, TX: Spring Pub., 1981.

Kael, Pauline. *Reeling.* New York: Warners, 1972.

Kammen, Daniel, and John Money. "Erotic Imagery and Self-Castration in Transvestism/Transsexualism: A Case Report." *Journal of Homosexuality* 2.4 (Summer 1977).

Kane, Ariadne. "The Ninth World Congress of Sexology." *Tapestry* 56 (1990).

Katz, Jonathan. *Gay American History. Lesbians and Gay Men in the U.S.A.* New York: Avon Books, 1976.

Kelley, Tomye, and Diana C. Kelley. "Self Protection and Self Defense for the Genetic Male, While in the Female Role." *Information Booklet.* Denver, CO: Gender Identity Center of Colorado, 1990: 39-41.

Kellis, Kyndal F.M. "The Berdache Tradition: A Model for Personal Growth and Cultural Acceptance." *Tapestry* 56 (1990).

Kenna, J.C., and J. Hoenig. "Transsexualism and Slater's Selective Vocabulary Test." *The International Journal of Social Psychiatry* 30.3 (Autumn 1984) 207-13.

Kennedy, Hubert. "The Third Sex Theory of Karl Henreich Ulrichs." *Journal of Homosexuality* 6 (1/2) (Fall/Winter 1980-81): 103-11.

Kessler, Suzanne. "The Medical Construction of Gender: Case Management of Intersexed Infants." *Signs: Journal of Women in Culture and Society* 16.1 (Autumn 1990): 3-27.

Kessler, Suzanne, and Wendy McKenna. *Gender: An Ethnomethodological Approach.* New York: Wiley-Interscience, 1978.

Key, Wilson Bryan. *Media Sexploitatian.* New York: Signet Books, 1976.

King, David. "Gender Confusions: Psychological and Psychiatric Conceptions of Transvestism and Transsexualism." *The Making of the Modern Homosexual.* Ed. Kenneth Plummer. Lanham, MD: Barnes and Noble Books, 1981. 154-83.

Kinsey, A.C., W.B. Pomeroy, and C.E. Martin. *Sexual Behavior in the Human Male.* Philadelphia: W.B. Saunders, 1948.

Kinsey, A.C., W.B. Pomeroy, C.E. Martin, and P.H. Gebhard. *Sexual Behavior in the Human Female.* Philadelphia: W.B. Saunders, 1953

Kirk, Kris, and Heath Kirk, eds. *Men in Frocks.* London: GMP Publishers, 1984.

Kitman, Marvin. *The Kitman Tapes: I Am a VCR.* New York: Random House, 1988.

Kockett, G., and E.M. Fahrner. "Transsexuals Who Have Not Undergone Surgery: A Follow-Up Study." *Archives of Sexual Behavior* 16.6 (1987): 511-23.

Kottak, Conrad. *Prime-Time Society: An Anthropological Analysis of Television and Culture.* Belmont, CA: Wadsworth, 1990.

Krafft-Ebing, DR. R.V. *Psychopathia Sexualis.* 1906. Rev. ed. New York: Physicians and Surgeons Book, 1922.

Kwan, Marie, Judy Van Maasdam, and Julian Davidson. "Effects of Estrogen Treatment on Sexual Behavior in Male-to-Female Transsexuals: Experimental and Clinical Observations." *Archives of Sexual Behavior* 14 (1985): 29-37.

Lacan, Jacques. *Feminine Sexuality.* Eds. Juliet Mitchell and Jacqueline Rose. New York: W.W. Norton & Co., 1982.

LaHaye, Beverly. *Who But A Woman: Concerned Women Can Make a Difference.* New York: Thomas Nelson, 1984.

Latham, Aaron, and Andrea Grenadier. "The Ordeal of Walter/Susan Cannon." *Psychology Today* Oct. 1982.

Laub, Donald and Norman Fisk. "A Rehabilitation Program for Gender Dysphoric Syndrome by Surgical Sex Change." *Plastic Reconstructive Surgery* 53.4 (Apr. 1974): 388-403.

Levine, Stephen B. "Letter to the Editor." *Archives of Sexual Behavior* 13.3 (1985).

Lily, Michael. "Through the Looking Glass—Cross-Dressing in American Indian Culture." *Tapestry* 54 (1989).

Lindemalm, Gunnar, Dag Korlin, and Nils Uddenberg. "Long-Term Follow-Up of 'Sex Change' in 13 Male-to-Female Transsexuals." *Archives of Sexual Behavior* 15.3 (1986): 187-211.

Lindholm, Charles and Cherry Lindholm. "The Erotic." *Science Digest* Sept. 1982.

Lopez, Nora. "Killing Burning of Transvestite Baffles Police." *San Antonio Light* 30 Mar. 1991.

Lothstein, Leslie. *Female-to-Male Transsexualism: Historical, Clinical and Theoretical Issues*. Boston: Routledge & Kegan Paul, 1983.

_____. "Sex Reassignment Surgery: Historical, Bio-ethical, and Theoretical Issues." *American Journal of Psychiatry* 139.4 (Apr. 1982): 417-26.

Lowe, Marian. "Sociobiology and Sex Differences." *Signs: Journal of Women in Culture and Society* 1.11 (1978): 118-25.

Lynn, Merissa Sherill. "My Workshop, The Tri-Ess Issue, Messed Up Kids." *Tapestry* 55 (1990 a).

_____. "Virginia." *Tapestry* 50 (1987).

_____. "What's Happening, How Many of Us are There? and Lead, Follow or Get Out of the Way." *Tapestry* 57 (1991).

Lynn, Merissa Sherill, Sr. Mary Elizabeth, David Lafontaine, and Ann Maguire. "Symbiotic Synergism with the Gay Community and the Women's Movement." *Tapestry* 56 (1990 b).

Madonna. *Sex*. New York: Warner Books, 1992.

Marcuse, Herbert. *Eros and Civilization: A Philosophical Inquiry into Freud*. New York: Vintage Books, 1962.

Mass, Lawrence. "Insight into Gender and Roles: (Some) Boys Will be Boys." *The Advocate* 26 (May 1987): 55-56.

Masters, W., and V. Johnson. *Human Sexual Response*. Boston: Little Brown and Co., 1966.

Mead, Margaret. *Male and Female: A Study of the Sexes in a Changing World*. New York: William Morrow & Co., 1949.

Mengert, Sheila. "The Politics of Transsexualism—Strategy for the 1990's." *Gender Euphoria* Oct. 1992.

Meyer, Jon, ed. *Clinical Management of Sexual Disorders*. Baltimore: Williams & Wilkins Co., 1976.

Meyer, Jon, and John Hoopes. "The Gender Dysphoria Syndromes: A Position Statement on So-Called Transsexualism." *Plastic and Reconstructive Surgery* 54.4 (Oct. 1974): 444-51.

Meyer, Jon, and Donna Reter. "Sex Reassignment." *Archives of General Psychiatry* 36 (Aug. 1979): 1010-15.

Meyer, Walter, Paul Walker, and Alice Webb. "Physical and Hormonal Evaluation of Transsexual Patients: A Longitudinal Study." *Archives of Sexual Behavior* 15.2 (1986): 121-38.

Millken, Donald. "Homocidal Transsexuals: Three Cases." *Canadian Journal of Psychiatry* 27 (Feb. 1982): 43-45.

Millot, Catherine. *Horsexe: Essay on Transsexuality*. Trans. Kenneth Hylton. New York: Autonomedia, 1990.

Minkowitz, Donna. "Weekend from Hell." *Village Voice* 29 Sept. 1992.

Mitroff, Ian, and Warren Dennis. *The Unreality Industry: The Deliberate Manufacturing of Falsehood and What it is Doing to Our Lives*. New York: Birch Lane, 1989.

Mobley, Donna. "Different Perspectives." *Fiesta Chapter Newsletter*. Farmington, NM, June 1990.

Money, John. *Love and Love Sickness: The Science of Sex, Gender Difference and Pair-Bonding*. Baltimore: Johns Hopkins UP, 1980.

_____. "Propaedeutics of Diecious G-I/R: Theoretical Foundations for Understanding Dimorphic Gender-Identity-Role." *Masculinity/Femininity. Basic Perspectives*. Eds. Reinisch, Rosenblum, and Sanders. New York: Oxford UP, 1987: 13- 29.

Money, John, and Patricia Tucker. *Sexual Signatures: On Being a Man or a Woman*. Boston-Toronto: Little, Brown & Co., 1975.

Money, John, and Paul Walker. "Counseling the Transsexual." *Handbook of Sexology*. Eds. J. Money and H. Musaph. New York: Elsevier/North-Holland Biomedical, 1977: 1289-1302.

Montagu, Ashley. *Sociobiology Examined*. New York: Oxford UP, 1980: 1-13.

Murphy, Timothy. "Freud Reconsidered: Bisexuality, Homosexuality, and Moral Judgement." *Journal of Homosexuality* 9 (Winter 1983): 65-77.

Murray, Linda. "Sexual Destinies." *Omni* (Apr. 1987): 100-28.

Nestle, Joan. *The Persistant Desire: A Femme-Butch Reader*. Ed. Joan Nestle. Boston: Alyson, 1992.

Newsweek Magazine. "Air Power Faces Its Biggest Test." Special report. 21 Jan. 1991.

Newton, Esther. *Female Impersonators in America*. Chicago: U of Chicago P, 1979.

_____. "The Mythic Mannish Lesbian: Radclyffe Hall and the New Woman." *Signs: Journal of Women in Culture and Society* 9.4 (1984): 557-75.

Oakley, Ann. *Sex, Gender & Society*. New York: Harper & Row, 1972.

Ornstein, Robert, and Paul Ehrlich. *New World, New Mind: Moving Towards Conscious Evolution*. New York: Doubleday, 1989.

Out Magazine. "News Flashes." July 1992.

Ovesey, L., and E. Person. "Transvestism a Disorder of the Self." *International Journal of Psychoanalytic Psychotherapy* 5 (1976): 219-36.

Parker, Wendy. "The Gender Community: Where are We Going in the 90's?" *Tapestry* 57 (1991).

Pathy-Allen, Marietta. *Transformations: Crossdressers and Those Who Love Them*. New York: E.P. Dutton, 1989.

Pauly, Ira B. "Gender Identity Disorders: Evaluation and Treatment." *Journal of Sex Education and Therapy* 16.1 (1990): 2-24.

Pauly, Ira, and Thomas Lindgren. "Body Image and Gender Identity." *Journal of Homosexuality* Fall 1976.

Perez, Emma. "Sexuality and Discourse: Notes from a Chicana Survivor." *Chicana Lesbians: The Girls Our Mothers Warned Us About*. Ed. Carla Trujillo. Berkeley, CA: Third Woman P, 1991.

Perry, Mary Elizabeth. "The Manly Woman: A Historical Case Study." *American Behavioral Scientist* 31.1 (Sept.-Oct. 1987): 86-100.

Person, E., and L. Ovesey. "Psychoanalytic Theories of Gender Identity." *Journal of American Academy of Psychoanalysis* 2 (1983): 203-26.

Phillips, Cynthia and Linda Phillips. Personal communiation 1991.

Picket Fences. "Christmas Special." CBS Aired on Dec. 1992.

Pierce, Wendy. "An Interview with Dr. Stanley Biber." *Tapestry* 54 (1989).

_____. "The Mechanics of Gender Perception." *Tapestry* 57 (1991 a).

_____. "There and Back Again: the Trinidad Experience." *Tapestry* 57 (1991 b).

Plummer, Kenneth, ed. *The Making of the Modern Homosexual.* Lanham, MD: Barnes & Noble, 1981.

Prince, Virginia. "Commentaries, Remarks, and Notes Pertaining to Sex Research: Sex, Gender and Semantics." *The Journal of Sex Research* 21.1 (Feb. 1985): 92-101.

_____. *Everything You Always Wanted to Know About Cross Dressing and Did Not Know Whom to Ask!* Unpublished manuscript. V. Prince Ph.D., Box 36091, Los Angeles, CA, 1992.

_____. "Homosexuality, Transvestism, and Transsexualism." *American Journal of Psychotherapy* 11 (1987): 80-5.

_____. *How to be a Woman Though Male.* Los Angeles: Chevalier, 1987.

_____. "The Life and Times of Virginia Prince." *Transvestia* 28.100 (1977).

_____. Personal communication, 1993.

_____. "Sexual vs. Genderal Identity: The Real Confusion." *Transvestia* 27.97 (1977): 80-91.

_____. *The Transvestite and His Wife.* Los Angeles: Author, 1967.

_____. *Understanding Cross-Dressing.* Los Angeles: Chevalier, 1976.

_____. "Yesterday, Today & Tomorow or Where We Were, Where We Are, Where We Might Go in the Future." *Tapestry* 50 (1987).

Prince, Virginia, and P.M. Bentler. "Survey of 504 Cases of Transvestism." *Psychological Reports* 31 (1972): 903-17.

Prior, Jerilyn; Yvette Vigna; and Diane Watson. "Spironolactone with Physiological Female Steriods for Presurgical Therapy of Male-to-Female Transsexuals." *Archives of Sexual Behavior* 18.1 (1989): 49-57.

Pritchard, James; Dan Pankowsky; Joseph Crowe; and Fadi Abdul-Karim. "Breast Cancer in a Male-to-Female Transsexual: A Case Report." *Journal of the American Medical Association* 259.15 (15 Apr. 1988): 2278-80.

Pruett, Kyle, and Kirstein Dahl. "Psychotherapy of Gender Identity Conflict in Young Boys." *Journal of the American Academy of Child Psychiatry* 21.1 (1982): 65-70.

Qualls, B.; J. Wincze; and D. Barlow. *The Prevention of Sexual Disorders: Theories and Approaches.* New York: Plenum, 1978.

Raymond, Janice. *The Transsexual Empire. The Making of the She-Male.* Boston: Beacon, 1979.

The Reporters. "Mistaken Identity." ABC. Aired 17 May 1989.

Ricketts, Wendell. "Biological Research on Homosexuality: Ansell's Cow or Occam's Razor?" *Gay Personality and Sexual Labeling.* John P. DeCecco. New York: Harrington, 1985. 65-95.

Romanyshyn, Robert D. *Technology as Symptom and Dream.* New York: Routledge, 1989.

Roscoe, Will. *The Zuni Man-Woman.* Albuquerque: U of New Mexico P, 1991.

Roseanne. "Halloween Special." ABC. Aired Oct. 1990.

Ross, Michael, and Julian Need. "Effects of Adequacy of Gender Reassignment Surgery on Psychological Adjustment: A Follow-up Study of Fourteen Male-to-Female Patients." *Archives of Sexual Behavior* 18.2 (1989): 145-53.

Roszak, Betty, and Theodore Roszak. *Masculine/Feminine. Readings in Sexual Mythology and the Liberation of Women.* New York: Harper & Row, 1969.

Ruan, Fang-fu; Vern Bullough; and Yung-mei Tsai. "Male Transsexuals in Mainland China." *Archives of Sexual Behavior* 18.6 (1989): 517-22.

Rubin, Gayle. "Thinking Sex: Notes for a Radical Theory of the Politics of Sexuality." *Pleasures and Danger: Exploring Female Sexuality.* Ed. Carol Vance. Boston: Routledge & Kegan Paul, 1984. 267-320.

Rudd, Peggy J. *Crossdressing with Dignity: the Case for Transcending Gender Lines.* Katy TX: PM Publishers, 1990.

_____. *My Husband Wears My Clothes: Crossdressing from the Perspective of a Wife.* Katy TX: PM Publishers, 1990.

Ruse, Michael. "Nature/Nurture: Reflections on Approaches to the Study of Homosexuality." *Journal of Homosexuality* 10.3-4 (Winter 1984): 141-50.

Russo, Vito. "A State of Being." *Film Comment* 32 (Apr. 1986).

Sally Jesse Raphael. "Billie Tipton Story." CBS. Aired August 1989.

_____. "Changing Sex for Success." CBS. Aired 28 Feb. 1990.

Saturday Night Live. "It's Time for Androgyny: Pat." NBC. Aired 16 Feb. 1990

_____. "It's Time for Androgyny: Pat." NBC. Aired Dec. 1991.

Savon, Leslie. "Miles to Go." *Village Voice* Summer 1991.

Seiter, Ellen; Hans Borcher; Gabriele Kreutzner; Eva-Marie Warth, eds. *Remote Control: Television Audiences and Cultural Power.* New York: Routledge, 1989.

Seward, John, and Georgene Seward. *Sex Differences: Mental and Temperamental.* Boston, MA: Lexington Books, 1980.

Shapiro, Laura. "Guns and Dolls." *Newsweek* 28 May 1990.

Shore, Elsie. "The Former Transsexual: A Case Study." *Archives of Sexual Behavior* 13.3 (1984): 277-85.

Simels, Steven. *Gender Chameleons: Androgyny in Rock N' Roll.* New York: Timbre Books/Arbor House, 1985.

Small, Meredith F. "Sperm Wars." *Discover* July 1991.

Socarides, Charles. "A Psychoanalytic Study of the Desire for Sexual Transformation ('Transsexualism'): The Plaster-of-Paris Man." *International Journal of Psycho-Analysis* 51 (1970): 343-48.

Solomon, Jack. *The Signs of our Time Semiotics: The Hidden Messages of Objects and Cultural Images*. Los Angeles: Jeremy Tarcher Inc., 1988.

Sontag, Susan. "Notes on Camp." *Against Interpretation and other Essays*. New York: Eyre & Spottiswoode, 1964. 275-92.

Steiner, Betty W., ed. *Gender Dysphoria, Development, Research, Management*. New York: Plenum P, 1985.

Stekel, Wilhelm. *Sadism and Masochism: The Psychology of Hatred and Cruelty*. Vols. 1 & 2. New York: Washington Square P Inc., 1968.

Stoller, Robert. *Presentations of Gender*. New Haven: Yale UP, 1985.

_____. *Sex and Gender*. New York: Science House, 1968.

_____. "Transsexualism and Transvestism." *Psychiatric Annals* 1 (1974): 61-72.

_____. "Transvestism in Women." *Archives of Sexual Behavior* 2 (1973): 323-28.

Stuart, Kim Elizabeth. *The Uninvited-Dilemma: A Question of Gender*. Lake Oswego, OR: Metamorphous P, 1983.

Summers, Jodi. "Lizzy Borden: Electro-shock Therapy." *RIP* 26 Oct. 1987.

Szasz, Thomas. *The Manufacture of Madness*. New York: Harper & Row, 1970.

_____. *The Myth of Mental Illness*. New York: Hoeber Medical Books, 1961.

_____. *Sex by Prescription*. New York: Anchor/Doubleday, 1980.

Talamini, John T. *Boys Will be Girls*. Lanham MD: UP of America, 1982.

Taubin, Amy. "The Demme's Monde." *Village Voice* 19 Feb. 1991.

Taylor, Alan. "Conceptions of Masculinity and Femininity as a Basis for Stereotypes of Male and Female Homosexuals." *Journal of Homosexuality* 9.1 (Fall 1983): 37-55.

Trebay, Guy. "Cross-Dresser Dreams: How RuPaul, a Black Man in a Platinum Wig and Platform Heels, Captured the Imagination of Mainstream Pop Culture." *New Yorker* 22 Mar. 1993: 49-54.

Trebbe, Amy. "The Manhunter Behind Lambs." *U.S.A. Today* 1 Mar. 1991.

Tripp. C.A. *The Homosexual Matrix*. New York: Signet Books, 1975.

Tsoi, W.F. "Developmental Profile of 200 Male and 100 Female Transsexuals in Singapore." *Archives of Sexual Behavior* 19.6 (1990).

Van Kemenade, Johannes, Peggy Cohen-Kettenis, Leo Cohen, and Louis Gooren. "Effects of the Pure Antiandrogen RU 23.903 (Anandron) on Sexuality, Aggression, and Mood in Male-to-Female Transsexuals." *Archives of Sexual Behavior* 18.3 (1989): 217-27.

Van Putten, Theodore and I. Fawzy I. "Sex Conversion Surgery in a Man with Severe Gender Dysphoria: A Tragic Outcome." *Archives of Gen. Psychiatry* 33 (June 1976).

Vidal, Gore. *Myra Breckinridge*. Boston: Little Brown & Co., 1968.

Von Saal, Fredrick S. "Variation in Infanticide and Parental Behavior in Male Mice Due to Prior Intrauterine Proximity to Female Fetuses: Elimination by Prenatal Stress." *Physiology and Behavior* 30 (1983): 675-81.

_____. "Variation in Phenotype Due to Random Intrauterine Positioning of Male and Female Fetuses in Rodents." *Journals of Reproduction & Fertility Ltd.* 1981: 633-50.

Wahl, Charles, ed. *Sexual Problems: Diagnosis and Treatment in Medical Practice.* New York: Free P, 1967.

Walinder, J., and B. Lundstrom. "Preoperative Evaluation of Candidates for Conversion Surgery." *Emerging Dimensions of Sexology: Selected Papers from the 6th World Congress, Sexual Medicine* Vol. II. New York: Praeger Scientific, 1984. 229-34.

Walker, Paul. Interviewed in *New York Times* 2 Oct. 1979.

_____. Interviewed on *What Sex Am I.* Film directed by Lee Grant, 1986.

Walsh, Andrea. *Women's Film and Female Experience, 1940-1950.* New York: Praeger, 1984.

Walters, William, and Michael Ross, eds. *Transsexualism and Sex Reassignment.* New York: Oxford UP, 1986.

Weeks, Jeffrey. "Movements of Affirmation: Sexual Meanings and Homosexual Identities." *Radical History Review* 20 (Spring/Summer 1979): 164-179.

_____. *Sex Politics and Society: The Regulation of Sexuality Since 1800.* London: Longman, 1981.

Weinreich, James. "A New Sociobiological Theory of Homosexuality Applicable to Societies with Universal Marriage." *Ethnology and Sociobiology* 8 (1987): 37-47.

Wells, Joel. "Sexual Language Usage in Different Interpersonal Contexts: A Comparison of Gender and Sexual Orientation." *Archives of Sexual Behavior* 18.2 (1989): 127-43.

Wheeler, Connie, and Leah Schaefer. "The Nonsurgical True Transsexual (Benjamin's Category IV): A Theoretical Rationale." *International Research in Sexology, Sexual Medicine* Vol. I. Eds. H. Lief and Z. Hoch. New York: Praeger, 1981.

Whitehead, Harriet. "The Bow and the Burden Strap: A New Look at Institutionalized Homosexuality in Native North America." *The Cultural Construction of Gender and Sexuality.* Eds. Sherry B. Ortner and Harriet Whitehead. Cambridge: Cambridge UP, 1981. 80-115.

Williams, L. Walter. *The Spirit and the Flesh: Sexual Diversity in Indian Culture.* Boston: Beacon, 1986.

_____. "Women, Men, and Others: Beyond Ethnocentricism in Gender Theory." *American Scientist* 31.1 (Sept.-Oct. 1987): 135-41.

Wilson, E.O. *Sociobiology the New Synthesis.* Cambridge, MA: Harvard UP, 1975.

Wise, Thomas, and Jane Lucas. "Pseudotranssexualism Iatrogenic Gender Dysphoria." *Journal of Homosexuality* 6.3 (Spring 1981): 61-67.

Woodhouse, Annie. "Breaking The Rules or Bending Them? Transvestism, Femininity, and Feminism." *Women's Studies International Forum* 12.4 (1989): 417-23.

_____. *Fantastic Women, Sex, Gender and Transvestism.* New Jersey: Rutgers UP, 1989.

_____. "Forgotten Women: Transvestism and Marriage." *Women's Studies International Forum* 8.6 (1985): 583-92.

Wrate, R.M., and V. Gulens. "A Systems Approach to Child Effeminancy and the Prevention of Transsexualism." *Journal of Adolescence* 9 (1986): 215-29.

Yard, Molly. Interviewed in *Newweek Magazine* 16 July 1990.

Yudkin, Marcia. "Transsexualism and Women: A Critical Perspective." *Feminist Studies* 4.3 (Oct. 1978): 97-107.

Zuger, Bernard. "Homosexuality in Families of Boys with Early Effeminate Behavior: An Epidemiological Study." *Archives of Sexual Behavior* 18.2 (1989): 155-65.